PRAISE FOR *WALKING THROUGH FIRE*

"It's not often you find a friend who will pray for you at 2:00 a.m. when they lie awake in pain, but Vaneetha Risner is that friend to me. And I am all the richer, all the stronger for it. It's why the book you hold in your hands is so powerful, for we all want to see someone in whom living for Christ and dying for Him is indistinguishable. We crave a visceral story that has meat on it. A story that soars and inspires. It's what you'll find in *Walking Through Fire*. Here is a true story that shows how God can turn tragedies into remarkable triumphs of faith and endurance. So, be inspired by Vaneetha's extraordinary story, and rest assured that the same God who sustained her will uphold you through every heartache and hardship!"

—Joni Eareckson Tada, Joni and Friends International Disability Center

"I must admit, over the last few years as I've gotten to know Vaneetha and her story, she has become one of my heroes. But in her book *Walking Through Fire*, Vaneetha doesn't present herself as the hero of her amazing story. No. She is careful to let you know her Lord is the hero. I know of no other book that more engagingly and graphically presents the deep heartaches of life in this fallen world and the comforting glory of the presence, power, and promises of the Redeemer. Walk through fire with Vaneetha and see her Lord in the flames. You'll be glad you did."

—Paul David Tripp, author of *New Morning Mercies*

"I have endorsed many books over the years, but I don't recall reading one from start to finish the day it arrived. It held me all the way. I've never met Vaneetha, but for years I've known and loved her through her writings. In *Walking Through Fire*, you will see her heart, her honesty, her pain, her eternal perspective, and her love for Jesus. As I read, my heart ached for Vaneetha's losses, identified with her hopes, laughed at her sense of humor, rejoiced in our King's redemption, and longed with her for that blood-bought home where our dreams will forever come true. Beautifully done."

—Randy Alcorn, *New York Times* bestselling author of *Heaven, Happiness,* and *If God Is Good*

"'Men of the breaking hearts had a quality about them not known to or understood by common men. They habitually spoke with spiritual authority. They had been in the presence of God, and they reported what they saw there.' This quote by Tozer describes the beauty and power of Vaneetha's memoir, *Walking Through Fire*.

I couldn't put this book down! Vaneetha writes raw with vulnerability and honesty about her past, her deepest pain, her biggest losses, and her God who faithfully held and transformed her through every broken chapter in her story. This book is a close-up and colorful reminder that life is full of suffering, but that God draws near to the brokenhearted."

—Ellie Holcomb, author and Dove Award–winning singer-songwriter

"John Bunyan said that believers are like bells: the harder they are hit, the better they sound. This is because believers sound more like Christ when afflicted. This mature Christian wisdom, winsomely and poetically rendered, is replete in Vaneetha's powerful memoir."

—Rosaria Butterfield, pastor's wife, homeschool mom,
and author of *The Secret Thoughts of an Unlikely
Convert* and *The Gospel Comes with a House Key*

"Is a life of suffering a life worth living? In her transparent and inspiring memoir *Walking Through Fire*, Vaneetha Rendall Risner answers that question with a resounding yes. Not because suffering is good, but because our God-with-us is faithful—even when, even if, even here. Vaneetha's story of excruciating losses and radiant hope reveals the glory of God in such a way that you might just find yourself removing your shoes."

—Sharon Garlough Brown, author of *Sensible
Shoes* series and *Shades of Light*

"The moment I finished reading this remarkable memoir, I was struck by the phoniness of much of what occupies my time. What we call ordinary life is often a form of unreality. Vaneetha had re-grounded me to see again the precious value of each human life, the gift of joy despite the sorrows, and the goodness of God over everything. This book will minister to anyone acquainted with the lacerations of a severed marriage, the chronic aches of a broken body, or the haunting flashbacks of a buried child. But it's a story for anyone who needs to be re-grounded in order to feel human again. I highly recommend it."

—Tony Reinke, author and senior teacher at Desiring God

"From the moment I started reading *Walking Through Fire*, I couldn't put it down. As Vaneetha recounts various trials and tragedies—disability, death, and divorce—she shares them with humility, honesty, compassion, and conviction. This book will encourage your faith, kindle your hope, and show you how to walk with God in the midst of life's unexpected hardships."

—Melissa Kruger, author and director of Women's Initiatives
for the Gospel Coalition

"It's one thing to serve God when things go right. But what does it look like to serve God when everything goes wrong, time after time after time? *Walking Through Fire* provides such a picture, showing us faithfulness in the midst of a lifetime of trial. This is Vaneetha at her finest: vulnerable, transparent, honest, and hopeful . . . always hopeful. It made me want to run the race with greater perseverance. I loved reading this book. Spectacular!"

—Brian Fikkert, coauthor of *When Helping Hurts*

"Whether we've endured childhood trauma or faced obstacles in adulthood that we never would have chosen, each one of us longs to make sense of our suffering. We wonder if God is with us and for us. Because Vaneetha Rendall Risner is the spiritual guide I have trusted to navigate my own suffering, I am thrilled to be able to share *Walking Through Fire* with all my friends. This book equips readers to trust God when we need God most."

—Margot Starbuck, author of *The Grown Woman's Guide to Online Dating*

"A friend of mine says that when anyone in his life suffers to a degree he can't even imagine, he likes to ask that person, 'Who is God?' Through the pages of the Bible we find a God who most beautifully reveals himself to and through the poor, the marginalized, and the suffering. Christ identified with the vulnerable, all the way up to the cross where, in his weakness, he mightily secured a victory of which we'll forever sing. We do well, then, to lean in when a sister like Vaneetha writes and, as we read, ask, 'Who is God?' In her page-turning memoir, Vaneetha doesn't merely tell us who God is. She masterfully shows us."

—Quina Aragon, spoken word artist and author
of *Love Made* and *Love Gave*

"Our brains need stories of how others have flourished within their constraints so that we might know our own hard stories can be ones of flourishing too. Vaneetha poignantly offers herself—and the valuable lessons she's learned—to us as a reminder that often life's most difficult struggles can be our most powerful assignments."

—Katherine Wolf, survivor, advocate, and author
of *Suffer Strong* and *Hope Heals*

"I had the incredible privilege of recording the powerful song "Held," written by Christa Wells, based on Vaneetha's story of the unimaginable loss of a child. This book beautifully and honestly tells a story of deep loss and redemption, and it is a must-read for anyone who's ever wrestled with the question of why a good God would allow such suffering in this world."

—Natalie Grant, recording artist, author, and philanthropist

"Every lamenter has a story. It's rare to be invited into the sacred places of the soul and hear the long and confusing struggle with pain. Grief is messy. Sorrow is humiliating. Doubt is discouraging. Yet Vaneetha Risner welcomes us into her journey. Not just to hear her story but to marvel at the redeeming grace of God. *Walking Through Fire* is more than a memoir. It's a memorial to hope in Christ for those who hurt."

—Mark Vroegop, lead pastor of College Park Church, Indianapolis,
and author of *Dark Clouds, Deep Mercy* and *Weep with Me*

WALKING
THROUGH
FIRE

WALKING THROUGH FIRE

A Memoir of

Loss and

Redemption

VANEETHA RENDALL RISNER

NELSON
BOOKS

An Imprint of Thomas Nelson

Walking Through Fire

© 2021 Vaneetha Rendall Risner

Published in Nashville, Tennessee, by Nelson Books, an imprint of Thomas Nelson. Nelson Books and Thomas Nelson are registered trademarks of HarperCollins Christian Publishing, Inc.

Published in association with the literary agency of Wolgemuth & Associates, Inc.

This is a true story, and I have told it as faithfully as I could, often using journals, letters, and emails. That said, these are my memories and none of the conversations are meant to represent word-for-word accuracy; rather, I've tried to retell them in a way that evokes the feeling and meaning of what was said.

Some names and circumstances have been changed to protect the privacy of the individuals involved.

Music and lyrics for "Held" by Christa Wells.

Thomas Nelson titles may be purchased in bulk for educational, business, fundraising, or sales promotional use. For information, please e-mail SpecialMarkets@ThomasNelson.com.

Unless otherwise noted, Scripture quotations marked ESV are taken from the ESV® Bible (The Holy Bible, English Standard Version®). Copyright © 2001 by Crossway, a publishing ministry of Good News Publishers. Used by permission. All rights reserved.

Scripture quotations taken from The Holy Bible, New International Version®, NIV®. Copyright © 1973, 1978, 1984, 2011 by Biblica, Inc.® Used by permission of Zondervan. All rights reserved worldwide. www.Zondervan.com. The "NIV" and "New International Version" are trademarks registered in the United States Patent and Trademark Office by Biblica, Inc.®

Scripture quotations marked NLT are taken from the Holy Bible, New Living Translation. © 1996, 2004, 2015 by Tyndale House Foundation. Used by permission of Tyndale House Publishers, Inc., Carol Stream, Illinois 60188. All rights reserved.

Any internet addresses, phone numbers, or company or product information printed in this book are offered as a resource and are not intended in any way to be or to imply an endorsement by Thomas Nelson, nor does Thomas Nelson vouch for the existence, content, or services of these sites, phone numbers, companies, or products beyond the life of this book.

ISBN 978-1-4002-1813-4 (audiobook)

Library of Congress Cataloging-in-Publication Data

Names: Risner, Vaneetha Rendall, 1964- author.
Title: Walking through fire: a memoir of loss and redemption / Vaneetha Rendall Risner.
Description: Nashville, Tennessee: Nelson Books, 2020. | Includes bibliographical references.
Summary: "The astonishing, Job-like story of how an existence filled with loss, suffering, questioning, and anger became a life filled with shocking and incomprehensible peace and joy"--Provided by publisher.
Identifiers: LCCN 2020015645 | ISBN 9781400218110 (trade paperback) | ISBN 9781400218127 (epub)
Subjects: LCSH: Risner, Vaneetha Rendall, 1964-| Christian biography.
Classification: LCC BR1725.R5785 A3 2020 | DDC 270.092 [B]—dc23
LC record available at https://lccn.loc.gov/2020015645

Printed in the United States of America

21 22 23 24 25 LSC 10 9 8 7 6 5 4 3 2 1

To Katie and Kristi, who have bravely
walked through fire with me.
And to Joel, who is even better than my dreams.
I love you more than words can say.

When you pass through the waters, I will be with you;
    and through the rivers, they shall not overwhelm you;
when you walk through fire you shall not be burned,
    and the flame shall not consume you.

—Isaiah 43:2

CONTENTS

Foreword by Ann Voskamp XIII

Prologue XIX

Chapter 1 Please 1

Chapter 2 Discoveries 3

Chapter 3 Vulnerabilities 11

Chapter 4 Paul 16

Chapter 5 Going Home 24

Chapter 6 Complications 29

Chapter 7 Empty 33

Chapter 8 Saying Goodbye 39

Chapter 9 Aftermath 46

Chapter 10 Experiencing God 55

Chapter 11 Dave 64

Chapter 12 Adjusting 84

Chapter 13 The Clinic 95

Chapter 14 Another Loss 102

Chapter 15 Directionally Challenged 113

Chapter 16 Surprised Again 121

Chapter 17 Reactions 132

Chapter 18 Accepting What Is 142

Chapter 19 Trying to Look Good 152

Chapter 20 Crazy Love 163

Chapter 21 Escalation 168

CONTENTS

Chapter 22 Two Steps Forward   173
Chapter 23 Three Steps Back   185
Chapter 24 A Different Story   191
Chapter 25 Not About Me   196
Chapter 26 Redemption   204
Chapter 27 Brave New World   212
Chapter 28 Winter Is Past   221
Chapter 29 The Way You Walk   226
Chapter 30 Looking Back, Walking Forward   232

"Held" Music and Lyrics by Christa Wells   243
Acknowledgments   245
Notes   249
About the Author   251

FOREWORD

Sometimes sitting in the ashes of your most cherished dreams would be a relief.

Because that would mean the fire's over. That would mean you have survived, and now there's only the rising.

But what happens when there seems to be no extinguishing of the fire you're trapped in? What happens when hungry flames leap from one dream to the next, and everywhere you seem to turn you get burned? What happens when the season you find yourself in isn't just a dumpster fire but a raging, wild inferno and there's no way to evacuate your one and only life?

No one tells you this in Life 101:

You've got to figure out more than putting one step in front of the other; you've got to master the art of walking through fire.

Because if you aren't walking through fire right now, someday you will be.

I can remember the day I first met Vaneetha Risner. When you're in the presence of giant faith, one is only awed by a far greater God. After you sit with this woman and her unforgettable story, you will never walk away from it. You will be carried away by her story. You will carry her story with you. And you will be forever changed, because you will have met the One who passionately burns within her.

Vaneetha Risner is a modern-day Job.

And this is the story of a woman who feared God enough to not be afraid to cut through the smoke of things and be howlingly honest with God, to say out loud what a whole world of us are thinking:

> *Don't You see us burning, dying, grieving, hurting alone here in our own skin? Don't You hear our heart-pounding begging in the midst of the flames when our prodigals run toward pits, when our people reel with diagnoses, when our veins scream with chronic pain?*
>
> *Where are You, God, when the very people who are supposed to hold our hearts next to theirs just get up and torch us and never look back, and our souls are scorched with shame? Are You around at all, God, when the people we sacrificed for turn around and sacrifice us on the altar of rejection, and all stack of our dreams, our days, go up in these mocking tendrils of smoke, and our lives end up being this stinging stench in the nostrils in ways we could never speak out loud?*
>
> *Do You not have power to heal? To avert this pain? Or do You just choose not to?*

Is God ultimately impotent or just plain indifferent?

The story in these pages will testify:

> God is not impotent—His very Word testifies how He kept a young girl from death, raised a middle-aged man from the dead, and gave eyes light and ears reverberation. The Wounded Healer can heal.
>
> God is not indifferent—He's wept over a grave and catches every single one of our tears in a bottle, because He can't bear to waste grief. The way Christ most moves is to be moved with compassion (Matt. 9:36). The One who stretched out His hands on the Cross, stretches out His arms to touch us now (Mark 1:41).

God is not impotent and God is not indifferent. God hates injury, infirmity, and injustice. God came to heal and relieve us from suffering, and He calls us to alleviate and decimate suffering. So if God allows suffering, it must be to allow something He loves even more than He hates suffering.

Sometimes God allows what He can hardly stand to accomplish more than we understand.

What seems like your story is but one line in His story.

In every one happening, the Word Himself is writing hope into a million other stories.

Our God, the One who walks on water and walks through fire, He rises. Our God never stops rising, and He never stops resurrecting—resurrecting tender hope and relentless love for you, the world, in a thousand unlikely places.

Fight through the flames and ask, *Where are you, God?* and you can see through the smoke.

He's in the rolling away of the stones. He's in the resistance against the dark, right there in your daily practice of resurrection. He's in the rising from the ashes. He has moved right in. He bent low and slipped in through the cracks of the surrendered broken heart. And He stays with us no matter the heat.

When you don't know where God is, know that this is exactly where He is:

He's fighting for you (Ex. 14:14), going right before you (Deut. 31:8), always making a way for you (Isa. 43:19), and carrying you (Isa. 46:4), so you can lean into the strength of the universe. He's the courage in your veins, the drumbeat of the brave in your heart, and the resilient grit in your every rising and your every step forward.

Jesus, the only man of perfection, was a man of sorrows. He perfectly understands your heartbreaking sorrow, and He stands heartbroken with you in it.

No one can truly withstand suffering unless they know God truly stands with them.

You have a Lover holding you together. You have a Comforter cupping His hands for every tear. And you have a Friend whose arm is around you, pulling you into the safest presence that won't leave you alone for one God-forsaken moment. This isn't trite cliché—this is your true reality.

I can bear witness to seeing it in the eyes of Vaneetha, in her voice, in the blazing, cruciform courage she loaned me when she sat across a table and told me this searing story and how she chose, no matter the burn, to stay in God's story. To live the story of Jehoshaphat, who was overwhelmed by a whole horde of trouble, and, though he didn't know what to do, kept his eye fixed on the Lord, which has a way of fixing the seemingly impossible things. Jehoshaphat didn't send out an army to fight but sent out a choir to sing. To sing truth into the face of everything: "Give thanks to the Lord, for his love endures forever" (2 Chron. 20:21 NIV).

Vaneetha told me how she grabbed her pen like a sword and daily wrote down God's gifts and His goodness, and she slayed flames with her praise: "That's how you walk through fire—with a grateful heart on fire for the praise of God."

Vaneetha testifies:

We can live bitter—*or we can live beloved.*
We can trust our changing feelings alone—*or we can trust in the unchanging love of God alone.*
We can feel abandoned in the flames—*or we can abandon ourselves to God.*

Turn the pages of Vaneetha's story. Every single one singed with the glory of God, and you will feel it burning in your bones.

When we think we might write our story differently, it's only because we don't know the same things the Storyteller knows.

No one knows why the sovereign Storyteller allows heat and heartbreak and fire. But the answer must be cosmically important enough that the Storyteller allows His heart to break too. And there He is, always walking every single step with us through the fire.

There is a Storyteller who writes Himself into our story, to raise us from the ashes—in His perfect time, in His perfect way, for His perfect glory—so our souls are always well.

Turn these pages and feel your own heart ignite for God.

Because that's the only way you will ever walk through flames. You've got to fight fire with holy fire.

Ann Voskamp,
Author of the *New York Times* bestsellers *One Thousand Gifts* and *The Broken Way*
16th of September in the year of our Lord, 2020

PROLOGUE

Can you tell us about your life?"

I look at the faces in the room. Each looks back expectantly. I take a breath, say a silent prayer, and begin to speak. I tell them about polio and bullying, medical mistakes and wrongful death. I describe abandonment, betrayal, and loss.

My words intrigue them—the way a car crash does. Sometimes it's best not to look too closely at the wreckage.

"But is there anything happy?" they ask. "Did you ever laugh with all the tears?"

And then, quietly, "Has your life been *good*?"

My eyes sparkle as I grin, my joy evident.

"Come and see."

Chapter 1

PLEASE

I hung up the phone, trembling. Moments before it had seemed like only a setback. Now I couldn't understand what was happening. I was terrified.

Turning from the phone, I limped to a nearby chair and carefully lowered myself until my knees touched the carpet. It was the only way I could kneel in prayer.

"I'll do anything, God," I sobbed. "*Anything*. I'll read the Bible every day. I'll serve in a soup kitchen every holiday. I'll give away all our money. Just . . ."

My voice was desperate.

"Please, please, please," I begged, "just *please* save Paul."

At some point there were no more words. No more tears. Only exhaustion and a growing sense of dread.

⁂

When I could think clearly again, my mind went back eight months to one of the chapter titles in a book I was studying with a group of women from my church: "God Never Makes a Mistake." I'd laughed when I read it. The words sounded naive, and I assumed that the author, Evelyn Christenson, must have had an easy life—until I learned she'd suffered three miscarriages, a stillborn baby, and an infant who died at seven months. My laughter turned to shocked curiosity.

How could she claim that? By that point in my life I'd already endured three miscarriages of my own, and I was eleven weeks pregnant, wondering if I'd carry our baby full term. So as I prepared to lead the book study, I flipped through the Bible for hours, searching for answers. At the study I confessed that it seemed unbelievable to me that God never makes a mistake or that God has control over everything that happens. There was simply too much pain in the world to believe that *all* suffering had a reason behind it. But then I read aloud a quote from the book:

> This is the place you reach when after years and years of trials and difficulties, you see that all has been working out for your good, and that God's will is perfect. You see that He has made no mistakes. He knew all of the "what if's" in your life. When you finally recognize this, even *during* the trials, it's possible to have joy, deep down joy.[1]

A frank discussion erupted. We were all anxious to share our experiences, our theology, or both. How could a good God purposefully allow all the suffering in the world? Perhaps God never *wants* suffering but couldn't stop it because of our free will. Someone quoted Romans 8:28—"And we know that for those who love God all things work together for good, for those who are called according to his purpose"— seeming to suggest that this single verse settled everything. Another person mentioned Genesis 50:20, in which Joseph, after having suffered immensely at the hands of his own family, told them, "You meant evil against me, but God meant it for good."

But as I continued to kneel, all these months later, I wondered about that Romans verse. About the idea that God doesn't make mistakes, and about whether God could or would change things. I had just begged God to save Paul. *Would he?*

A knock at the front door startled me. Knowing exactly who it was, I rose slowly back to my feet and steeled myself for whatever was about to happen.

Chapter 2

DISCOVERIES

Just six months earlier, life had been good.

My marriage was better than it had ever been, in part because of the hard road Dave and I had walked. Our daughter, Katie, was a typical energetic two-year-old. I hadn't miscarried and was well into the second trimester of another pregnancy. Lingering effects of childhood polio still showed in my distinctive pendulum-like limp, my weak arms, and my tiring from walking too much, but that was nothing new.

Dave and I were excited to learn the sex of the baby at my twenty-week ultrasound. As the technician set up the computer and smeared gel on the probe, she asked, "So do you want to know if you're having a boy or girl?"

"Definitely." I grinned at Dave. I knew he'd love a son, but I wanted a sister for Katie.

She slid the probe back and forth across my abdomen as she concentrated on the image on the monitor. "Well, everything looks good so far. Lots of amniotic fluid, strong heartbeat, positioned head down, two eyes, and . . . hang on . . . great! He moved for us. Looks like you're having a boy."

"Yes!" Dave pumped his fist in the air. "It'll be fun to have a boy, Van. You'll see."

Suddenly the ultrasound tech's back stiffened as she leaned closer to the monitor. All we could hear was the sound of the computer keys as she clicked them, and then she pressed the probe harder into my stomach. "I'm trying to figure something out," she said in a quiet monotone. "I . . . I need to get someone else to look at this."

"Is everything okay?" I asked.

"I'm not sure. I'll get the doctor." She stood up to leave, and as she was closing the door she turned around and whispered, "I'm so sorry."

What did that mean? Dave and I held hands and waited. Neither of us knew what to say, and the silence stretched.

When our OB finally returned after an agonizing wait, she sat at the monitor without a word and immediately redid the ultrasound. Then she turned to face us. "So here's what's going on," she reported. "It looks like your baby has a heart problem. A hypoplastic left heart, which means he may only have half of his heart. But we'll do another ultrasound to confirm, so don't panic yet. After you get dressed, we'll talk about next steps."

Thirty minutes later we were in the car, pulling out of the hospital lot. I tried to push down my panic. *Maybe the next ultrasound will clear everything up and our baby will be fine.*

The drive home to our north Raleigh suburb took half an hour. Mostly we drove in numb silence. We talked a little about whether we had the strength to begin telling people what we had learned. All I wanted at the moment was to crawl into a hole and try to process what we'd heard, but I knew that wasn't an option. Our family knew about the ultrasound appointment and would be calling us if we didn't call them.

At home we sat in the living room and called our families.

My older sister, Shalini, listened and promised she'd pray.

Dave's parents, Maxine and Jerry, listened supportively and didn't say much.

My parents, Dave and Suku, listened, and then my mother asked a few questions. "I think it'll be fine, don't you? Doctors are wrong all the time. But what exactly did they say? When will you know more? How are you feeling? Are you worried?" I knew the questions were her way of loving and supporting me.

Each time the person on the other end answered, we tried to sound upbeat. The diagnosis was preliminary, after all, and most things I worried about never happened. But with each call, the knot in my stomach pulled tighter. We hated forcing our family into limbo with us. But we knew they'd want to know, and we absolutely needed their support.

When Dave and I collapsed into bed that night, Katie sleeping peacefully in her crib, we were too tired to speak. The effort of trying to be positive, to think positively, to believe and say the right things, had drained us. Worse, there was no clear finish line. We wouldn't know anything definitive until the next ultrasound, scheduled for the following week.

We held hands in silence until our exhaustion crumbled into fitful sleep.

⚜

The more detailed level II ultrasound made the diagnosis definitive. Our baby boy had hypoplastic left heart syndrome (HLHS), a rare condition in which the left side of the heart, which does the majority of the heart's work by pumping out oxygenated blood, was severely underformed.

Our main obstetrician, Dr. Wilson, whom we loved, told us we had numerous options. We could attempt a heart transplant at birth, but there was a waiting list. There was a three-step surgery we could try, but different hospitals had varying rates of success. Abortion was an option, technically, although not for Dave and me. Or we could do nothing and simply love him for however long he lived, which would likely be less than two weeks.

"I'm not an expert in these choices, though if you call me later I can put you in touch with a pediatric cardiologist and some other resources," Dr. Wilson told us kindly. "But at the end of the day, the two of you are in charge now. The decisions will be yours to make."

It was bewildering. I felt as if most medical crises had a set path and that, however difficult, there was at least a clear direction. But in our baby's case, it sounded as if there were several paths, and Dave and I had no idea which one to choose.

We decided to start by giving our baby a name: Paul. And then the middle name flowed naturally: David. Both Dave and I admired the relentless passion for God that the biblical Paul and David had modeled throughout their lives, and so it seemed fitting to name him after them.

Once we had a name, we felt more ready to tackle what was in front of us. I called a high school friend, Jon, who was a pediatric cardiologist, and he volunteered to talk us through our medical options. That helped us feel less overwhelmed.

Soon we began to tell our friends. Most were sympathetic and kind, but a few asked probing questions that almost implied Paul's condition was my fault. Had I done something wrong early in my pregnancy, like using a new medicine or drinking alcohol? One person even asked me if I'd ridden my exercise bike too vigorously. And each time I defended myself, my unspoken fears grew.

Especially since I'd been asking myself the very same questions.

When I shared the news with my book study group at church, one woman asked, "You look so calm, but aren't you afraid? Do you still think that God never makes a mistake?"

Startled by the question, I nodded. I was terrified to express even the slightest doubt. I honestly didn't *know* what I thought about that. I was too dazed to feel much of anything. But I whispered, "Yes. I still believe that," as I silently prayed for more faith.

It was a prayer I would repeat over and over in the following days, though I was conflicted. Could a person who questioned how God could let this happen *also* pray for more faith? Could hope and anger sit side by side or would one of them eventually devour the other?

The weight of doubt and judgment was already heavy the night Sam, a Christian friend from Dave's work, arrived with his wife, Kathy, to talk with us. They brought a beautiful potted violet and a stack of Christian books and tapes.

Dave put everything on the coffee table as the four of us settled in the living room. Sam spoke first, saying, "We've been praying every day for you. We brought these books and tapes because we wanted you to know that Paul can be healed, born without any heart defect."

"Thanks for praying," Dave said. "We're praying that Paul will be healed, too, but we don't know what God's plan is for him."

Kathy and Sam exchanged glances, and then Kathy said, "Prayer is more powerful than you think, but the key is believing your prayer will be answered. *If* you believe, it will."

"I believe in prayer, but what if God has a different plan for Paul's life?" I asked, remembering the quote from my book study. "I think that God can use hard things for our good, don't you? I'm trying to trust that God doesn't make mistakes."

Sam leaned forward and his voice sharpened. "You need to understand that God's will is always to heal. If you truly believe it and pray with faith, Paul will be healed, but it's up to you." He sat back, and his voice softened as he asked, "Why don't you read the books and listen to the tapes?"

They mean well, I reminded myself.

"Thank you," I offered in a cheerful voice. "We'll be sure to take a look at these."

❦

In the wake of Sam and Kathy's visit, Dave was confident that we should continue praying as we had been doing. While he appreciated their concern, Dave felt we should keep trusting God with the outcome rather than trying to manipulate God into healing Paul.

Most of me agreed, but my fear motivated me to explore Sam and Kathy's material. So in addition to my usual prayers, I began praying for Paul's healing dozens of times a day, inserting his name into scriptures about healing. I read book after book on healing and listened to tapes while working around the house. Instead of finding hope, however, I became increasingly unsettled with what the authors were claiming. The thought struck me: *They're trying to force God to give them something, as if they know what's best, instead of trusting that God knows what's best.*

As the days passed, my prayers for Paul's total healing became mechanical. I would say them without thinking, and sometimes I caught my mind wandering while praying.

The idea of faith-based healing wasn't new to me. Back in college at the University of Virginia, during the spring of my first year, a traveling faith healer came to town. Signs advertising his ministry were plastered all over the grounds, and at the insistence of some well-meaning friends, I reluctantly agreed to attend the event. We were all hoping that God would heal me from the residual effects of my polio.

Leading up to that night, I prayed almost nonstop for healing. I knew that God could do it. But would he? I was nervously excited but still dreaded the thought of being on display—especially if I wasn't healed.

When my friend and I arrived, the lecture hall was already packed. People even stood along the walls. We were immediately greeted by a ministry staffer who assured us he had seats in the front row. As he escorted us up the aisle, I realized there was no way I could remain anonymous.

I limped toward our seats. I was so used to the burning stares I could almost ignore them.

Almost.

The message from the traveling evangelist was about faith and healing. When he finished speaking and closed his Bible, a guitar began to play. "If anyone, and I mean *anyone*, needs to be healed of *anything*," he crooned over the gentle guitar, "come on up here. God wants healing for all of you."

I watched person after person step up onto the stage. The healer asked what people needed, then touched legs, ears, stomachs, eyes, fingers. Every single person reported healing—but not one that was visible. I slumped back in my seat. Part of me was relieved that the long line meant there wouldn't be any time for me, while the other part wondered if I really could be healed. But the whole service seemed a little too slick, and something about the healer made me uncomfortable.

Did that mean I was being too skeptical? Or that I lacked the necessary faith? As I thought and prayed, the ministry staffer who had taken me to my seat tapped my shoulder. "We want you to go up now. Don't worry about the line."

I hesitated, but my friend looked at me pleadingly. "I think you should go, Van. Why not?"

The question had been answered for me when the staffer pulled me to my feet. Before I could process what was happening, I found myself helped up a set of four steps and placed directly in front of the faith healer.

The auditorium, which had been filled with the hum of whispered conversations, grew eerily still. The back of my neck confirmed the stares.

"What can I do for you?" the man asked as he turned to face me.

"I had polio as a child," I answered, sitting on the chair he gestured to, "and all four of my limbs are weak. I'd like to be healed of my paralysis."

"Okay," he said, kneeling in front of me.

Now I was *begging* God to use this man to heal me. I desperately wanted this. The man prayed a brief prayer, put his hands on my legs, and declared that one leg was longer than the other. He pulled it toward him and confidently said, "I fixed that."

I didn't feel different, but he quickly followed up with, "Now, what else can I do?"

"Well, my arms and legs are weak."

"Okay, so why don't you walk for me right now to make sure I didn't already take care of that."

I stood carefully and walked across the stage with the same back-and-forth limp I always had. The crowd murmured.

"Hmm. I thought lengthening your leg would have fixed that," the man said as I returned. "Maybe this requires more prayer." He motioned for me to sit again. He prayed, touching my arms and ankles, then asked me to walk the stage again.

Still no change in my limp. The murmurs grew.

The healer's hands were on his hips when I returned. He frowned at me. "I need to ask you, do you have the faith to be healed?"

"I *think* so," I answered. "I love Jesus, and I know he can do anything. And I really want this."

"Well, I *know* I can heal everyone who has enough faith," he responded, "but I don't think you do. You should pray and ask God to give you that faith. I'll be doing a healing service about twenty minutes from here tomorrow night, and if you pray and get the faith you need, you'll be healed then. I'm sure of it."

I struggled to find the words, any words, to answer, but his attention was already on the next person in line, and I was already being helped back down the four steps. At the bottom the staffer left me, and I returned to my seat, humiliated.

I sat down, alternating between feelings of anger and embarrassment. *How dare that man pin his failure on me—or is it true that I really lack faith? I want to be healed, and I know God can heal me—but what if that isn't part of God's plan? And what is everyone else thinking of me?*

⁂

Now, as I prayed daily for Paul's healing, I was feeling that same conflict. Was there a right way to pray? Back in college I'd been praying only for myself—and I hadn't been on the verge of death. But now I was praying on behalf of someone vulnerable, someone who could die. The stakes were far higher. And I still didn't have answers.

Chapter 3

VULNERABILITIES

If Paul wasn't healed before he was born, Dave and I needed to evaluate our options.

If we did nothing, Paul would die within two weeks of birth. With help from a cardiologist friend, Jon, we settled on pursuing a series of three surgeries, the first one within days of birth. These operations, if successful, would give Paul the best long-term chance of survival. There were risks involved with each surgery, so the infant mortality rate was high. But if Paul did survive, he would have a decent chance of living a relatively normal life, albeit with some limitations, well past middle age.

Jon suggested we contact Dr. Bove of the University of Michigan hospital system, who had one of the highest surgical success rates with HLHS. The fact that Dave's parents lived in Michigan was a plus as well. Dr. Bove agreed to perform the procedure, and our insurance company approved it. We just needed my OB to sign the final paperwork and send it in.

With Dave at work, I went to the appointment alone. Because patients had to rotate through all the obstetricians at the practice, on this visit I needed to explain the situation to a doctor I'd never met.

"Do you mind signing these papers while I wait?" I asked Dr. Taylor after she had finished my exam and I'd explained Paul's condition. I took a manila folder from my bag and extended it toward her. "We need to set this up as soon as possible."

"A hypoplastic left heart is a serious problem," she said, putting on her reading glasses and leafing through the report. "You realize that if your son lives he'll have a tough life, and so will you. Is it worth it?"

"I know he might have a hard life," I answered. "But having a hard life doesn't mean it won't be meaningful or worthwhile. We want to do all we can to give him the best chance for a full life."

Dr. Taylor raised her eyebrows at me, then resumed reading the papers. When she reached the final page, she looked at me over her reading glasses and said, "Have you thought about terminating your pregnancy? You're not too far along to do that."

I stared at her, shocked. "You mean an abortion? I'm twenty-eight weeks, you know. And we *want* this baby."

"It may sound noble to you," she replied, closing the folder, "but it's cruel to do this. Terminating your pregnancy would be easier for you and your baby. It doesn't mean you aren't a good parent. It makes you a better parent, because you're doing what's best for him in the long run. Why would you bring a child into the world knowing he will need multiple surgeries and may have long-term problems?"

My body was shaking in anger, but she didn't seem to notice. "Obviously you can do what you want," she concluded. "But personally and professionally I'd recommend an abortion."

I wanted to scream, "I didn't ask you what you would do! I don't want your opinion! You have no right to question me like this or speak about my baby like this."

Except I didn't.

Alone, dressed in a thin gown that was missing a tie in the back, talking to a fully dressed doctor in her examining room, I felt powerless. And I couldn't risk making her so angry that she would refuse to sign the authorization. I needed her.

At last I managed to speak. "Human life is precious to me, and I'd never want to kill an unborn baby. People would say that *I've* had a hard life because I had polio as a child, but I like my life, and I think it's worthwhile. I know there are huge risks and no guarantees with this condition, but we want to do all we can for our son." I paused. "So would you mind just signing the forms?"

Without hesitating she said, "I'll need to look them over in more detail to make sure I know what we're signing. I'll get back to you." She whipped off her reading glasses, stood, and walked out.

I struggled to contain my tears as I got dressed. What she had said about Paul, that some lives just weren't as important as others, really, had been about me too. The cruelty stung as I staggered out of the office and back to my car.

For two days I prayed Dr. Taylor would sign the papers.

On the third day I called the office and spoke with Dr. Wilson. She found the folder on Dr. Taylor's desk, unopened and unsigned. And it needed to be at the insurer within three days for the surgery to proceed.

"I am so, so sorry, Vaneetha," my doctor said. "I'll send out the forms today, before I do anything else. And you can see *me* each time you come in, okay? You won't have to see Dr. Taylor again."

I realized I had been holding my breath. "Thank you," I said. "You have no idea what this means for us."

⚜

Before we traveled to Michigan from North Carolina, my doctor scheduled a final fetal echocardiogram at Duke University Medical Center since it had the most powerful equipment. Dave went with me to the appointment and was sitting by my side holding my hand when the doctor entered.

"It's nice to meet you," she said, looking down at me. "I'm Dr. Brown. I've looked at your chart, and I'm familiar with what's going on. I'm double certified in pediatrics and cardiology."

She immediately set up the monitor, gelled the probe, and went to work, her hand guiding the cold metal back and forth across my protruding belly as she scanned Paul's body. "I can see his heart issues right now," she said, staring at the screen. "And I concur with the initial diagnosis."

Dave squeezed my hand tighter.

Then Dr. Brown's voice brightened. "I can also see he has a perfect liver and healthy kidneys." She continued to probe the rest of his body, reporting each healthy organ as she identified it.

"Why are you checking all his organs for us?" I finally asked.

She paused her scan and looked at me. "Well, you already know that your son will die without surgery. And even with surgery, he'll have a limited and probably difficult life."

Cold spread down my back. I hoped I was misunderstanding her.

"So if you don't operate at birth," she elaborated, "they can harvest these organs as soon as he passes away, which will give other children a chance to live. It's your choice, of course, but personally I think it's the most humane option."

I'm not sure what I would have said if Dave hadn't spoken first. "So you're saying we should do nothing. Just let him die and then give his organs to someone more deserving?"

"I wouldn't look at it exactly that way. But yes. I think bringing children with disabilities into the world is cruel. And you could help other children who are less disabled and could be more functional. Your son could have cognitive problems as well, which is a common comorbidity with heart babies. But it's your choice."

It's your choice. The words felt as if she was telling us, *It seems like you two aren't smart enough to make the right one.*

Once again I was exposed, vulnerable, horizontal, and half-naked on a table while a double-board-certified doctor lectured me about how it would be humane to let my child die. I'd heard that line of thinking before, and not just from Dr. Taylor and Dr. Brown. Some people assumed that certain lives were more worthy than others and that a life of suffering was automatically in the latter category. That assumption implied that nothing good could come from suffering, and that people who were less able—and who might be a drain on society—were undoubtedly less important.

Hot, angry tears blurred my vision. Dave saw my expression and took over the conversation. He knew we needed this doctor, just like we'd needed Dr. Taylor. As she finished the echocardiogram, Dave made small talk about her board certifications and hobbies. As I continued to lie on my back, she talked about her work for several minutes, during which I desperately tried to feel human again. I prayed. Tears ran from the outer corners of my eyes and into my ears.

"I don't have time for many hobbies because work is all-consuming," I heard the doctor tell Dave. "But I love my dogs. They're almost like my children."

"I like dogs too," Dave offered. "So how many children do you have?"

"Oh, I don't have any. My husband and I don't want kids. We're too busy with our careers, and besides," she confessed, "I see enough children at work."

Chapter 4

PAUL

Our daughter Katie and I arrived in Michigan two weeks before my scheduled C-section. We stayed with Dave's parents, Maxine and Jerry, who lived forty-five minutes from the hospital where the surgery would be performed. Dave planned to join us closer to the date, when his work allowed. And my parents, Dave and Suku, who lived near us in Raleigh, would fly to Michigan before the birth.

I was scheduled to deliver Paul on the morning of August 15, 1997. A team of specialized doctors was stationed in the delivery room with us, ready to evaluate Paul and to help us fight for his life.

Dave sat in a chair near my head and squeezed my hand while we waited for my epidural to completely numb me—except it never did. There was a curtain between us and the doctors, but we could hear them muttering impatiently to each other. One suggested redoing the epidural, but no one liked that plan because of the extra thirty minutes it would take. They didn't want me to have general anesthesia because it would make Paul less alert, which his doctors wanted to avoid.

The obstetrician poked my abdomen with something sharp.

"Ouch!" I said.

"You felt that?" he clarified. "Did it feel sharp, or just pressure?"

"Sharp. Definitely sharp!"

He poked me again in a slightly different spot.

"Ouch!" I said again.

"Hmm," he said, and then peeked around the curtain. "The

epidural has probably numbed you somewhat, and it's better for your baby not to get any anesthesia. This isn't ideal, but I'm going to go ahead and do this, since all these specialists are waiting."

I thought, *Go ahead and do what?* Then the unfathomable pain told me exactly what was happening: he was performing a C-section on me without full anesthesia. I started screaming, but mercifully the unbearable pain lasted only a few seconds. The moment Paul was delivered, powerful medication was pushed through my IV, and the agony disappeared.

I saw Paul for an instant—his wriggling little legs and curly black hair—before the anesthesia knocked me out and he was whisked away to the PICU (Pediatric Intensive Care Unit) for tests. I woke up in the recovery room and was soon wheeled to my own room.

"You need to rest up," a nurse told me before closing the door. "You'll see your baby soon enough."

I tried to settle into the bed. I closed my eyes, then opened them. Concentrated. But it didn't help. I still could not bring a picture of Paul's face to my mind.

⁓⧉⁓

The next afternoon nurses arrived to help me out of bed and into a wheelchair. Paul had been in the PMCU (Pediatric Moderate Care Unit) ever since the doctors finished their extensive postdelivery evaluation.

When Dave and I entered the PMCU, it felt strangely cozy. The large room featured rocking chairs, quilts, and warm lighting on an open floor, with sliding curtains separating the beds from each other for privacy. Paul rested in a plexiglass Isolette the size of a microwave oven. Electrodes and sensors connected him to a machine that beeped as it measured his oxygen saturation levels. Supplemental oxygen—warmed and humidified—arrived through a cannula taped into his tiny nose.

"Can I hold him?" I asked. I assumed the answer would be no.

"Of course you can," the nurse said, glancing at the small sign above his bed. "He's a strapping seven pounds, eleven-and-a-half ounces, and twenty inches long."

Tears welled in my eyes as Dave helped me into the rocking chair beside the Isolette. The nurse scooped Paul up and placed him in my arms. I studied his precious face, smelled his fresh baby smell, and felt the warmth of his tiny body against mine. His curly, dark hair stuck out at wild angles. When he opened his eyes and looked at me, I melted. This was the child I'd waited and prayed for.

Afraid I might pull the tube or sensors out, I held Paul rigidly for fifteen minutes, afraid to move. Then it was Dave's turn. By then Maxine and Jerry had arrived with Katie, followed closely by my parents. Paul was gently passed from arm to arm, and the whole time Katie held tight to one of his tiny hands and said, over and over, "Katie loves you, baby Paul. Katie loves you."

oeff~

The surgery wasn't scheduled until four days after Paul's birth.

"Now that you know the setup," one of the nurses told us, "you can come and see Paul anytime you want."

And so we did. Times and days blurred and drifted into each other. Dave and I stayed at a hotel attached to the hospital, and we never had to step outside. Already done with the wheelchair, I walked through a fog of sleep deprivation from hotel to PMCU and back again. I pumped milk for Paul and tried to eat. I visited with friends who surprised us by flying up from North Carolina. And I talked to Dave about Paul's future. The doctors had told us about potential genetic issues that were associated with Paul's heart condition, but we wouldn't know anything with certainty until the tests came back in several weeks.

I rarely saw Katie during this time. She was staying with Maxine and Jerry, who brought her to the hospital every day. But Katie quickly grew restless in the hospital setting, so Dave would frequently take her outside to play. My world was Paul. I sat beside him or held him, continually surprised by how perfect his body appeared on the outside while on the inside the left side of his heart was severely underformed and threatened his life.

In a normal heart the left side is responsible for pumping oxygen-rich blood into the body. But Paul's heart was unable to supply enough of that blood, a situation that would stress both his heart and his lungs and, if left untreated, would kill him. The surgery would, as one of the doctors put it, "redo some of Paul's plumbing," taking much of the workload away from the weaker left side.

"I love you, Paul," I told him as I sat by his side. In response, he simply kept breathing, and I simply watched his chest move up and down.

⚜

The day before Paul's operation, we were all on edge. The normal exhaustion of caring for a newborn was magnified by the hospital setting, by being so far from home, and by the knowledge that Paul would soon be on an operating table and might not survive the surgery.

I was at Paul's side in the PMCU when Maxine arrived to visit him. I knew several viruses were going around, so I didn't want anyone getting close to his face. When Maxine leaned forward to kiss him, I panicked. Snapped. "Don't get too close, and don't breathe on him," I demanded. "And definitely don't kiss him."

As soon as I spoke, I regretted my words. She spun to face me, and the pain on her face was obvious. Before I could attempt to explain, she turned and walked out. "I'm not going to take this anymore," she said over her shoulder. And then I was alone with Paul and a feeling of guilt.

That night in our hotel room, I told Dave about what had happened.

"Don't worry about it," he offered. "She's probably over it already. We're all under a lot of stress."

But I couldn't not worry. Maxine had looked furious. After our room-service dinner—an elegant pairing of rubbery chicken and wilted spinach—I decided to call her. I sat on the edge of the bed and dialed her number from memory.

"I didn't mean to hurt you, I promise," I told her. "I'm sorry for what I said, Mom. Will you forgive me, please?" I was pleading.

Maxine didn't say anything for a long moment. When she finally spoke, I felt a weight wrap around my shoulders as I tried to process her words. "Honestly, your words don't mean anything right now. And, no, I won't forgive you. Not now."

By the time I hung up the phone I was sobbing hysterically. I let myself fall backward on the bed, then rolled over and pounded my fists into the bedspread. *Now I won't forgive you for hurting me—and for adding more pain to my anxiety!*

When I could finally talk to Dave about it, he defended his mother.

Shock and sadness settled into the room with us. Twelve hours before Paul's surgery, Dave and I lay on the far edges of the king-size bed, trying to find sleep beneath the layers of anger and self-justification.

⸎

The next morning, right before surgery, my mom, Maxine, and I visited Paul in the PMCU, while the men took Katie to the surgical waiting room. None of us said much. Maxine and my mom held Paul briefly, and then the nurse settled him into my arms for a few minutes. I held him close, smelling him, staring at him, trying to memorize every detail. Would this be the last time I saw him alive?

Too soon the nurses lifted Paul onto a stretcher. I hugged him one last time, then watched as he was wheeled through the doors. Impulsively the three of us stood and followed the nurses into the hallway, escorting Paul to the elevator. We waited until the doors closed. Now it was out of our hands. Now our job was just to wait and trust.

We'd been told the operation would most likely take six hours but that we shouldn't worry if it took longer. We knew our surgeon, Dr. Bove, had a high success rate with this procedure, at around 80 percent. Comforting as that was, eight out of ten sounded better in the abstract. Inadvertently I pictured ten Isolettes, then shook my head and forced myself to think of something else.

We picked at food from the hospital cafeteria and tried to make small talk in the waiting room. But the effort was too great, and mostly we sat in silence. My parents took a walk outside, and Dave took Katie out to play in the grass. I walked back and forth to the chapel to pray, often passing Jerry, who was pacing the halls. Maxine mostly stayed in the waiting room, knitting something for a charity supported by her parish. From time to time we'd all find ourselves back together, but all we could manage to talk about was the weather. Maxine and I kept as far apart as possible without making our estrangement obvious to others.

At last Dr. Bove entered the room. He was a tall man, confident but not cocky. "That was a complicated surgery," he reported. "But Paul did great. The surgery could *not* have gone better."

I exhaled, feeling as though I'd been holding my breath since they wheeled Paul away. Dave and my father crossed the room and shook Dr. Bove's hand. "Fantastic news," my father said in his slight accent, his upbringing in India still coloring his speech.

"I'm so thankful," I said. "And so relieved."

My mom folded her hands and said, "Thank you, Lord." Then she looked up and said, "And thank *you*, doctor."

Maxine whispered, "I'm so glad."

Soon a nurse told us we could see Paul, two at a time. Dave and I stood to follow her. She led us to a secure room, opened it with a code, and ushered us inside. There we meticulously washed our hands and put on hospital gowns over our clothes.

When the nurse gave the okay, we entered a large room with several beds, each separated by a sliding curtain. I took one step and stopped. *Paul*. My baby lay splayed on his back at the center of a storm of machines, each blinking and beeping and humming. The smell of antiseptic hung like a fog in the cold room. Paul's entire chest was covered with bloodstained gauze, and tubes protruded from beneath the bandage as well as both wrists and both ankles. He reminded me of a tiny boat on a dangerous sea.

I shivered. If I'd had a blanket with me, I would have covered him.

A nurse approached us and said, "Hi, I'm Shannon, and I'm going to be taking care of Paul." She was calm and professional. "I'm going to be with him my entire shift, and then another nurse will take my place, so you don't need to worry about anything."

I closed my eyes, trying hard to not worry. I reminded myself that this nurse had taken care of countless babies like Paul before.

"Your son *is* doing well," she said sympathetically. "Though I'm guessing this looks a bit shocking."

Shocking was exactly the right word. I couldn't even think as I stared at my baby, alone on the bed.

"Can I touch him?" I finally asked. I couldn't understand what I was seeing, but maybe Paul's skin would understand his mother's touch.

"Not yet, but soon," the nurse said. She was genuinely sorry. "You're both welcome to stay as long as you want."

I slumped into the single plastic chair at the end of the bed. Clearly we were not supposed to get too comfortable in this room. Dave stood by my side, and we stared at Paul as he lay sleeping.

I wanted to stay until he woke, until he opened his eyes and saw me. I wanted Paul to know he was not alone. That we loved him desperately. And that we would never leave him. But he was sedated and couldn't know any of that.

As I listened to the monitors beep and the machines whir, I wondered how I would make it through the next five minutes, let alone whatever lay ahead.

Chapter 5

GOING HOME

It was a bright afternoon when we pulled onto our street in suburban Raleigh. After the surgery, Paul had been in intensive care for three days and moderate care for five days. Then all four of us had been sent home. Katie was awake in the back seat, chattering about how she was going to take care of Paul and tickle his toes. She reported that her friends in preschool were going to be very excited. Paul was starting to fuss after napping on the drive from the airport.

"Vaneetha, check it out!" Dave said. I looked where he was pointing. A giant cardboard stork perched on our front lawn, its beak holding an announcement about Paul. A large bunch of blue balloons waved in the breeze. We parked, and entered an immaculately clean house. A dozen red roses glowed on the counter. The fridge and pantry were stocked with food. A notepad on the island showed a list of dinners for the next three weeks.

Katie clapped her hands in excitement. Dave and I cried. We weren't in this alone.

In the eight days following Paul's surgery, I'd gone outside only once, and the light had nearly blinded me as I walked around, stunned. I'd almost forgotten what grass and trees looked like and what fresh air smelled like. My world had shrunk to gazing at Paul, staring at the oxygen levels on his monitors, and trying—mostly failing—to read my Bible and write in my journal.

I'd been anxious to go home, yes, but the discharge procedures had been terrifying. Dave and I had attended seminars and received pamphlets with frightening titles, such as "The Warning Signs to Watch for at Home with Your HLHS Child" and "When to Call 911." I was afraid that I wouldn't remember everything in an emergency. Paul couldn't yet nurse or even be bottle-fed, so they'd given us a stethoscope and taught us how to insert his nasal gastric (NG) tube into his nose, checking to make sure we hadn't punctured his esophagus. It was nerve-racking to do that, so I had wanted to stay at the hospital longer to gain more confidence.

I also knew I'd have to teach our nanny what I was learning. She'd been with us ever since Katie was born. She arrived each day when Dave left for work and left when he returned, ensuring there would always be someone who could lift and change Katie since my weak arms couldn't manage it. Now she would have an extra responsibility: helping care for a newborn with special needs.

"You'll be just fine," more than one nurse had assured us at the hospital.

And so we'd brought our fragile family back to Raleigh.

⁕

Those first few weeks at home were packed with adjustments as Dave and I learned to be Paul's sole caregivers. It meant digital timers in every room to make sure we remembered his medicine. It meant becoming comfortable with the tiny syringes we used to draw up countless medicines. It meant washing and sterilizing the syringes after each use and stationing them on the counter, a constant reminder of what we had to do next. The NG tube was always frightening. But with the help of a lactation consultant, Paul was nursing after two weeks, and we threw away the tube. It was a huge relief.

It seemed like Paul cried constantly the first three weeks at home, and he lost weight. The doctors and nurses had drilled into us that if his oxygen desaturated, his lungs would have to work overtime to compensate for his weaker heart. So if he was getting so upset that he gasped for breath, we needed to calm him down. "He can cry, of course," they'd said. "Just don't let him get so hysterical that he turns blue."

That had sounded easier in the hospital than it did in our bedroom at three in the morning.

Dave spent hours walking the halls with Paul, holding and rocking his tiny, bawling body. But often we couldn't calm him down. We repeatedly asked each other whether he looked like he was turning blue.

Katie spent most of her time with Paul when he was awake. She'd position his little bouncy seat in front of the television and tell him what Barney the purple dinosaur was doing. Each morning when she woke, she'd run to find me and ask how baby Paul was, and if she could hold him on her lap while she sat in the big leather chair in the corner of the living room.

We had a routine—we *had* to have a routine—but, still, Dave and I struggled to hold it together. Dave's parents asked to visit, but I refused, saying it wasn't a good time. I was still angry. Besides, Dave and I were exhausted and the tension was constantly ratcheting upward. We existed on isolated fragments of sleep between Paul's crying and his medical care.

Then, just when we thought we couldn't take it any longer, Paul started to gain weight.

He began to cry less often, and he started to smile and sometimes laugh, especially when he saw Katie. When he kicked his chubby legs in delight, his thick curls would shake. Katie would play with him for hours at a time and sing "Jesus Loves Me" when he got fussy. I'd been hesitant to order birth announcements, but now we took an adorable picture of Paul and sent it off to be printed.

Dave's parents asked again when they could come visit, and I grudgingly set a date for a few weeks later. I wasn't sure how the visit would go, but I believed Maxine and I could reconcile—or at least be civil. At six weeks old, Paul was finally strong enough to leave the house, and we even attended a neighborhood baby shower for him. Getting ready to welcome guests and visit friends in the neighborhood helped to lift my postpartum fog. I began to see that life might be good again.

Before the shower we went to our regular appointment at UNC (University of North Carolina) Medical Center for a checkup. Our normal pediatric cardiologist was out of town, so we saw a substitute. He picked Paul up, pulled him close to himself, and said, "You are a beautiful, healthy little boy, aren't you?"

Dave and I grinned and held hands. The doctor thoroughly examined Paul, and the nurse ran some tests. With the results in hand, the doctor declared, "This little guy looks amazing. He's in the seventieth percentile for weight and height, and all his vital signs are excellent. He's going to be just fine."

"Thanks so much," we told him, zipping Paul back into his fleece sleeper.

The doctor tore a few sheets from his prescription pad and handed them to us. "He is doing so well that I'm not refilling *all* of his prescriptions. He doesn't need them anymore, and I don't think it's good to overmedicate infants."

When we arrived home, Paul's birth announcements were in the mailbox. They were beautiful. Propped up in his striped mint-green sleeper, Paul looked so happy, almost as if he was laughing. We couldn't wait to send the announcements to people who hadn't met him yet.

That evening, while Dave was dressing Paul and Katie was watching him, I decided to call my cardiologist friend, Jon, and share the good news that Paul had finally turned the corner.

"He's even off some of his medication," I gushed, "because he's doing so well."

"Wait, tell me again. What exactly did they take him off of?" Jon's voice was tight and angry.

"I don't remember," I fumbled. "Let me see." I ran to get the bottles and told him what we still had and what wasn't being refilled.

"That's okay, right?" I asked. "Do you think something's wrong?"

"I don't know who this guy is," Jon said, "but he's too aggressive. Paul is too young. He can't come off those medications yet. You need to call this doctor and get that taken care of right away. What he did was so irresponsible. It's as if he doesn't understand Paul's condition."

The pit that had opened in my stomach during the call became a chasm. I looked at the clock. It was 6:05 p.m., and we were supposed to be at the shower by 6:30 p.m.

"Do we need to do this now? It's Friday night, and the office is probably closed. Do I need to go straight to the emergency room, or can I just leave a message on the office answering machine if they don't pick up?"

"You can maybe wait until Monday. But don't let this go. It's important."

"Okay. I promise."

Relieved that I didn't have to take care of the problem immediately, I hung up and dialed the doctor's office, leaving a message for the cardiologist. Meanwhile, Dave finished dressing Paul in a cozy cream-colored sleeper, and Paul and I left for the nearby shower.

When we arrived at the home of our friends Jim and Ann, their living room was already crowded. Everyone was anxious to see Paul and gathered around his carrier.

"Here's the beautiful baby we've all been praying for," a neighbor gushed. "And look how *handsome* he is."

I smiled, and Paul fell asleep.

Chapter 6

COMPLICATIONS

Two days later, very early on Monday morning—the clock by my bed said 3:00 a.m.—I woke to nurse Paul.

Dave lifted him from the bassinet beside our bed and positioned him for me to nurse lying down. I was exhausted, and Paul seemed tired as well. After several futile minutes, Dave picked Paul up to burp him, thinking maybe he had a little gas that was preventing him from nursing. I watched through half-closed eyes as Dave walked Paul around the bedroom, gently patting his back. I was so tired I'd almost fallen back asleep when I heard Paul let out a piercing scream. My eyes jerked open, and I could see that Paul was limp in Dave's arms. We stared at each other in total shock for a long moment, waiting for a sign that our baby would be okay.

But when the total silence continued—no cries, no whimpers, no movement—we were jolted into action.

I picked up the phone in our bedroom and dialed 911 while Dave held Paul to his chest. When the dispatcher answered I tried to sound coherent. "Our son, our baby, has a heart problem, and now he's gone limp. He's . . . he's not breathing." I glanced at Paul and Dave to see if anything had changed in the ten seconds I'd looked away. Nothing had. I turned my attention back to the phone and pleaded, "Please come now. Right now. Hurry! Here's our address."

I hung up and followed Dave toward the kitchen.

"Do you think we can do anything?" I asked, hoping Dave would have some ideas. But he shook his head. I needed to try something, so I suggested, "Let's put a wet washcloth on his face to maybe startle him awake." I turned on the sink, wet a cloth, and placed it on Paul's cheeks, one at a time, whispering to him, "Paul, you'll be okay. Hang on. Mommy and Daddy love you so much. Don't forget that."

I needed him to smile, open his eyes, somehow acknowledge me, but instead he lay lifeless in Dave's arms. Both of us stroked his cheeks and kissed his face. He looked strangely peaceful. Dave stood and walked slow laps around the kitchen. I followed. And we alternated between staring at Paul and looking out the window for the lights of the ambulance.

"It's going to be okay, right?" I asked.

"I hope so. He was fine last night," Dave answered. He leaned down and kissed Paul's curls. "I'm praying that this is nothing and they can figure it out at the hospital."

"This feels like forever," I said, and we both looked at the clock. It had been almost fifteen minutes. "Where's the ambulance? It shouldn't take this long."

"I was thinking the same thing," Dave said. "I wonder if they just can't find the house because it's set back from the street. I'm going to run outside to the curb so they can put him in the ambulance right away." Dave hadn't put Paul down since he'd screamed, so he was still in shorts.

"Wait. Put on some jeans and a sweatshirt at least," I said. "I'll hold Paul."

I sat down on the couch, and Dave placed Paul in my arms. As Dave ran to the bedroom, I realized I should have already called someone to come stay with Katie so we both could go to the hospital. Within a minute Dave returned, scooped Paul out of my arms, and headed for the door.

"I want to go too," I said. "I don't want to leave him."

"Call Ann. As soon as she comes over to stay with Katie, you can leave."

Both of us heard the wail of the approaching ambulance. Dave looked for his shoes but gave up when red light began to strobe through our front windows. He ran out the door barefoot, cradling Paul.

I dialed Ann, who answered immediately. "Hello?"

"It's Vaneetha. An ambulance just took Paul and Dave to the hospital . . ." My voice trailed off.

"I'm pulling my clothes on right now," she said. "I'll be right over."

I realized I needed to get dressed as well, so I went into the bedroom and put on the clothes that were draped on the bedroom chair. *Probably just a scare,* I told myself as I buttoned my jeans. *Things like this happen all the time.*

Except I couldn't forget my earlier conversation with Jon. So while I waited for Ann, I decided to call him. It was the middle of the night, but I was out of options. I wanted to know what to tell the doctors in the ER who might be unfamiliar with Paul's condition, and I needed a dose of hope, however small.

The phone rang three times before Jon's wife answered. She told me he was visiting friends and gave me their number. "I promise he won't mind if you call," she assured me. "He'd want you to."

I hung up and hesitated, wondering if it was too much of an imposition to wake Jon up at a friend's house. But, no, I desperately needed reassurance. I dialed the number, and Jon's friend immediately brought him to the phone.

He listened until I finished describing what had happened. "I was afraid of this," he said. "I'm so sorry."

I choked up and had to catch my breath before continuing. "I feel so bad I didn't take him to the ER after we talked. But what should I do now? What should I tell them at the hospital? Do I need to bring his medicine?"

"I don't know, Vaneetha. I'm just not sure what happened exactly. I'm so sorry." He sounded defeated. Hopeless.

No answers. I hung up the phone more afraid than ever. What was taking Ann so long? I decided to pray until she arrived and lowered myself onto my knees by using a nearby chair.

"Please, please, please," I begged, "just *please* save Paul."

The knock at the front door startled me. I got off my knees and walked to the front door. Ann and Jim stood on the porch. "I'm so sorry it took us this long," Ann said, stepping inside. "But we waited for Jennifer to come and watch our kids so we could both leave. Jim will take you to the hospital, Vaneetha. Katie and I will be fine here."

"I can drive myself," I said, "I just . . ." I was shaking too much to speak. Too much to drive.

Jim offered me his arm. "Let's go," he said. "I'll take you."

When we pulled onto the main road, Jim asked if we could pray. We took turns asking God to heal Paul and to give the doctors wisdom as they worked on him. I felt a spark of hope inside. And as the lights flicked past outside the car, I continued to pray, trying to kindle that hope.

Chapter 7

EMPTY

Jim dropped me off directly in front of the emergency room entrance before parking his car, and I walked as quickly as I could to the front desk. I hadn't had any contact with Dave, so I had no idea what was happening.

"My husband and our baby came by ambulance about thirty minutes ago. Do you know where they are?"

"Just a minute. Let me check for you," the woman said.

She disappeared down the hall, returning less than a minute later with a nurse in scrubs. The nurse walked around to the front of the desk where I stood. "Hi, I helped treat your son," she said softly, stretching both hands to take hold of mine. "I'm so sorry."

I stepped back in shock. *Sorry for what?* Pulling my hands from hers, I asked, "But where is Paul? Can I see him now?"

The nurse took another step toward me, this time folding her hands at her waist. "I'm so sorry," she repeated. "But your son is dead."

The words made no sense at first. They simply ricocheted around inside my head, carrying no meaning. And then something twisted inside me, suddenly, like I had been kicked in the gut. I grabbed the desk to steady myself.

I had been prepared to see Paul hooked and wired to a battalion of machines. Prepared to stay up all night, all week, keeping watch. But not for this. Never for this.

After a moment the nurse asked quietly, "Do you want to see where your husband and son are now?"

I nodded, unable to speak.

"This way," the nurse said.

We walked along a bright hallway, passing doctors and nurses in scrubs, and stopped in front of a set of double doors. The nurse opened the doors and held her hand out, inviting me to enter. I passed through another door and into an operating room: tile floor, bright overhead lights, and a single metal table.

Dave sat on the table, still barefoot, cradling Paul in his arms. He looked up and found my eyes. His were red, and tears ran down his cheeks.

I walked to the operating table, and Dave used one arm to help me up so I could sit beside him. I leaned into his body, and he lifted Paul into my lap. I couldn't stop shivering. I cradled my baby, wanting to take in every detail. His tiny, frail body, his familiar baby smell, his face crowned with a shock of dark, curly hair. He looked almost serene. He wasn't even two months old.

The nurse left us alone with Paul. I had questions about Paul's final minutes but knew I wouldn't be able to absorb the answers just then. There was no reason to speak in that sacred moment. Time simply stopped as Dave and I held each other and Paul—a still life of loss.

Eventually the nurse tapped on the door and cracked it open. "Take as long as you want in here," she said. "The doctor said we don't need an autopsy."

By then we didn't want . . . anything. We were numb. Uncomprehending. We signed some papers we didn't read and made our unsteady way to the lobby. We found Jim, and he walked us to his car.

On the way home I glanced at the time: 5:51 a.m. My body was ready to nurse Paul again. We'd been feeding him every three hours, like clockwork. Now? I had no idea. I shook my head and stared out the window.

We walked into the same house, but it felt like it belonged to a stranger. Every familiar object seemed foreign, as if I were seeing it for the first time, detached from whatever my previous life had been.

Jim pulled Ann aside and talked to her quietly. Then she ran over to me and hugged me as we both cried, holding tightly to each other. There were no words. When we pulled apart, she took Jim's hand and they stepped out the front door, closing it quietly behind them.

I looked at the entry, the living room, the kitchen. Paul's things were everywhere. On the counter were the small syringes for dosing his medicines. The living room floor was littered with toys and blankets, and his bouncy seat rested near the television. Two piles of gifts from the shower were stacked in the corner. On the kitchen counter, one hundred birth announcements sat untouched in a cardboard box.

Katie was still asleep. What would I tell her when she woke?

I asked Dave what had happened in the ambulance and at the hospital.

"They just kept trying to get him to breathe again," he said, standing with his head down and shoulders slumped. "But he never did. They kept trying and trying."

Dave combed his fingers through his hair as I stared at the back of his head.

"They kept trying," he said again, "and I hoped they could do more at the hospital. All I could do was pray."

His arms went slack at his sides, and then he walked toward the bedroom.

Alone, I dragged the kitchen chair out from the table and sat. I'd been on my knees in front of this chair just hours earlier, begging God to save Paul.

God hadn't. Paul was dead.

I remembered a neighborhood gathering I'd gone to when Katie was an infant. A woman named Shirley, who had lost her daughter to cancer years before, had shared her story. We'd all sat spellbound as Shirley described what it was like to say goodbye to her young child. She shared a list of dos and don'ts for grieving parents, and I'd written them down to help me become a better friend. Now they kept running through my mind.

> *Don't* wash the deceased child's clothes without permission,
> since parents may want to smell the last thing their
> child wore.
> *Do* go to the funeral.
> *Don't* offer trite sayings, like "Heaven needed another angel" or
> "This is all for the best."
> *Do* send cards or letters, even weeks or months later.
> *Don't* box or get rid of any of the child's belongings without
> asking the parents.
> *Do* mention the child's name whenever you can. ("I promise
> it won't upset the parent," Shirley had said. "Believe me,
> they're thinking of their child all the time anyway. And it
> helps to know other people haven't forgotten either.")

When I arrived home after Shirley's talk, I'd gone straight to the nursery and knelt beside Katie's crib. As I watched her sleep, staring at the rise and fall of her chest, making my own breathing match hers, I felt my heart fill with gratitude. Life had thrown some hard things my way, but never anything like Shirley had experienced.

Thank you for not asking me to bury a child, I'd prayed while watching Katie. *You know I could never handle it.*

I was about to test the truth of that statement.

I pushed myself to my feet and crossed to the kitchen counter. Four different sizes of syringes sat prepped for Paul's use, each beside its corresponding bottle of medicine. One was so small that it held only one milliliter. Dave and I had designed a reliable system for Paul's care so that no matter how tired we were, he never missed a feeding or a dose of medicine.

I stared at the syringes. Then I found a large Ziploc bag and placed each syringe into the bag—one at a time, carefully, in ascending order of size—and stuffed it into a kitchen drawer. I didn't know what would happen in the next hour or the next day, but somehow I knew I needed to protect Paul's syringes so that no one threw them away.

I looked outside. It was still dark. I considered crawling back into bed beside Dave. I thought maybe I might wake up and discover it had all been an awful dream.

But when I walked into the bedroom, I saw Paul's bassinet. It was the last place he'd slept. It was the room where I'd spent what felt like countless nights holding him, nursing him, patting his back, and praying he would stop crying and fall asleep, and that his oxygen levels would stay constant. Just two nights earlier I'd fantasized about sleeping through the night. I'd felt like one night of uninterrupted sleep would reset me to normal.

Instead of getting into bed, I wandered aimlessly through the silent house. When the sky began to lighten, I sat at the kitchen table and stared outside.

I saw Katie the second she skipped out of her room and into the hall. "What are you doing, Mommy?" she asked as she entered the kitchen, holding her teddy bear's paw in one hand and swinging it. I was usually nursing Paul when she got up, and he was always happy to see her.

Katie knuckled her eyes and pushed her long hair away from her face. "Where is baby Paul?"

The dark and silent minutes had provided no answer. I paused. I wasn't sure how to tell her what had happened. "Baby Paul's not with us anymore, Katie," I blurted. "Jesus came and took him last night."

"Oh," Katie said, her head tipping to one side. "But when can I see baby Paul again?"

I beckoned to Katie, then struggled to pull her onto my lap to settle her as I considered my answer. "Oh, sweetheart, you can't see Paul again. Paul died. We've talked about death before, but it's hard to understand."

No one had told me what to do in this situation. Nothing I said would be helpful to a two-and-a-half-year-old. But I had to say something, even if it was something I didn't understand myself. I felt Katie shifting in my lap, trying to look up at me.

"Jesus took Paul to heaven," I said, "and we can't see him again until we go to heaven."

Katie understood. She screamed and wriggled out of my grip and back to the floor. Standing, she faced me and demanded answers. "Why didn't Jesus come to my room and let me say goodbye to Paul?" she asked in a high voice. "Why didn't you tell him to knock on my door before he took him?" She was stamping her foot with every question and crying in earnest.

Her questions felt like accusations. Maybe they were.

I leaned toward my baby girl. "I'm so sorry, Katie," I sobbed, pulling her into a hug that I desperately hoped might communicate what my words hadn't, couldn't. "I'm so, *so* sorry."

Where did this fit on my list of the dos and don'ts of grieving? My only certainty was that I was doing it wrong—and that I didn't know how to do it any other way.

Katie let me hug her.

And then I watched as she retreated to her room to play with her dolls.

Chapter 8

SAYING GOODBYE

I called my parents and my sister, Shalini. Dave called Maxine and Jerry.

Since my parents lived nearby, they asked when they could drive over. I told them to come anytime but not to expect me to be good company. Shalini hung up so she could race to the airport and grab the next flight from Toronto to Raleigh. Maxine and Jerry booked a flight and a hotel. It was the first time they wouldn't be staying with us. We hadn't had a real conversation since we'd left Michigan.

Jim and Ann had told our network of friends, and the first call came just after seven that morning, as the sun was rising. Then came another and another and another and another. I let the answering machine handle each one until the pediatric cardiologist's office called and I heard, "We got your message on Friday that you were concerned about your son's medication. We weren't sure from the message what exactly the problem was, and we wanted more information for the doctor. So if you could please call us at . . ."

I grabbed the phone and answered. "Yes, I called Friday, but my son, Paul, died this morning. I'm not sure what happened, what medicine he needed . . ."

My voice faltered, and the woman abruptly said, "Oh, okay. I'll let them know," and hung up. I expected her to sound sad or surprised or at least say, "I'm so sorry," but I didn't even get that.

Ann returned around nine, and by midmorning people began to

stop by. Ann spent the day in the background, taking food, assigning jobs, and sharing what had happened so we wouldn't need to relive it. She made conversation when I initiated it but otherwise said very little. I loved knowing that she was there.

When my friend Patti arrived, I felt a strange wave of relief. Her husband had died a few years earlier, and I'd seen her laugh since then—full-body, head-back, tear-inducing *laughter*. I hoped maybe I could laugh again too. Paul's lactation consultant brought a fragrant camellia bush that would bloom each year in October. Our pastor offered to go with us to the funeral home and help us make the unfamiliar decisions.

Throughout the day food arrived. Casserole dishes and Tupperware containers full of soup and cold cuts and salads and sliced fresh fruit. Ann labeled each dish with a Sharpie on masking tape and stored them away in the appropriate place.

I was grateful I wouldn't have to think about food, but I was unable to eat.

I was grateful for the presence of our friends, but I didn't know what to say or how to act.

I was grateful that Patti said I would survive this, but I had no idea how.

My body felt like it belonged to a stranger.

And that day, that night, the next day and night, every minute I managed to sleep was a nightmare, and every moment spent awake was worse.

⚜

"I'm sorry for your loss."

Those were the first words we heard from the funeral director. And we would hear them over and over again as we did things no parents should ever have to do.

Schedule a wake.

Plan a funeral service.

Find a cemetery and a plot.

Write an obituary.

Choose a newborn-sized casket.

I couldn't imagine being physically separated from Paul by the wood, the dirt, the grass. Being kept from the precious baby I'd nursed and held and prayed for seemed impossible.

The funeral director walked us through everything. We decided on an open casket for Paul since most people who would be attending had never met him.

The night of the wake—the third night after Paul had screamed—the funeral home parlor was lit by crystal lamps and sconces and decorated with antique knickknacks and oil paintings. The oriental rugs soaked up the light and sound.

The room was warm when Dave and I approached the tiny white casket an hour before the mourners were scheduled to arrive. Katie was at home with a babysitter.

When I saw Paul, I clutched Dave's arm.

Dave gasped.

"I know," I managed. "It doesn't even look like him."

Paul's hair had been parted and styled flat, following the contours of his skull. I had never seen him look that way. Dave's body deflated at the sight, and he walked away from the casket. I followed. There was nothing we could do.

Just before the mourners arrived, the funeral director stationed Dave and me at the front of the room. From the corner of my eye I could see the white of Paul's casket off to the left. I walked over to look at him again. My hand went to my mouth—his hair! We would learn later that our nanny had arrived early to say goodbye to Paul. She immediately noticed his slicked-down hair and asked the funeral director if she could restyle it. She then spent thirty minutes removing the product from his thick black locks and teasing them back into vibrant curls.

Our son looked so peaceful now as he lay with his stuffed doggie on his chest. My eyes traced his long eyelashes, and the pale skin of his cheeks, his nose, and his tiny mouth made him resemble a beautiful china doll.

Then it was time. We stood at the front of the funeral home parlor for two hours. Friends and family filed in, forming a line that stretched through the building and out onto the front steps. Each mourner passed a table covered with pictures of Paul before they reached us. We appreciated everyone who took the time to show up, but some were easier to appreciate than others.

"I'm sorry," a friend would say, and we'd hug each other tight.

"He was so . . . *is* so beautiful," another friend would say, and Dave and I would almost dare to smile.

But others chose to offer advice or theological reflections.

"This is probably for the best. His life would have been hard anyway."

"Don't forget Romans 8:28."

"God is going to use this, and you'll be grateful."

"I guess heaven needed another angel."

I couldn't imagine that God would kill babies because heaven was underpopulated, and I didn't believe people would become angels in heaven anyway. But I kept my opinion to myself.

After it was over and we were home, Dave and I collapsed into bed. I hadn't stood for that long, ever. My legs and back flared with pain. In some ways our grief had increased as we'd been forced to relive and question our most painful moments. Should we have gone to the ER on Friday night? Could we have done anything different, anything sooner?

And worse: How would we talk to Katie? A grief counselor had recommended we leave her at home for both the wake and the funeral. She was simply too young to understand, but she wasn't too young to question or act out or be permanently hurt.

That felt true for me as well. But with the funeral the next day, I needed to look and act—and be—strong.

⁘

The next morning every chair in our church was filled. People stood along the walls and in the back.

I'd put Paul's birth announcements on the table outside the sanctuary because I wasn't sure what else to do with them. Dave and I had chosen our favorite music. Jerry read Scripture and my dad prayed. When he ended with the line, "See you in heaven, Paul," I could hear people crying.

Dave and I both spoke. We told of how much we loved Paul, how convinced we were that God was using his life, and how thankful we were for God's faithfulness. We reiterated our conviction that God never makes a mistake. We both felt the need to reassure people that God was still good and that we were not falling apart.

Immediately after the service, the funeral director ushered Dave and me down the center aisle and out through the front doors toward the waiting hearse. Autumn sunlight filtered through the trees that lined the road, and white-and-gray clouds drifted across a deep blue sky. How could such a perfect day coincide with Paul's funeral? Or maybe it was better that way—better than laying him to rest in damp and cold darkness.

While we waited for the pallbearers to load the casket into the hearse, I heard a familiar voice call out behind me, "Van, wait a second!"

I turned and saw Maxine and Jerry. Before the service I'd seen Dave talking to them, but I'd only waved from a distance. Now

Maxine was hurrying toward me, and without waiting for me to say anything, she reached out and pulled me into a hug. I returned it immediately, automatically, as if my body and maybe my heart had already been expecting it. When we pulled apart, she was smiling.

"I'm so sorry, honey," she said. "I was under a lot of stress. I'm sorry for everything."

"I'm so sorry too," I said. "I'm sorry I hurt you and was thoughtless, and that I didn't let you visit earlier. I'm glad you're here now."

And then we held on to each other, family again, until the pallbearers arrived and more people began to spill from the church. Once the casket was loaded, Dave and I climbed into the limo, which was parked behind the hearse. As we talked about my reconciliation with Maxine, I immediately regretted not having let them come earlier—my bitterness had prevented them from being able to hold their grandson again.

The drive to the gravesite felt longer than I'd expected as our snaking line of vehicles with headlights on crawled through town. We passed people out walking their dogs, stores that were opening up for the day, the crowded parking lot of a nearby urgent care facility. All these things were familiar yet strangely foreign. I caught myself wondering if we were creating a traffic jam behind us.

At last we reached the countryside. We'd chosen the cemetery because it was peaceful and out of the way. A massive willow tree shaded the children's section, which overlooked a pond. At the gravesite, Dave and I were seated under a canopy. Jerry and Maxine sat to our left, and beside them sat my parents and Shalini.

I heard our pastor's words. I heard them the same way I heard the sound of the water feature at the center of the pond or the branches of the willow rustling. I heard everything—every sniffle, every polite cough, every "amen"—as background noise. Because the only thing I could do was stare at Paul's coffin.

When the service ended, Dave took my hand and we walked to

stand in front of the coffin. I was glad they were not lowering it into the grave while we were there. Seeing Paul go into the ground would have been too much to take in. I knew he wasn't really there—that he was in heaven with Jesus—but I didn't want to leave the casket.

White roses covered the top, and several had cascaded into the grave. Dave took one, and hand in hand we walked back to our car.

Then it was done.

Chapter 9

AFTERMATH

After the graveside service our families and some close friends came with us back to the house. Our fridge was overflowing with food—the entire kitchen table was covered with containers and plates—and we stayed with each other for hours and hours. Nobody knew what to say, but everyone there had loved Paul and still loved us. Whatever words emerged took on a sort of holiness, and slowly processing the previous week was cathartic. Friendships felt deeper, family felt tighter, and God seemed present in every conversation and every hug.

When everyone eventually left, though, the house became eerily quiet. We'd put Katie down for the night already, and Dave distracted himself with work. I knew I should go to bed, but I couldn't. I drifted from room to room, unsure of what to do. The hospital had told us what to do if Paul cried too long. They'd taught us how to insert a breathing tube into his tiny nostrils, how to dose and deliver syringes full of medicine.

But this? I felt devoid—of purpose, of thought, and even of feeling.

ఇ

All too soon, the fabric of support and love we'd felt at Paul's funeral began to unravel. It started with the piles of gifts I'd opened at Paul's baby shower. *Can I return these? Should I?*

The familiar feeling of obligation began to creep into me. One by one I reopened the boxes and made a list of thank-you notes to write. I forced myself to write at least one card a day. In neat ink I told friends and coworkers and neighbors that we were doing okay. I thanked them for their support and promised them we would save their lovely gifts and find a use for them.

The task occupied my body, but my mind began to darken. Each time I added a verse to the bottom of a note or composed a new way of communicating how well we were doing, something dimmed inside me. The truth was that *I* didn't even know how I was doing.

At the funeral days earlier, in the company of our whole congregation, and at home afterward, surrounded by the loving presence of family and friends, I *had* been doing well—or at least I had been busy enough to make that assumption possible. Everyone had said the right things, including me. But on the blank page of my thank-you notes, the truth was messier.

I presented the calm exterior of someone who could praise God through the worst situation. That was what faithful Christians did. And I was a faithful Christian, wasn't I? My faith seemed to fade, card by card, replaced by a sense of numbness.

"By God's grace we are doing well," I wrote.

Meanwhile I thought, *Where is God, and who have I become? How can I trust a God who just let my son die?*

⁂

I kept trying to call our pediatric cardiologist's office to talk to someone about Paul's death. I wanted to understand what had gone wrong, and I wanted to hear them say they were sorry about what had happened. I needed closure. I couldn't remember the substitute doctor's name, however, so I was forced to leave messages with the nurses.

Each time I'd tell them who I was, who Paul was, what had happened, and that I'd like to hear from the doctor, *any* doctor, at the practice.

Each time I was promised a call back. But it never came.

I fought against bitterness and anger. Part of me knew they were protecting themselves from a lawsuit, and for good reason. Dave and I thought we'd have a good chance of winning. We talked about it and prayed for wisdom.

Suing for malpractice might get an incompetent or grossly negligent doctor off the street. But strangely, we felt that particular doctor was neither; we all make mistakes, even doctors. And we knew a lawsuit could fuel further bitterness, forcing us to relive all that had happened while doing nothing to bring back our baby. We certainly understood why other people chose to sue in similar situations, but we decided it wouldn't be the right decision for us. We wanted to be in the healthiest emotional place we could be, especially for Katie, who was grieving in her own way.

One week after Paul died, I loaded Katie into our minivan and drove her back to preschool. I wanted her to return to something familiar. Her teacher had already told the other parents about Paul's death to spare me from having to explain it. When we arrived I unbuckled Katie from her car seat and took her hand as we walked through the front door. A mom from Katie's class was leaving just as we entered, but she looked at the floor and didn't speak as she walked past. That stung. But I kept walking, hoping I'd see a friendly face.

The teacher usually greeted the arriving families at the classroom door. Today, however, she was inside the classroom pinning something to the bulletin board. When she saw us, she waved and called, "Katie, come on in." Then she immediately turned back to her project.

Katie ran into the classroom and began to play with her friends while I lingered in the doorway. Was the teacher really not going to ask me anything—or even acknowledge Paul's death? But I couldn't try to attract sympathy. What was I supposed to do, limp to her side and wait for her to offer condolences?

I watched the teacher's work become busywork as she fidgeted with rehanging an art project for the third time. Finally I turned and left, just as another mother approached the classroom with her little boy. Our eyes met briefly, and then she dropped her gaze and walked past without a word.

Outside I felt a cool October breeze tickle my face as I walked to the minivan. The moment I climbed in and closed the door, I slumped forward and cried. Did anyone care? No, it wasn't that. I had my own network of people who truly cared for me, like Shalini and Jennifer and Ann. I didn't need Katie's preschool staff to take care of me, I needed them to *acknowledge* me. One word even. Or one kind touch on the shoulder that communicated, "We see you. We're sorry. And we know that your life has been forever changed."

But Katie's preschool wasn't an aberration. A neighbor pretended not to see me as I walked toward her in the canned-soup aisle of the grocery store. She turned her back and walked away quickly. We hadn't made actual eye contact, so it was possible she truly hadn't seen me—except that the same scene repeated itself nearly every time I ran errands around town. People probably hoped I hadn't seen them, but I always did, and it always hurt.

Perhaps worse, however, were those who did acknowledge me, but without acknowledging what had actually happened. In my better moments I could assign good motives to those who ignored me. *She probably doesn't know what to say, and she doesn't want to make things worse.* Some people truly seemed unaware that they were making things worse.

Two weeks after Paul died, I attended a Pampered Chef party, hoping to take my mind off my grief for a few hours. It worked, but imperfectly. Part of me felt guilty that I was trying to do something fun instead of mourning Paul. As I considered buying a cute sandwich cutter, a woman beside me tried to start a conversation.

"How many children do you have?"

"Two," I said without thinking, which led to a lengthy and uncomfortable talk about Paul.

When the woman politely moved on to a different area of the party, I found the guest bathroom and took stock of myself. There was no way I could repeat that conversation, which had brought up emotions I wasn't ready to deal with. I was supposed to be forgetting about my emotions at the party, not delving deeper into them with strangers. Except how could I forget Paul or my grief?

Back at the party, another woman asked how many kids I had. "One," I said. And then I immediately excused myself and left the party. I realized I would have to respond to that question for the rest of my life, and there was no right answer. I couldn't deny Paul's existence, yet I couldn't keep explaining his death at every social gathering.

Before Paul was born I'd been working part-time as a marketing consultant, and I'd been partway through a major project. Heading back to the office for the first time since Paul's death, I stepped off the elevator and almost bumped into a coworker waiting to go down. He paused, acknowledging me and looking me in the eye. Then he said, "Hey, it's good to see you. I'm glad you're here, back at work. I'm glad you're over this."

I looked at the carpet and counted the seconds until I heard the elevator door shut behind me. *Over this.* What did that even mean? I walked into my office and gathered some papers, organizing them into folders. After a few minutes my manager, Jeff, stuck his head in the door. "It's good to have you back. I'm so sorry for your loss. We were all so upset when we heard."

There, is that so hard? I was thankful he cared. His simple words acknowledged what had happened. I was about to thank him when he added, "Every time my wife and I have put a dog down, it's been really hard. When we'd walk back into the house, it felt empty. But after a few weeks it always got better. So I know it'll get better for you."

I forced myself to nod and say, "Thanks, Jeff," as I looked away and went back to sorting papers. I knew no one was *trying* to hurt me, but knowing that didn't lessen the pain. Back home, in the silence of our house, I found myself reliving these moments in my head more often than I wanted to—more often than was probably healthy.

⟡

I was fortunate to have close female friends who continued to walk with me. When I was tempted to detach, to pull back into a shell of private grief, these women were there to pray and cry and sometimes even laugh with me.

My neighbors Jennifer and Lisa were especially helpful during this time. I went regularly to Jennifer's to meet with them. Jennifer would put a pot of tea at the center of the table, and Lisa would prompt, "Tell us what's going on with you. How are you doing?" When I looked uncertain, she'd often say, "Maybe that's too broad a question to answer. I mean how are you doing *today*?" There was no judgment, no pressure to say the right things, and I appreciated the specificity of *today*. I had no idea how I was really doing in general, but I knew about today. And comfortingly, Jennifer and Lisa also shared their own problems with me. It was a relief to have a social situation that wasn't focused entirely on Paul.

One day a new friend, Christa, who went to our church, brought me a meal, which led to a deep conversation about Paul and how I was processing his death. She came over frequently after that, and her visits sometimes lasted for hours.

But there was a solitary part of my grief that longed for written words over those spoken. Every day I'd walk out to the mailbox and carry back stacks of cards and letters about Paul. I appreciated the wonderful cards, but I learned to love the letters most. I always opened them alone, when I had time to savor the words, however painful they sometimes were to read. If someone took the time to write a letter, it usually meant they would be including memories of Paul or telling how his life had touched theirs in some way, even if they'd never met him.

My friend Patti, who had lost her husband years earlier, wrote a letter that I read so many times I nearly memorized it. My fingers would rub the soft corner of the paper as I willed her words to burn their way into my heart.

I want to tell you how much little Paul's life affected me and how much your faith in God's goodness has inspired me.

I did not want to wrestle again with my faith in this God who was supposed to love us as his children. But until you and Dave walked into the sanctuary, I was wrestling. Then, when you and your family came in and we all stood and began to sing, all that changed.

By the time you walked up to the front and talked about the verse in John 9 where Jesus tells the disciples this happened so that the work of God might be displayed, the hope of eternity and the anchor-weight strength of your trust in God had taken over the room. Although there were tears, they were not tears of anguish and despair—they were tears of hope and thanksgiving for the little one who had brightened our lives if only for a moment.

Patti wasn't entirely right—or perhaps she was only right about that moment. The tears at Paul's funeral *were* tears of hope and thanksgiving. But that was not true of every tear I'd shed since. I read her words again and again, longing to return to that certainty.

We cut out the announcement about Paul David (I hate the "O" word) that was in the newspaper, and we still have it on our refrigerator. Paul's hands and face seem to have been captured in the act of expressing his joy. It reminds me of the joy that awaits us and of the great reunion that is coming. I will keep Paul's picture up for a very long time, and I will not forget him.

As remembrances arrived and I sorted them into growing piles on the kitchen counter, I decided to make a scrapbook about Paul—a place for letters like Patti's and for any other threads of hope that might someday be stitched into something bigger. I spent weeks gathering and organizing pictures, the funeral program, Paul's obituary, and the letters and cards that had touched me. I made trip after trip to Michaels, the nearest craft store, walking up and down the aisles looking for the right paper and embellishments.

I knew I had every picture of Paul that I ever would, so I planned the book around them. I organized the pictures by location: the hospital in Michigan, the baby shower, and our home. Then each night, when Katie was asleep, I stationed myself at the dining-room table and worked. While Dave played solitaire on the computer, I cropped pictures, glued backing on them, and affixed them to acid-free paper. I wrote comments about Paul underneath each.

Every page had a theme and was decorated to match. One page was labeled "Cute as a button" and had pictures of Paul laughing, with buttons arranged in an abstract design around the pictures.

I included the letters too. Somehow opening a box and unfolding letters seemed more painful, and more of a commitment, than glancing through pages of a book. So I photocopied each letter, shrank it down, and affixed it to the pages of the scrapbook.

The book, with each page an elaborate work of art, took over two months to complete. This instrumental grieving, processing loss through a physical outlet, didn't just stop with Paul's scrapbook. A friend took me to a paint-your-own-pottery studio where I painted a bowl in Paul's honor. I kept going back, eventually ending up with a painted set of dishes. My last piece was a "You Are Special" plate that I hoped would help us celebrate birthdays, special events, and even everyday triumphs.

"I love it," Dave told me when I gave it to him, as he turned the plate around and around in his hands. "I think it might help us heal."

⚜

Soon afterward, the cemetery called to tell me Paul's marker had come in. I barely remembered picking it from a catalog at the funeral home. At the time I had been so engulfed in grief that it seemed like just another necessary detail. Dave and I drove to the cemetery, and when we arrived at the marker I was startled by how small and insignificant it looked: nothing more than Paul's name, along with our names, etched into a plain little stone.

Looking to the left and right of Paul's tiny plot, I saw beautiful tributes on marble markers and vases filled with flowers. Why hadn't I paid more attention or visited cemeteries before choosing? I felt certain that those who saw Paul's marker would assume we didn't care. I sobbed as we left, unsure why I cared so much about what strangers might think—but I did.

Back at home I got out my watercolors to help me process. As I swirled my brush across the paper, I tried to focus on the great reunion that was coming, when none of this would matter. Right now it was hard to believe, but I thought maybe I could take it one slow step at a time.

Chapter 10

EXPERIENCING GOD

Inevitably the mailbox emptied.

Not completely. There were still the usual notices and bills and credit-card offers. But the box was empty of cards and letters about Paul. It seemed that everyone had gone back to their normal lives. Somehow the empty mailbox symbolized what I feared most: that *we* were expected to go back to our normal lives as well.

But of course that whole idea was meaningless. I could never go back to the way things were. My new normal was that I'd buried my baby son.

When Paul died, I wanted to honor God in my response. I prayed that God would use Paul's life to bring people to faith. And in the immediate aftermath of his death, God had felt close, ever present, as if he was walking beside me through the day. Sometimes it even felt like I was being carried.

That season of faith had been a flare that faded all too soon. Even as the daily routines of life began to return, the only routine of my spiritual life was a daily litany of doubts and questions. Alone with the quiet at my kitchen table—Katie at preschool, Dave at work, the house straightened, and dinner already prepped—I would stare at nothing, remembering again and again that I had begged God to save Paul's life, and God hadn't.

Why?

Why had God let us travel to Michigan for Paul's birth and

successful surgery only to let him die? Why had God not saved Paul even after I begged him? Why had God let me feel so much *hope* if all along he was going to crush it?

My Bible sat opened and ignored on the table.

I had been so concerned about other people's faith that I hadn't paid attention to my own. Whenever I went out and saw parents with babies, I asked myself if God loved them more than he loved me. I was embarrassed that I had proclaimed God's faithfulness in front of everyone at the time of Paul's death and now felt . . . nothing. Indifference was easier than the pain of trying to trust. God felt like a stranger behind a double-locked door.

I had thought my faith in God would shield me from pain. But now I understood that anything could happen to me or anyone I loved at any time. No one was safe.

I wrote sporadically in my journal:

> I asked God to use his life
> and he did
> at the funeral.
> Did Paul die to help other people?
> Is he more of a principle
> than a person?

Many days I would just sit at the kitchen table and stare off into space until Katie needed something, which would jolt me back into reality.

Katie's constant questions also added to my doubts. "Is Jesus bringing baby Paul back soon? Why did he take him anyway?"

Dave and I tried to answer her, but after dozens of times we gave up. No explanation stuck with her—probably because there wasn't an explanation that stuck with us.

One afternoon I decided to take a drive. Katie was with our nanny and would be fine without me. All I'd been doing was sitting at the kitchen table, restless and unhappy, unsure of what to do with myself. So I thought I would just go out and do something. Anything.

It was almost a mistake. As I pulled onto the main road, still driving aimlessly, I realized I'd lost any desire to live. I was empty. Depressed. Life felt pointless. I considered accelerating and then crashing into a power pole, not caring whether I lived or died. The muscles of my right leg tensed, but then . . . *No. I have to stay alive for my family.*

I continued driving at the speed limit and turned off the radio. I had felt distant from God for so long I'd forgotten how to talk to him. Something had to change. But I didn't know what or how. I hesitated, unsure about what to say, so I just blurted out what I was thinking.

"Jesus, I don't understand why Paul died," I said out loud. "But I need you right now. I can't live like this anymore. I can't. I want to feel your presence again and know that you love me."

Nothing happened. I drove randomly for several minutes until the silence became uncomfortable. *Maybe it's time to go back to the kitchen table.* I popped in a random cassette tape and turned the volume up. The tape featured a worship band, and as the music flooded the minivan, I started to sing. Soon I was singing at the top of my lungs. Something inside me *needed* to sing, to praise God, almost as if I couldn't stop the words from flowing out of me.

Then—suddenly, in the middle of a chorus—something happened. Inexplicable joy arrived or bubbled up or was unleashed. I turned off the music, and into the sudden silence, I laughed.

I laughed! A laugh that began somewhere close to the core of my being. A laugh that went on and on, a laugh that brought such tears that I had trouble seeing the road, a laugh that began to cramp my stomach. Every emotion I'd ever experienced—*every* emotion—seemed black-and-white compared to this explosion of color.

The realizations came one after another, like familiar friends pulling me into an embrace.

Jesus is feeding me.
God's promises are true.
God will never leave me and will walk with me through everything.

Then my eyes widened.

God has never left me.

That was the purest moment I had ever lived. God's presence surrounded me. I kept driving as the joy made its way through my body to my toes, my fingers, almost reaching the tips of my hair.

My hair! I suddenly thought. *I need to get a haircut if I'm going to be out in public again!*

The laughter rolled back. I was thinking about something ordinary! I knew how to get a haircut, and I would. And then I would figure out what to do next, knowing that whatever happened, God would be there with me.

☙

God's presence was a feast, and I was a famished soldier returned from an exhausting campaign. I couldn't stop reading the Bible or asking God to fill me with his Spirit and presence.

I still cried every day, but instead of crying into a void, I was crying to God, holding nothing back. I wrote furiously in my journal, asking God questions and telling him how angry and hurt I was. But every sentence, every tear, drew me toward God and not away. My silence since Paul's death had raised walls, and now it felt as if every word was helping to tear them down.

It wasn't the first time I had truly encountered God. My hunger for the Bible reminded me of the night in high school when I had whispered, "God, I don't know if you exist. But if you are real, please show me." When nothing happened I'd rolled over and gone to sleep, sure that God wasn't real after all.

The next day I woke up earlier than usual and remembered my prayer from the night before. I said it again just to be sure. Then I opened my nightstand drawer and pulled out a Bible I'd been given years earlier. I didn't understand why other people read this book when it didn't make any sense. I asked out loud, "So why did all this happen to me anyway, God? If you are so loving, why did I get polio? Why have I had to struggle all my life? How could you possibly be good?" I began flipping through the Bible, wondering if my words had been heard as I aimlessly read random verses from the Old Testament.

I skipped ahead, and the Bible opened to John 9. I read, "As he went along, he saw a man blind from birth. His disciples asked him, 'Rabbi, who sinned, this man or his parents, that he was born blind?'" (vv. 1–2 NIV).

Finally, something relevant. I understood that question because it was similar to my own. I wanted to know whose fault it was that I got polio. So I kept reading.

"'Neither this man nor his parents sinned,' said Jesus, 'but this happened so that the works of God might be displayed in him" (v. 3 NIV).

I read the words again and wondered what it meant to have the works of God displayed in someone's life. Could God use my life and disability for something good? Was God telling me that my polio had a purpose? That it wasn't senseless or random? As I rolled these thoughts around in my head, something changed inside me.

I smoothed out the pages of the Bible and wondered what had

happened. It was almost as if the Bible had previously been written in a foreign language, one I couldn't understand without a translator, but now it was written in everyday English. The words made sense for the first time.

As the sun streamed into my window, I knelt by the side of my bed and committed my life to a God whom I didn't know but was certain knew me. I believed he had created me for a purpose, and I wanted to understand it.

Now, seventeen years later, I felt that same sense of commitment and presence. I was pulled toward the Psalms. Lament became the language of my love for God. I no longer avoided God because of my pain but offered my pain to him, and I discovered he was already there, waiting and listening.

> Be gracious to me, O LORD, for I am languishing;
>> heal me, O LORD, for my bones are troubled.
> My soul also is greatly troubled.
>> But you, O LORD—how long?
>
> . . .
>
> I am weary with my moaning;
>> every night I flood my bed with tears;
>> I drench my couch with my weeping. (Ps. 6:2–3, 6)

I could *pray* this! I was already living it—the languishing, the trouble, the weariness, the tears—and now I could be honest with God about how I was feeling. I didn't need to pretend I was in the mood to be thankful. God didn't need my empty words; he wanted my real emotions.

As I said these raw words, I felt a newfound freedom to be authentic with God. Every day I discovered pain on the pages of my Bible, and every day I offered it back to God. I yelled it, whispered it, cried it through tears.

Why, O Lord, do you stand far away?
>   Why do you hide yourself in times of trouble? (Ps. 10:1)

I say to God, my rock:
>   "Why have you forgotten me?
Why do I go mourning
>   because of the oppression of the enemy?" (Ps. 42:9)

My soul is bereft of peace;
>   I have forgotten what happiness is. (Lam. 3:17)

Save me, O God!
>   For the waters have come up to my neck.
I sink in deep mire,
>   where there is no foothold;
I have come into deep waters,
>   and the flood sweeps over me. (Ps. 69:1–2)

I no longer felt I needed to push my pain down or only focus on the good things when I talked to God. He opened my eyes as I read the Psalms, and I realized that he wasn't waiting for the pain to disappear. No, he was already inside it. Pain and lament were not opposed to praise—after voicing my lament, praise naturally followed. It happened to the psalmists. And it happened to me.

Why are you cast down, O my soul,
>   and why are you in turmoil within me?
Hope in God; for I shall again praise him,
>   my salvation and my God. (Ps. 42:5–6)

These scriptures of lament and praise became balms, promises, whispers of hope.

A friend from church gave me a cassette tape about suffering. I could have piled all the grief theology books I'd been given into a ten-foot stack, but I hadn't been able to get into any of them. They were too impersonal, too abstract, too prescriptive. I couldn't take any more *theories* about grief. I needed something practical.

One afternoon in the minivan, on my way to the grocery store, I picked up the cassette and pushed it into the player. Reading theology felt like a big commitment, but I could listen to a tape while doing something else.

The speaker's enthusiasm instantly disarmed me. His love, even his devotion, for Jesus radiated through his voice. He talked about worshiping God out of delight rather than duty, with a passion resembling the way we love our spouses. To him, delight was an important element of enduring faith. I'd never heard anyone speak about God with that type of enthusiasm, and I wanted to know more. I, too, wanted my love for God to change the shape of my very voice.

The speaker told a story about the nineteenth-century British evangelist Charles Spurgeon, who struggled with severe depression throughout his life and died of gout and kidney disease at age fifty-seven. Yet Spurgeon believed that his suffering was directly from God's hand.

I drifted out of my lane. *Pay attention to the road!* I reminded myself. I drove more cautiously but listened even more carefully. Those words sounded radical.

The speaker quoted Spurgeon directly:

It would be a very sharp and trying experience to me to think that I have an affliction which God never sent me—that the bitter cup was never filled by His hand, that my trials were never measured out by Him, nor sent to me by His arrangement of their weight and quantity.[2]

Wait. *That the bitter cup was never filled by his hand, that . . . ?*

I rewound the cassette. *It would be a very sharp and trying experience to me to think that I have an affliction which God* never *sent me?*

I rewound the cassette again. *Nor sent to me by his arrangement of their weight and quantity.*

I continued to drive. Just another minivan in suburban Raleigh, appearing to everyone else like I was carpooling or running errands.

Their weight and quantity.

The words staggered me. Weight meant severity. Quantity meant frequency. Spurgeon—a man who suffered from deep depression and agonizing pain—was suggesting that his suffering would be *worse* if he thought it hadn't come from God.

This idea was radically disorienting. Of course I knew that God ordered the universe. But did he order every part of my life too? I had never before felt the impact, the collision, of God's sovereignty with the life of Vaneetha, age thirty-three.

I wanted to believe—not just in theory but with all of me—that the suffering in my life wasn't random or meaningless, but that God was using it all for good. That it all had a God-ordained purpose.

"Is that even possible?" I whispered.

Chapter 11

DAVE

The idea that my personal pain wasn't random comforted me. But it also introduced difficulties.

I'd been a teenager when I accepted the truth of John 9—that my polio wasn't someone's fault or an accident but had happened so the work of God might be displayed in my life. Since then I'd known that my polio had a purpose, but I hadn't assumed there was a purpose to *all* my suffering.

My story contained other sharp pains as well. Wounds that remained raw. I'd suffered a miscarriage before Katie was born and two others between her birth and Paul's. But the deepest and most personal wound was created several years before Paul was born.

Dave had been unfaithful to me.

He told me at breakfast one morning. We had a fight the night before, and I was hoping to talk about the distance between us. But I never expected him to mention another woman. Delaney, he called her. She worked out at our gym, and he'd been spending a lot of time with her—time he claimed he'd been working late or going for a drive to "clear his head." He even said he thought he might be in love with her.

I began to dry heave. I was almost seven months pregnant with Katie at the time, and as my thoughts drifted into the future, I felt afraid. Almost terrified. I couldn't raise a child by myself with my disability. I didn't want to be a single parent. I wasn't great with babies.

More than that, I couldn't picture my life without Dave, and I didn't *want* to. I wanted us to stay together. But after an affair?

I questioned everything, especially my judgment. I thought we were happy. I thought our marriage was good. I thought this could never happen to us.

⚜

Dave and I had been together since 1990. That was the year I turned twenty-five and had left a great job at Bank of Boston, where I'd worked for four years. My banking career consumed me, and I was promoted quickly. I was enjoying all the trappings of success in a big city.

I felt I deserved this prosperous life. After all, I'd paid my dues growing up with a disability. I was involved in Park Street Church but often missed services to go to the beach or to explore New England with my friends from work. Then I packed up and moved from cold Massachusetts to sunny California when I was accepted to Stanford's MBA program.

On the first day of class, the provost informed us that we were a diverse class that included "a physician with a twenty-year established practice, a United States Navy submarine commander, a professional model, and, last but not least, a guy from Domino's Pizza." Everyone laughed. Diverse indeed.

Several days later I was eating lunch in a courtyard with four other women, including the one who was *clearly* the model, when a tall guy in a sweatshirt and shorts asked if he could join us. After he sat down, everyone ignored him. So when the other students left for class, I asked him a few questions, and he moved his tray beside mine.

"I have a confession," he stage-whispered. "I'm Dave, the infamous Domino's Pizza guy."

My eyebrows shot up, and Dave laughed.

"It's true," he said. "But I worked for corporate, and I never delivered pizza!"

I laughed back, and we ended up talking for almost three hours. We became fast friends and met daily to chat about absolutely everything: assignments, family, faith, books, music, movies, and favorite restaurants. While I was a former banker interested in marketing, Dave was a former CPA interested in general management. Ironically, Stanford seemed like the perfect program for both of us.

Dave first asked me out on a date after noticing how beautiful I looked (his words, not mine) while I was researching in the computer lab. He told me he was falling for me, and I was attracted to him too. Besides being genuinely nice and really smart, he was handsome. But I had dated several guys in Boston and wasn't sure I was ready for a new relationship. And Dave was still figuring out where he was with Jesus. So I told him we needed to wait.

Except we drifted into dating anyway.

We spent hours studying together and usually went out to eat afterward, always agreeing on which fun restaurant to try. We talked on the phone every night before bed about our strengths, fears, and dreams. We even laughed about the same crazy things that no one but us thought were funny, and endlessly repeated lines from the movie *Caddyshack*, like "Buddies for life, I think."

Then one night after dinner, Dave was walking me to my apartment door when he impulsively kissed me.

Every day I prayed that God would intervene and break up our relationship if it wasn't right, but I knew that was a cop-out. I felt guilty about dating someone who didn't share my faith, but at the same time I wanted a boyfriend. All my friends were getting engaged, and I hated being single. Plus, Dave seemed perfect for me, and I loved every moment we were together. So when Dave told me he'd decided to follow Christ, I was relieved, feeling God would now bless our relationship.

A few days later I caught myself staring at a gorgeous stranger on campus, only to discover it was Dave. Dressed in a dark suit and tie with a white shirt, his suit jacket tossed casually over his right shoulder, he must have been on his way to a presentation. I stared at him as if I'd never seen him before. At six-foot-four with broad shoulders, brown hair, a strong jaw, and hazel eyes, he stood in stark contrast to my five-foot-two frame and mocha skin. My heart skipped more than a few beats when I saw him that day. Dating him seemed like a dream.

Dave proposed in May, much to my surprise. We'd been dating less than five months and had just finished studying for a test in my apartment. As I closed the textbook, he asked in a joking tone, "So, would you marry me?"

I laughed and responded, "I hadn't really thought about it before. But, yeah, I guess I would."

"No, Van, I'm seriously asking you," Dave said softly as his eyes met mine. "*Will* you marry me?"

We married between our first and second year of business school, less than a year after we'd met. At the wedding I overheard one of my mom's Indian friends say, "I'm so glad she's marrying an American. An Indian would never marry her with that limp, which is such a pity because she is so fair and has a pretty face."

We moved into married student housing—a complex called Escondido Village—and soon discovered what stress really was. Dave was committed to studying and learning, while I was committed to procrastinating, cramming, and forgetting. He kept his socks in neat rows, folded and organized by color, while I never knew where all my socks were. He wanted to work out at the gym daily, while I wanted to go out with friends daily. Still, we made it through our final year at Stanford. Dave graduated in the top 10 percent of our class, and I was happy just to graduate.

After graduation we moved to Winston-Salem, North Carolina, where I took a job as a product manager at Hanes, and Dave started his own sports-drink business. We both immersed ourselves in our careers but made sure we had time together. After a few years, we felt ready to expand our family.

I got pregnant quickly, then told everyone we knew and even people we didn't. I excitedly started planning the nursery and read *What to Expect When You're Expecting* each day to know how my baby was developing. At twelve weeks, though, on a business trip in New York, I began bleeding heavily. Alone in a hotel room, I kept telling myself that everything would be fine, that this was probably normal, and that there was nothing to worry about.

When I returned home, I called the doctor, and he told us to come in for our regularly scheduled ultrasound that week. A few minutes after the ultrasound began, the doctor told us that our baby wasn't alive anymore. He was kind but clinical, and I felt foolish as I sobbed while scheduling the D&C (dilation and curettage).

"You'll have more babies," the doctor reassured me. "This is really common and probably for the best. It's nature's way of preventing you from having a nonviable pregnancy." Then he added, "At least you know you can get pregnant."

That was supposed to be reassuring, and in many ways it was, except it also felt as if he was minimizing what had happened. His words didn't make the loss any less painful, but they did make me less likely to openly grieve about it. For days after the D&C I was depressed, obsessing over what I might have done wrong. *Was this my fault?* I wondered. I felt defective somehow, awash in grief, but no one seemed to understand.

When I got pregnant again, we didn't tell anyone until my second trimester, all too aware that it could happen again. Nothing felt safe anymore. At twenty weeks along we learned we were having a girl and decided to name her Katrina and call her Katie. Though my job was bringing in better income than Dave's, we jointly decided that I would stay home once Katie was born, and that Dave would accept my dad's offer to be CFO of his telecommunications consulting firm in Raleigh.

After we moved to Raleigh, I spent most days alone in the house, wondering how to fill my time. I missed being a product manager for girls' underwear at Hanes. I'd loved everything about that job, from designing and sourcing the product to negotiating licenses with Mattel to overseeing commercials. I called a friend from Stanford to commiserate. After she listened, she said, "I think what you're doing is super noble, seriously. I'm so impressed that you can give up your entire career to stay home with kids. I couldn't do it. But I really admire you."

I hung up the phone and went shopping.

Our move to Raleigh frustrated Dave as well. He was learning a new industry on the fly, and after years of working for himself, he found having a boss—particularly his father-in-law—challenging.

The third trimester of pregnancy was miserable for me. I just sat at home all day while my body swelled up. I would wait for Dave to come home so I'd have someone to talk to, but then wouldn't have much to contribute to our conversations.

One afternoon I decided to make a great dinner. I'd been too tired to cook for a while, but I went to the grocery store and picked up a few items to make one of Dave's favorite Italian dishes. I worked for several hours to prep everything and was excited to hear the garage door go up. I washed my hands and went to the door to greet him.

Dave seemed surprised when I opened the door to the garage. "Wow. You never greet me at the door," he said, walking past me and putting his keys on the table. He then glanced at the cutting board and food on the kitchen counter and pans on the stove. "It looks like you've been busy today."

"I wanted to make your favorite dinner tonight. And afterward I thought we could talk for a while. It seems like we haven't connected in forever."

"Thanks, that's sweet," Dave said as he grabbed the folded

newspaper off the edge of the counter. "Let me read the paper for a little bit, and then we can talk."

I felt deflated. I had gone to so much effort, but he didn't seem very enthusiastic. "Maybe you can help me prep a few more things," I said as I chopped peppers. "We can talk about your day at the same time."

Dave was engrossed in the paper. "I'll help in a minute, okay?" he said, looking up. "It's been a tough day. Sometimes I feel like you don't give me any room to breathe."

His irritation fueled mine. "You know what it's like for me to feel horrible all day, then go out and get stuff for your favorite meal, and then have you ignore me? I already feel unimportant, and now you're making me feel even worse. Like talking to me is just another obligation!"

Dave got up from the table. "I'm going back to change my clothes. I don't want to talk about this. This is exactly what's wrong with us. You don't give me any space."

I stood there, fuming, as I watched him walk away. When he came back he seemed more cheerful and helped with dinner. We didn't talk about anything in particular as we ate. I wanted the meal to be peaceful, so I avoided talking about my frustrations. Dave cleaned up the kitchen after dinner, and I asked if we could sit in the living room and finish our earlier conversation.

"I'm not in the mood for talking, Van. Not now. I appreciate the great dinner, but I just need to think and let off some steam." He grabbed his keys and headed out the door to the garage. "I'm just going to drive for a little while."

This wasn't the first time he'd gone out driving late at night to clear his head. After a few hours, I finally went to bed but couldn't fall asleep. I kept staring at the red digits on the clock: 12:00. 1:00. 2:00. 3:00.

I was wide awake when Dave returned at 3:30 a.m. I listened to him undress quietly in the dark. "Where were you?" I whispered. "I've been worried and haven't been able to sleep."

My voice startled him. "You shouldn't have waited up for me!" he snapped. "I was driving around because it helps me think. I realized I'd driven almost back to Winston-Salem when I noticed the time and turned around."

I waited.

His voice softened. "I'm sorry it's so late. You can go to sleep now." He pulled back the covers and got into bed.

"Dave, what's bothering you?" I whispered. "I know something's wrong, but I have no idea what it is."

"I don't know what's bothering me," he answered, sighing. "A lot of things, I guess. I hate not working for myself. And I just don't know about us . . ."

What? The second item on his list was *not* like the first.

"I mean, I know I should be excited about this baby, but I'm not. Ever since we moved to Raleigh, I've felt different about you. I remember being excited when I saw your car in the driveway, knowing you were home. But now that's all changed."

Terror. I tried to make sense of Dave's words. I was seven months pregnant. I'd given up my career, my life, and now he didn't know how he felt about me? I was glad he couldn't see me as tears rolled down my cheeks.

I was quiet for a minute, praying. Then I said, "Maybe we should go to marriage counseling. I know a lot of people say it's helpful. And we've just gone through so many transitions. A new job, a new city, our first house . . . expecting a baby."

"I don't want to go to counseling. Right now I don't want to work on anything, particularly our marriage."

There was no point in arguing. My mind was going in a million directions, and I was too exhausted to figure out what to say next, so I stayed quiet. Finally I asked, "Are you going to leave me?"

Dave grabbed my hand, and his voice softened. "No, of course not. I won't leave you."

We both lay there for a minute, neither of us saying a word as we stared into the darkness. Then Dave rolled over with his back toward me, and I rolled the other way.

When Dave returned from work the following day, dinner was cordial. After we finished eating, Dave cleared the table and said he was going to a bar with friends from the gym. I naturally assumed we were going together and went to go change. As I was getting ready, Dave walked in and clarified that he wanted to go alone because it would be too hard for me to stand. I was sure I could find a barstool to sit on, but Dave insisted on going by himself.

The next morning Dave told me about Delaney.

⁓

I felt like an idiot. A fool.

I called Shalini, and we talked for hours. She suggested seeing a counselor, so I picked a Christian counselor at random from the yellow pages. Dave agreed to meet Bill with me, and Bill agreed to see us separately as well as jointly. As a precondition, Bill insisted that Dave end his relationship with Delaney and cut off all contact with her. Dave reluctantly agreed.

And so we officially began marriage counseling.

Dave was in what Bill termed "a fog," which he said was common for most men who have affairs. Dave agreed, saying he felt numb and didn't care about *anything*. According to Bill, that meant Dave couldn't focus much on me, even though *I* was the one who'd been wronged. I didn't like the sound of that.

Bill advised Dave to answer all my questions truthfully. Then he warned me not to ask anything I didn't need the answer to, because the answers could trigger unexpected pain later. Once I knew them, he said, that information would be emblazoned in my mind. I understood what he meant, because I'd asked Dave the name of the restaurant he took Delaney to, and now I could no longer drive down that street.

"I feel like I'm losing my mind, Bill," I said. "When will this get better?"

He told me there was no way to know and, in the interim, I needed to think about what was best for me.

Dave and I both went to Bill individually for weeks. I felt like I was slowly recognizing Dave again, but doubts would resurface without warning, and I would wonder whether he still thought about Delaney.

"I think we're making progress," I told Dave one night as we were getting ready to go to a movie. "But then I wonder if it's all in my mind. Do you still think about Delaney?"

Dave sighed. "Yes, we're making progress. You're the best person in the world for me, and I know that. I'm sad that I almost threw it all away. But, yes, I do occasionally think about Delaney, though she wasn't good for me. Sometimes I'm drawn to things that aren't good for me. Delaney was like ice cream. I crave ice cream, but I know it's bad for me. You're like broccoli. It's my favorite vegetable, and it's really good for me. But I don't crave broccoli."

"Broccoli? Really? You're saying I'm like broccoli?"

"Maybe that's a bad analogy, but you know what I mean. I don't think you need to crave someone you love."

I'd brought it up, and I could tell he genuinely wasn't trying to hurt me. Nevertheless, the hurt came hard. I replayed this conversation for days. Everything negative I'd ever believed about myself felt true. I was unwanted and unchosen. My body was unattractive, huge with my pregnant belly. And my husband craved another woman more than he wanted me. I felt trapped, sentenced to stay in a loveless marriage out of necessity.

⸎

I hated being pregnant.

My once petite frame became a bloated mass as I retained water all over. Since I struggled to walk with the extra weight, I spent my days at home, relieved that I could avoid seeing women with beautiful bodies everywhere I looked. I'd envied them even before my pregnancy, and now, with Dave's infidelity, I couldn't even look in the mirror without crying. He liked sexy, athletic women who worked out at the gym, not doughballs like me.

I called Shalini in tears. "I feel ugly and undesirable, and I'm sure there's no hope for our marriage. Should I just file for divorce?"

She paused. "Well, to begin with, you're not ugly. You're beautiful. You certainly could file for divorce. He did have an affair. But is that what you want? I thought things were getting better after counseling."

"I don't know what I want. One minute I hate him, and the next minute I have hope. I want our old life back, our life before all this happened. But I can't have that."

"Yeah, I get that. I wish you didn't have to go through all this. Sometimes I hate Dave, too, and want you to divorce him, and other times I have hope he'll get right with you and God and that your marriage will be stronger for it. But what *I* think doesn't matter. What's happening now?"

"Our marriage is getting a little better, but I don't trust myself, or anything, to be honest. Sometimes I still feel that Dave doesn't want me back, like he's just staying because he feels obligated. Besides, Dave and I started dating when he wasn't a Christian, and I wonder if maybe God wants me to get out of this marriage so I can find someone else who would be better for me. Someone who really loves God."

Shalini hesitated and then said, "Vaneetha, I get that you're discouraged, but that's not how God works. Just because you think you made a mistake in marrying Dave, that's not a reason to divorce him and find someone else. You can't correct a first mistake, if it was one, with a second. You have grounds for divorce, but you'll regret it if you file rashly in anger and don't do it for the right reasons."

"The right reasons?" I interrupted. "I have every right to do whatever I want! I'm the one that was wronged, remember? It feels like you're lecturing me, and I can't handle that."

"I'm sorry. I'm not trying to criticize you. Maybe you can tell me what's on your mind." Shalini listened to me rant until I calmed down and she had to go.

I sat at the kitchen table long afterward, feeling defeated and hopeless. I picked up my open Bible and started reading, asking God for direction. I'd ignored the Bible for years, but after Dave told me about Delaney, I began reading it every day because I knew I needed to connect with God. I prayed for wisdom and almost immediately read Luke 1:37: "Nothing will be impossible with God."

For now, that would be my answer.

⁂

I delivered Katie a few weeks later, on April 21, 1995, and Dave carried her out to our parents, who were gathered in the waiting room. She was the first grandchild on either side. Katie, with her olive skin and dark hair, was a beautiful blend of our heritages. Later that day my mom told me Dave had been beaming when he brought Katie out to meet them. He'd said it was the most incredible day of his life, and that he had no idea he could love a little person so much.

We hired a nanny, Goldie, to help me during the day. She worked until Dave got home, at which point Dave took care of everything from changing Katie's diapers to giving her a bath to rocking her to sleep. Since I couldn't get her out of the bassinet by myself, Dave had to get up, even in the middle of the night, to put her beside me to nurse. He never complained about the extra work, saying it was a privilege.

Dave and I continued counseling with Bill, both individually and jointly. But Dave felt frustrated that it was taking so long for me to trust him and move forward. He wanted to put the past behind him.

"I know I caused this," he said. "But I want to have some fun in our life again."

Clearly he didn't understand the pain I was feeling. I was dealing with the fallout of his choices every day. Why should he get to put a timetable on that?

Bill pointed out to Dave that there was no magical way to fix what had happened.

"I can accept that to a point," Dave said. "But for how long? It seems like it's taking forever."

"It's not taking forever, Dave," Bill replied. "It's only been four months. And my best answer is that it takes as long as it takes. It's like when you're sick with a stomach bug and you don't want to throw up, but you'll keep feeling nauseated until you do. If someone were to ask you how many more times you needed to throw up, you wouldn't know. No one knows that beforehand."

⟋⟋⟋

Katie continued to bloom. Two months, three months, four months. She was happy and healthy.

Dave and I continued going to counseling, and our relationship seemed to be improving. In fact, our home seemed peaceful enough that I signed up for a local marriage seminar. I'd lost my baby weight, so I felt more attractive and wanted to rekindle our spark.

On the second night of the conference, our homework was to talk about our physical and emotional relationship. I assumed Dave's romantic feelings toward me had changed, but I was shocked when he admitted he had never been very physically attracted to me. It wasn't just my pregnancy weight—which in itself seemed wrong to hold against someone—but also that my body was covered with scars and my legs were skinny. If he were being completely honest, he confessed, I just wasn't very sexy to him.

When he said that, I wanted to cover every inch of my body and never let him see it again. But after a minute I was brave enough to ask, "So why did you marry me if you're not attracted to me?"

"I love you, that's why. But I can't change the fact that I don't *want* you that way. We both need to accept that. I accepted it a long time ago."

I struggled for words but couldn't think of a coherent response. I had worked so hard to accept my body. "You have no idea how hurtful that is," was all I could manage.

Dave shrugged. "I'm sorry, I'm not trying to hurt you. But I want to be honest. I don't think it's fair for you to be mad at me for that."

I couldn't figure out what to do with what he said, so I ignored it. I couldn't survive another conversation on that topic, so I shoved Dave's words down as deep as I could and moved on with life.

❦

I was excited when Ann, a friend from church who lived a few streets over, invited me to a neighborhood book study because I wanted to get to know people in Raleigh. I soon made other friends, like Jennifer and Lisa, who got me hooked on scrapbooking. That neighborhood group was where I also met Shirley, who had lost her daughter to cancer.

Dave and I continued to go to counseling.

"I'm trying to figure out if Dave's affair was a one-time thing or if it might happen again," I told Bill at one of our individual sessions. "I don't want to trust Dave if he's going to do this again."

"Do you think you can ever have that kind of assurance?" Bill asked.

"It's not that I need an ironclad guarantee, but I don't want to do all this work for nothing."

"I know it's hard right now. But, unfortunately, you may have to take a risk because there are no guarantees. With anyone. What's precipitated this?"

"I was going through old boxes in the attic and found one with love letters to a woman he dated before me. She returned them for some reason, and he saved them. Bill, these letters are more passionate than anything he's ever written to me."

"Well, I can see why that's prompting your doubts. But you've got to understand, sexual activity outside of marriage is an exciting fantasy, like Coney Island. The excitement is in the illicit. I want you to know this has never been about you. It's about something in Dave that's broken. Don't think you need to change yourself physically for him. That's not what this is about."

"I want to believe you, Bill, but I can't. This *is* about me not being attractive enough. A month ago, Dave said . . ." Stopping midsentence, I didn't know whether to go on, because recounting our conversation felt vulnerable and humiliating. I waited for a minute, and neither of us spoke. Then I continued, "I can't believe I'm telling you this, but Dave said at a marriage conference that he wasn't attracted to my body. So I know that if I were sexier, we wouldn't be in this place."

Bill leaned forward. "I'm so sorry about that, and I understand why you've concluded it's about you. But trust me, Dave is trying to understand himself. This is *his* issue, *his* battle. And it has very little to do with you, Vaneetha. The roots of his struggle started long before you. He's chasing the airbrushed and the illicit. It's how Satan twists a good and beautiful thing into something wrong and hurtful. But Dave needs to truly repent and turn to God in this for your marriage to work. You'll see fruit from repentance that's sustainable if it's real."

I was grateful that Bill had said true repentance had fruit. I knew I couldn't trust myself to make the right decision in a vacuum, so I began to look for signs of repentance in Dave, even though I wasn't sure exactly what the so-called fruit would look like.

Over the next few months, I did see changes in Dave. He was kinder and more loving. He continued to care for Katie. I grew cautiously hopeful as we talked about the future and our marriage.

We often discussed how we both were feeling, though I had determined never to revisit the conversation about my attractiveness. I had buried those words so deeply that eventually I either forgot them or decided they didn't reflect Dave's true feelings. Either way, I moved on. But I also still dreaded the one-year anniversary of Dave's affair. He had told me about Delaney in late February, and all month I kept mentally revisiting where we'd been the previous year. February was torturous.

Then, on March 1, the doorbell rang, and a florist delivered a dozen long-stemmed roses with a card that read, "February is over! I love you, sweetheart." Though I hadn't told Dave of my struggle with the whole month, he somehow knew it was on my mind. That small gesture made me see that he was paying attention.

That night when he got home from work, he told me he'd made reservations at our favorite restaurant and arranged a babysitter. At the restaurant he said, "I can't tell you how sorry I am for all I put you through. I'm so grateful to you for not only staying, but for being as kind and gracious as you were. I didn't deserve that. I know God did that in you, and I know he's changing me too. You're the most precious thing in my life, and I can't believe I almost lost you because of my sin and selfishness." He then handed me an envelope with a long letter, handwritten on both sides of lined yellow legal paper, reiterating how much he loved me and how sorry he was for all he had done.

From that night on the way we related to each other changed. I felt loved and attractive again. We read books together, talked about everything, had regular date nights, and invited friends over for long dinners. Dave wanted to have people holding him accountable, so he started a men's group with weekly meetings. I saw a new passion for God fill him as he read the Bible more, shared what God was teaching him, and listened to my pain without being defensive.

Then one day I realized our marriage was stronger and deeper than it had ever been. Bill had promised that Dave's repentance would bear fruit if it was real.

And it was.

❧

I couldn't wait to tell Bill about it.

"We're doing so much better! You were right. I see clear evidence of repentance, which makes—"

"Do you mind if I bring up something that's been on my mind then?" Bill asked, interrupting me. "I've been praying a lot about this session, and I was wondering if you've thought about forgiving Dave?"

"Are you *kidding*? Forgive him after what he's done?" I took a deep breath. "Maybe I should clarify, what do you mean by forgive?"

"I think to forgive someone is to refuse to hold what they did against them."

"That's kind of what I thought, and I don't want to do that. Dave is sorry, but I'm still not positive it won't happen again. I'll always hold this against him."

Bill shifted in his chair. "I think we've all seen evidence of repentance, which is why you could reconcile and restore your marriage. Without repentance, I wouldn't advise reconciliation or restoration. But forgiveness is different because it doesn't even require that the other person be sorry. It's a unilateral act between you and God."

"You're saying we need to forgive people when they aren't even sorry? That doesn't sound right, Bill, but I don't want to keep belaboring something theoretical. Dave is sorry. But forgiving him feels like I'm saying that what he did wasn't bad. That I've forgotten about it and moved on. Even though things are better, I'll never forget. Never."

"Well," said Bill, "I know this sounds impossible right now, but I'd like you to pray about it. Christ calls us to forgive. Forgiveness has to do with your relationship with *God*, not with Dave."

"Bill, it feels like you're taking his side. And it sounds so churchy. You're acting like I owe Dave forgiveness, which infuriates me. We're just starting to put things back together, and now you're telling me to forgive him? Do you have any idea what you're asking of me?"

"Actually, I do," Bill said matter-of-factly. "But this isn't about me. I'm just asking you to pray about this. Will you?"

I reluctantly agreed and then spent the next two weeks wishing Bill had never brought it up. His suggestion had been *annoyingly* biblical.

The next time I saw Bill I said, "I'm not ready to forgive. Not at all. But I want to know how you think I should do it."

"Well, first, God needs your willingness. Even if you don't have the feelings of forgiveness, you can still forgive. It starts with an act of your will. It's a decision you make, and then the feelings follow, because God does the rest. You're asking Jesus to come into the process."

"It seems crazy that I can forgive even if I don't feel like it. Are you saying that I just need to say, 'I forgive,' and that's all?"

"Well, that's not exactly all. But that's how it starts. And Jesus bears all the cost in forgiveness, so it's not painful once you invite him into it. It's actually freeing. Here's a handout that might help you."

Bill handed me three sheets of paper, stapled in the top left corner, that had been copied from the book called *Set My Heart Free*. He watched me as I skimmed the first page. When I turned the page, he said, "Here's a prayer you can use to forgive. It gives you the words to use, so just put Dave's name in the blank space."

I looked down at the page and started reading.

Father God, as an act of my will I forgive _____ right now. I release all anger and resentment toward _____ and I allow your forgiveness to flow through me to him/her. Thank you for taking my anger away and replacing it with your peace and love.[3]

I looked up. "Of course I could do *this* . . . but it seems too simple. Wouldn't I need to do something else?"

"Saying it sincerely is the most important step, Vaneetha. It begins with a decision, but it's an ongoing process, because other offenses will come to mind, and you'll need to keep repeating this prayer or something like it. And you'll need to keep asking God to help you do it. But when you do, you'll be amazed at how much Christ's love and forgiveness will flow through you, and how much closer you'll be to the Lord."

❦

I took the paper home, and it stayed untouched on my desk for weeks.

I didn't want to forgive Dave, but I couldn't articulate the reasons, even to myself. It took a long time to realize what was holding me back: once I forgave, I could no longer bring up that issue in anger. And I wasn't yet ready to give that up.

I needed to know what I was forgiving before I forgave. So I wrote in my journal all the ways Dave's betrayal had hurt me:

> He made me feel unloved.
> He made me cry every night.
> He lied to me.
> He made me feel I wasn't good enough.
> He made me lose faith in myself.
> He wasn't sorry right away.
> He made me feel undesirable and unexciting by comparing me to broccoli and Delaney to ice cream.

I spent hours and filled pages as I wrote about all the ways I was hurt. But even when I'd exhausted my list, I knew there was more to add. I still wasn't ready to forgive Dave.

I looked at the journal daily, adding items whenever I thought of them. At first I'd focused on what Dave had done, but then I let myself notice some of the day-to-day consequences, the longer-term impact of what he'd said and done. Writing them down freed me. I carried less of that pain inside me and left more on the page.

Finally, a month after receiving the handout from Bill, I couldn't think of anything else to add to my journal. So I pulled out the handout and read it aloud, asking God to use it.

Over the next several months, I started to change.

I asked God to keep me from bringing up old memories or throwing Dave's past in his face, even during an argument. And God did. Bill had been right. Forgiving Dave brought an exhilarating sense of freedom.

Dave and I rediscovered each other. We restored our marriage. We laughed again. And almost two years after the affair, with two miscarriages in between, I got pregnant with Paul. When Dave had first told me about his affair, I wondered if we would make it. His infidelity could have irredeemably crushed our marriage.

But we *had* made it. We'd learned how to move through a crisis by talking, really talking to each other. At the time I didn't know how much of that good communication we'd need to survive the death of our baby boy.

Chapter 12

ADJUSTING

I discovered I was pregnant three months after Paul died, and I was terrified I'd miscarry again. I didn't know if I could handle any more dashed hopes.

Thankfully, the following months passed without incident—that is, until I was seven months along, on my weekly expedition to the drugstore to pick up photos of Katie for my scrapbooking. I tripped in the least dramatic way possible, stubbing my toe on an uneven square of sidewalk, and collapsed ungracefully. The pain was searing and immediate across the underside of my abdomen. I found myself sprawled on the cement and nearly passed out from the agony.

"Help, help!" a passerby screamed. "We need help right now! This is an emergency! Woman in labor! Someone call an ambulance!"

Fortunately no one listened to the ambulance part, because I quickly discovered I wasn't in labor. I was in pain, yes, but not in labor. As a crowd gathered, the blinding pain faded, replaced by the sharper sting of embarrassment. Several strangers offered to help me to my feet. Once I was standing, I realized the pain felt unrelated to my pregnancy. I took a tentative step, and then another.

"Can I help you to your car?" someone offered.

"Thank you so much," I said. "But I'd like to go inside first and get my pictures."

Dave was out of the country on a business trip, but a friend and her husband had invited me and Katie for dinner to keep us company.

While we were eating, the blinding pain in my abdomen returned, and now it rivaled the severity of when I first fell on the sidewalk. I dropped my fork and gasped in pain.

My friend jumped to her feet. "This is *not* getting better the way you said it was, Vaneetha!"

I was in too much pain to say a word.

She and her husband lifted me into the car, and she stayed with Katie while her husband drove me to the ER.

Five hours later a doctor approached. "Now, I know you're in pain," the physician said, "and I know you're pregnant. But we don't *exactly* know what we're looking at yet, injury-wise. The x-rays aren't conclusive. So let's get you on some Advil. It's an *amazing* painkiller!"

I smiled as I envisioned choking him.

Apparently my multiple hip surgeries had confused the doctors, and it wasn't until they called in my normal orthopedist to read the x-rays that I was given a diagnosis: a complete pelvic separation of three centimeters.

Which meant a Velcro brace—a bit like a corset, but lower—wrapped tightly around my abdomen.

And a week in the hospital to monitor the separation and my pregnancy.

And sleeping in a recliner at home for over six months, because lying on my back or side was too painful.

And a wheelchair.

But it was all worth it when Katie and Dave and I welcomed Kristi into our family on October 30, 1998—a little over a year after Paul's death.

❦

Those were good years. Hard at times, and busy, but good. We did what every family did: hid Easter eggs for our growing girls, discovered the joys of potty training, and laughed while playing Candyland and Go Fish. Most of what we did was ordinary, but some things were unique to us. Dave ventured out on his own as a consultant. Dave and I took a wonderful trip to Hawaii together. The girls and I volunteered at a nearby retirement community. At the community, we wheeled a little cart around to deliver mail to the residents and ended up befriending many of them, even getting invited to private family events.

I remember my mom inventing "Grandmother Day" with the girls. They would bake cookies and read books, and she would tell stories about India. My parents sometimes kept the girls overnight so Dave and I could be alone. Often we would just sit on the couch and watch TV shows we'd taped during the week. Dave would eat a huge bowl of ice cream and save the last little bite with all the chocolate chips for me. On a business trip to Hong Kong he'd bought a porcelain figurine of a Chinese couple on a bench. "That's going to be us when we get older," he told me.

One day when Dave and I were walking through my favorite craft store, I pointed to a scrapbooking guide and said, "That's my favorite. It's very innovative."

He raised his eyebrows.

As we continued to shop, I pointed to a row of paint bottles. "I really like that new glass paint. It's actually revolutionary."

"Van," Dave said, turning me toward him and smiling, "you need to get out more."

Instead of taking his advice, I became consumed with a new creative project: a scrapbook about my family heritage. From my mother I learned that, back in India, my grandmother had been a friend of the missionary Amy Carmichael, and that made me want to learn more about my ancestors on both sides. I solicited stories from dozens of family members about how they had come to faith in Jesus. My plan was to piece together a family history with testimonies and pictures.

Whenever letters or pictures arrived, I'd organize them into piles on the dining-room table—including a pile labeled "needs to be translated." I even dreamed about the book.

While I was still in the early stages of working on what I knew would be an incredibly complex project, I realized there should be a book about Dave's family too. But Dave was an only child, so we—meaning me—would have to work on his book if we wanted the girls to know more about their dad's heritage. As I considered it, I knew I wouldn't have the motivation to begin his family history after my massive family history project was complete, but I'd always come back to my family project. So I paused working on my album and began working on Dave's.

I worked for months researching Dave's ancestors and found stacks of pictures of his extended family when we visited his parents, Maxine and Jerry. I used ancestry software and made countless calls to the Bureau of Vital Records in the county where his father's family lived. For months I sent them queries for information as I gathered the data I wanted, including birth, marriage, and death certificates. I discovered that Dave's grandfather, whom we'd always thought was an only child, actually had six siblings who died in infancy.

The dining room became a Michaels craft outpost as I dutifully relocated items from the store to our house several times a week. One of the managers even offered me a job, saying, "Employees receive a 50 percent discount, you know. You could probably use that." On the next trip I was invited to a private staff party—after all, I was on a first-name basis with everyone who worked there. Dave was right. I did need to get out more, or at least to somewhere other than Michaels.

Maxine and I began to talk more often on the phone, mostly about the details of the scrapbook. We were growing closer by degrees, but I was still inwardly reserved. As perhaps typical for an overly sensitive daughter-in-law, I often interpreted her observations as criticisms. If she commented on how inquisitive the girls were, I would smile and agree but wonder why she thought the girls talked too much. We *were* close, but not as close as we could have been.

One morning as I was reading the Bible, I was struck by 1 John 4:20: "He who does not love his brother whom he has seen cannot love God whom he has not seen." I stopped reading immediately. I felt God was speaking to me. I'd been kind to Maxine, and I called her regularly to keep in touch, but I was a long way from really loving her. I asked God to help me love her more, whatever that looked like.

Several weeks later, I noticed that Maxine's voice sounded uncharacteristically depressed on the phone. "Mom, you sound sad. Is everything okay?"

"Nothing really. It's been a hard week. Lots of little things keep happening, and I'm not sure what to do with them."

"Do you want to talk about it? I have time right now."

"No, honey, I'm fine. Really. I'll get past this. So tell me what's going on with you."

It wasn't typical for Maxine to be that quiet. After we hung up I wanted to cheer her up and wondered if a package might brighten her day. So I headed off to Michaels (naturally) and filled a small box with a cute little sign, a small candle, a quilting book, and some candy.

A week later I received a card written in Maxine's cursive handwriting with her favorite blue pen.

Dear Van,
Still getting over the terrific *surprise* package. My eyes water (tiny tears) when I see and use all the different items. You made more than just my day. You made many, many days. Can't begin to tell you how I feel. It puts a smile on my face and joy in my heart. You are a very special person. May God bless you with all the special things you do for others.

Love,
Mom

After reading the note, I found myself more excited to talk with Maxine on the phone. Obligation began to transform into desire and delight. One tangible act of love changed our relationship.

And just in time, because tangible acts of love—at least of the creative type—soon became much more difficult for me.

⸙

Dave and I were driving to visit some of my college friends in Virginia for the weekend when a bolt of agony shot through my right arm as I reached for the seatbelt. I screamed and slumped forward in my seat, trying to make sense of what had just happened. Dave got out his cell phone to call our friends and cancel, but I insisted we should keep the date. "It'll go away soon, I'm sure. We've been planning this for months. There's no way I'm going to cancel now."

We were about two hours down the road in Emporia, Virginia, when the pain became unbearable. "Just stop by Walmart," I said through gritted teeth. "I'll get a pillow to rest my arm on. Maybe that will take the pressure off."

The pain intensified over the weekend until I couldn't even lift my arm. By Sunday morning Dave had to cut my food and feed me. When we got home on Sunday night, I decided I'd rest my arm completely. But the pain didn't subside, so I called the doctor first thing Monday morning. After examining my arm, he said it looked like medial epicondylitis—commonly called golfer's elbow—and should get better with rest.

Except it didn't. Two weeks later I was still in agony and couldn't use my arm. When I told Jennifer and Lisa the next time we met, they asked if it could be related to my polio.

"Of course not," I said quickly. Aside from my limp and the limited strength in my arms, I hadn't really *suffered* from polio since I was a little girl.

Truthfully, I didn't know much about polio, though I did know the story of how I'd gotten it.

It had all started late Sunday afternoon in Madras, India, when my mother realized her baby—me—had a 105-degree fever. She immediately dialed the pediatrician, but after ten long rings, she finally hung up. After a minute she called again. The compulsive dialing gave her something to do, but with each unanswered ring, she grew more anxious. As she waited, wondering where the doctor was and when he would be back, she wet a cloth and pressed it against my burning forehead. Then, knowing that a fever this high could cause brain damage to a baby, she scooped me off the bed and ran to visit a friend who was a doctor.

The young physician was exhausted from caring for her husband who was recovering from typhoid, and she quickly deduced that I was suffering from typhoid as well. She told my mother there was no point in taking me to the hospital because there would be a long wait, and I needed medicine quickly. She hurriedly wrote two prescriptions, one for an antibiotic called Chloromycetin and the other for the steroid cortisone.

My mother faithfully dosed me, and by the next day my fever had broken. She finished the course of medicine over the next week. At first each bitter dose caused me to squirm and kick, but with each passing day I reacted less. By the end of the week I lay motionless, eerily still.

No one paid much attention, assuming I was exhausted from fighting off the fever. But when my grandmother's friend, a physician in her sixties, came to visit, she knew something was wrong. Typhoid shouldn't cause lethargy. She asked if I'd been vaccinated against polio, and my mother told her I was due to get the vaccine in a few months.

Within minutes my mother and grandmother put me in a car and sped to the doctor's office.

"Why didn't you bring her in before this?" exclaimed the doctor.

My mother explained what had happened. "After her fever broke, I assumed she was out of danger. What's wrong with her?"

"I know your friend thought she was doing the right thing, but what she did was, well, unwise. She should have ordered the traditional tests to confirm it was typhoid before prescribing the medicine, especially to an infant."

My mother wrung her hands. "Please don't blame her, doctor. She was doing me a favor. But how did the medicine make it worse? What exactly is wrong with my baby?"

"Your daughter has polio, and the medicine the doctor prescribed allowed the polio virus to spread unchallenged. The physician who saw her was probably young and had never seen polio before. Your daughter originally had a mild case, but now she's going to be paralyzed, essentially a quadriplegic, for the rest of her life. The most she'll do is sit in a wheelchair, and that is even doubtful. She may have some movement on her right side, but her left side will never recover."

It seemed impossible. My mother had planned to rejoin my father soon, returning to the town in northern India where he was a professor of electrical engineering. She had come to Madras to deliver me and stay with her family for a few months. How could she go back now?

The doctor interrupted her thoughts. "I'm sorry to give you this hard news. You probably can't even take it all in right now." He hesitated, and then added, "I don't want to add to your pain, but you need to know that, if you stay in India, there is little we can do here. If you want more for her life, maybe Western medicine can do something."

Six months later, in the fall of 1965, our family of four arrived in England. My father was forced to take the first job he could find, installing telephone systems in London. Our small flat stood in stark contrast to my mother's family estate in south India. Five servants had attended to our every need there: a full-time cook, a driver, a gardener, a housekeeper, and a nanny. Since taking money out of India was forbidden, my parents now lived on a laborer's salary, furnishing our apartment with secondhand lawn furniture, sleeping on a used mattress on the floor, and using only cold water.

Though we came to England knowing no one, my parents immediately found a church that embraced us and helped organize medical care for me. Through various surprising connections, I was seen by the finest doctors in London, including Sir Herbert Seddon, an orthopedic surgeon who had been knighted for his contribution to polio research and treatment. I had my first surgery, the Yount procedure, at seventeen months old, in hopes that I'd one day be able to walk. Despite the prediction that I would be a quadriplegic, soon I was scooting from room to room on my bottom.

My father's supervisor at work recognized his capabilities and helped him transfer to a new position in Montreal, Canada, as an electrical engineer. In April 1967 I had my second operation at the Royal Victoria Hospital. This resulted in full casts on both my legs, which were spread apart in the V-shape and connected by a bar at the knees.

My next surgery the following year was at the Shriners Hospital for Crippled Children (now known as Shriners Hospital for Children—Canada), which I would almost call home for the next five years. I lived there for several months at a time after each surgery and was once there for nine months straight.

I was placed on a ward with a rotating group of about twenty other girls. Each side of the room had ten beds. The walls were painted mustard yellow, and there were two small TVs on either end that we watched a lot. In the middle was a small wooden table with a few chairs. Only the girls who could walk sat there, eating lunch or playing games while the rest of us watched.

My parents were only allowed to visit on weekends, and Shalini had to stay in the waiting room. Since some children there had been practically abandoned, the staff chose to limit the number of times girls like me—with loving families—could receive visitors. That way the disparity wouldn't be as difficult to bear.

The doctors at Shriners believed I could learn to walk without braces, and after I had recovered from more than a dozen surgeries, it was finally time to try. A nurse wheeled me into a room with railings on either side and a mirror on one end. "When you can reach the mirror on your own, you can go home," she told me.

If I can reach the mirror, I thought, *I'll be able to hold my daddy's hand and cross the street.* For some reason that was what I wanted more than anything else. But I couldn't even stand up from the wheelchair.

I looked down at my skinny, scarred legs, and at the ugly lace-up boots that made my legs look even worse. The nurse helped me stand, supported me as I took a step, and picked me up when I fell. An hour of this exhausted me, but the next day I returned to the mirror room and tried again.

Three-and-a-half weeks later I touched the mirror with my right hand, and a week after that I walked out of the ward on my own. Shalini was waiting in the lobby, and as soon as she saw me, she ran to me and hugged me tight. I remembered how much I'd missed her.

When we reached our house, Dad carried me up the stairs to the second floor where we lived. He put me down and smiled. Then I walked inside by myself, my limp causing my whole body to tilt from right to left. I still had to hold on to the walls for balance, but I could manage.

I was a girl who would always walk with a limp—but at least I was a girl who could walk.

⚜

Ever since that day, almost three decades earlier, I tried to do almost everything myself—and I mostly succeeded. That was why the ongoing pain in my right arm was so concerning to me. It threatened my hard-won independence.

When the pain remained intense and the doctor was unable to offer a clear solution, he gave me a cortisone shot in my elbow. The shot eased the pain tremendously, though the doctor warned the effects would eventually wear off, and three shots were the absolute limit. He referred me to other specialists, but they couldn't agree on what to do. One surgeon suggested operating on my elbow but couldn't offer any guarantees. Another doctor suggested complete rest. Still another wanted me to try physical therapy. The only thing everyone agreed on was that the pain was mystifying. At times I felt hopeless, wondering why no one could figure this out.

When the doctors couldn't help me, I searched for answers on my own. At the same time, I refused to consider that my pain could be hinting at a bigger issue. I was a wife and a mother with children to raise. Working around my pain, I continued living my life as I had before. If I found an answer, great. If not, I'd manage somehow.

Around this time I discovered I was pregnant again. I called Shalini, who was living in Toronto with her husband, and learned she was also pregnant and due two weeks after me. Our phone bills ballooned as we constantly discussed names and plans and morning sickness. We decided our kids would be best friends.

But when I was ten weeks along, I miscarried once again. My fourth. Another D&C and yet another loss. We hadn't told many people I was pregnant, so mostly I grieved alone. I was happy for Shalini, of course, and pretended her pregnancy wasn't hard for me. But I couldn't help but feel that all her milestones should have been mine as well.

Months later I mentioned the miscarriage to my orthopedic surgeon at my annual visit. "I'm so sorry, but you shouldn't get pregnant again," he told me. "Your separated pelvis from your last pregnancy will never go back together. It was dangerous then, and it would only get worse. You need to realize that if you carry another child, you may not be able to walk again."

I cried on the drive home. Not because there was anything wrong with our family of four—there wasn't—but because four was the only size it would ever be.

Chapter 13

THE CLINIC

Six months of shooting pain in my right arm completely baffled the doctors. Nothing was broken or torn, physical therapy was unhelpful, and the cortisone shots led to only minimal—and temporary—improvement. And so I was finally forced to consider my polio. I doubted it was the reason, but I needed to check off every box. I made an appointment with the International Rehabilitation Center for Polio in Framingham, a world-renowned polio clinic outside Boston. When I told Shalini, she agreed to go with me.

She met me at the Boston airport, looking chic in a new jean jacket that seemed more versatile than the five different sweaters I'd packed. Over dinner we planned our trip: restaurants, shopping, and coffee in the Back Bay neighborhood.

"And maybe the clinic?" Shalini joked.

"We'll see if we have time," I laughed. I had appointments on three consecutive days.

Maria, a cheerful physical therapist with dark, curly hair, was my first appointment at the clinic. She led Shalini and me into a workout room for my strength assessment test. Such evaluations always felt humiliating to me because they highlighted how weak I was. This one was no different.

Maria glanced up at me as I was squeezing the grip calibration. It registered almost zero, indicating I had no strength in my left hand. "You compensate so well I wouldn't have guessed how weak you are," she said. "You have basically no shoulder muscle on either side, so getting ready in the morning must be challenging."

I nodded.

Maria finished filling in the rest of the chart and said, "So my main job today is to figure out how things are going. Tell me about your family."

"I'm married, and I have two girls, ages four and eight. We had a nanny to help with the girls when they were babies, but we haven't had anyone in years."

"Great," she said, getting out a notepad. "So, tell me about your typical day, every single movement, starting in the morning."

"*Every* movement? You're kidding, right? This has the makings of a riveting conversation," I said, laughing. Shalini chuckled.

Maria didn't even attempt a smile.

I sighed. Over the next fifteen minutes I was interrogated about every movement I made throughout the day. I was sure the Spanish Inquisition would have been easier. When we finally reached the point in the evening when I went to bed, she turned to a fresh page of the notepad and asked, "Now to an atypical day. Do you have any hobbies?"

I exhaled loudly. "Yeah, right now I'm working on a heritage scrapbook album for my husband's family, tracing them back to the mid-1800s."

Shalini added, "Her scrapbooks are gorgeous and intricate. She could win awards."

Maria looked unimpressed. "How often do you work on your scrapbooks and for how long?"

"I don't work on them every day, but when I do, I usually work for two to three hours after the kids go to bed. It relaxes me, even when my arm hurts."

Maria nodded. "What else do you do? Do you like to cook?"

"Yeah, I really like cooking."

Shalini interjected, "She's an amazing cook. More like a gourmet chef."

Maria finally smiled. "So you're a gourmet cook and a scrapbooker extraordinaire. Anything else?"

Before I could answer, Shalini jumped in. "She makes jewelry and sells it at a boutique store." She motioned to her necklace and said, "She made this one for me. She also does watercolor painting and paints dishes."

I looked at her in shock.

Shalini turned to me. "What?" she laughed. "I knew *you* weren't going to tell about everything you do, so I'm going to."

"She makes it sound like I'm a psychotically compulsive artist, which I probably am," I told Maria. "But I like creating things with my hands. It's been getting harder with this arm, though. I've had to stop almost everything when the effects of the cortisone shots have worn off, so I'm hoping you can fix that."

Maria's smile was definitely forced. "I'm pretty sure you have postpolio syndrome, and we'll talk extensively about what that means over the next few days. Essentially, about thirty or forty years after someone first contracts polio their body goes backward, and their progress starts unwinding. The muscles affected by polio that were overused eventually stop working."

"What do you mean by overused? My whole body was affected by polio, except maybe my right hand. What does that mean for me?"

"It's complicated, but when you contract polio, your motor neurons die. That's why you were immediately paralyzed. Then your body sprouts something like secondary motor neurons, but they eventually wear out. So the more you use your muscles, the weaker you get. Down the road you'll probably use up your energy and be left as you were when you first contracted polio."

She paused, then finally added, "You were a quadriplegic."

As I was absorbing her words, she added, "From your evaluation, your right hand was affected too. It will wear out as well. So you need to start saving your hands and arms now by limiting your activities, especially your hobbies. I'm sorry to throw all this on you now, but do you have any questions before I take you back to the waiting room for your next appointment?"

Do I have any questions? I have a million!

One month after Paul died, one of my doctors suggested I join a post-polio support group because of some carpal-tunnel issues I was experiencing in my right hand. I didn't even know what post-polio was, so I called and talked to the moderator of the group. "I want to die," she told me, as a way to spark a friendly, supportive conversation, "because the pain is just mind-blowing." That didn't sound like a group I wanted to be a part of, so I never joined.

"How long do I have?" I finally asked Maria. "And what happens if I don't make any changes right away?"

"Well . . ." Maria paused again, trying to choose her words carefully, "you don't need to cut out everything immediately. But if you don't make any changes, someone will be feeding you in ten years."

My mind went blank. I was thirty-eight. This could *not* be happening to me. It was almost like contracting polio all over again, being forced to give up the life that I'd struggled to achieve.

I looked over at Shalini. She was furiously taking notes. She glanced up and smiled weakly and then went back to writing.

"I know this is very hard news," Maria said. "You're going to see a lot of people in the next few days, and then our team will make collective recommendations."

I nodded and whispered, "Thanks," as Shalini excused herself to go to the restroom.

The remainder of the day was filled with specialists, each person telling me how weak I was and what I needed to eliminate. When Shalini and I walked out of the clinic at 3:00 p.m., I felt as if I'd been inside for three full days.

In the car, neither of us knew what to say. Finally Shalini offered, "We can talk if you want. But if not, let's go shopping. We deserve a little retail therapy, and you can look for a jean jacket like mine."

We got to Macy's and separated to begin our hunt. Life was normal for everyone around me. People were shopping and laughing, trying on clothes and talking about their lives. I froze in the middle of the store. My world had stopped. I pulled out my cell phone and dialed Dave, but by the time he answered I was crying so hard he couldn't understand me.

I hung up and bought two different denim jackets. What else could I do? I had to try something, anything, to distract myself and numb the pain.

Back in the car, Shalini and I discussed our purchases as we drove to the hotel, comparing how much money we'd saved. The conversation was completely typical and utterly bizarre at the same time.

"It's a good thing I brought a huge suitcase, because I'm always prepared to find bargains. And I love the jackets. They'll look great with my Keds," I said.

"They are great jackets," Shalini agreed. "But I don't think you'll ever be wearing Keds again. They said you'll need special shoes for better support. I think you need to listen to that."

As she was speaking, my body filled with rage.

"Do you have *any* idea what I'm dealing with? You can wear any shoes you want!" I screamed. "Life is easy for you, and it always has been. My entire life is crumbling in front of me, and you have the nerve to tell me I can't wear the shoes I want?" Sobbing, I faced the window and stared out miserably until we reached the hotel.

When we parked, Shalini turned toward me. Tears were rolling down her face. She said, "I only understand a little of what you're dealing with, but I'm trying. I went into the bathroom after our meeting with Maria because I knew I was about to cry uncontrollably. This is horrible and completely unfair. You've been through enough already."

I turned back to face her. By now we were both sobbing.

"I know you love your Keds, your only normal shoes, because you used to wear those ugly orthopedic shoes when we were kids. You always wanted to wear cute shoes. But I want to help you do what they're suggesting now because it's best for you."

Her words deflated my tension and anger. Somehow I felt safe again. Shalini did understand—and she had already spent several hundred hours of her life in hospital waiting rooms because of me. We talked for a few minutes about adjusting to these changes, about processing the staggering loss before me, about trusting God in the dark. I told her how I felt blindsided and terrified.

The whole time my sister listened and nodded, holding my hand.

⁕

The next day, Dr. Silver, the head of the clinic, performed an electromyography procedure to get a precise reading on the condition of my muscles and ran additional tests, which lasted for hours. Then, on the third day, we met with the entire staff, led by Dr. Silver.

She began by saying, "It's been great having you here. I know we've drilled into you the importance of conserving your energy. Your energy is like money in a bank. Whenever you expend it, you're making a withdrawal, and you need to make sure it doesn't run out." She paused, then continued, "Unfortunately, this intense pain in your arm is part of post-polio syndrome and will never fully resolve. You need to get a brace made for your arm, and then stop using your arm as much as possible. I'm going to prescribe stronger pain medication and massage therapy, which should help a little. But you need to get used to less activity and increasing pain."

Everyone nodded. That information alone was overwhelming, but I had to pay attention to the rest of what she was saying, so I mentally pushed it aside.

"As your sister testifies," Dr. Silver said, "you are a remarkable person. In all my years in this field, I've never seen anyone walk with as little muscle as you have. On paper, what you've accomplished is impossible. But you have to protect what you have."

Shalini took notes as the doctor listed the team's recommendations:

Don't move hands when talking.
Limit all hobbies.
Use voice recognition software to type or write.
Use an electric wheelchair.

Every recommendation felt like another blow, another loss in a series of endless losses, another painful reminder of what I would be giving up. Before long we were saying goodbye to the staff. I wondered if they knew what it felt like to be given such life-altering news.

In the car on the way to the airport, I stared out the window, watching houses and trees rush past. I broke the silence. "It feels like life is rushing past me faster than before. Everything is about to change. I thought the pain was a temporary problem and would get better soon. But instead it's the start of a new normal, one where every day will be harder than the day before. I can't do this, Shal—"

"I know, Vaneetha. I'm so sorry. I'm here for you to do whatever you need." Her eyes were fixed on the road ahead, but her cheeks were wet.

I couldn't talk about it anymore. The weight of the last meeting had shut me down emotionally, and I needed to shift the mood. "You know, now that I'm looking at your denim jacket and mine in the light of day . . ." I said, drawing out the moment, "I agree with your opinion that *mine* is cuter than *yours*."

Tears became shaky laughter as we drove toward the airport and whatever my new normal would be.

Chapter 14

ANOTHER LOSS

I didn't tell Dave what a diagnosis of post-polio meant until we were face-to-face because it seemed too complicated and too painful to explain over the phone. But when I got back from Boston, I told him everything the team at the clinic had said, and he immediately wrapped his arms around me and held me as I cried.

"I'm so sorry about this," he said. "After you figure out what you need, just get it, no matter what it costs."

I appreciated his words and support, but there was something I needed that no amount of money could buy: my identity.

We had recently changed churches, a decision that threw some of the changes in my life into sharp relief. At our old church I had headed up crafts for Vacation Bible School, taught Bible study, and usually been the first to sign up to take someone a meal. I loved cooking for others so much that when Katie was in preschool she had listed my favorite hobby as bringing meals to new babies. We didn't know many people at our new church, so I wasn't being called on to volunteer as much. But it didn't matter. I would never be that person again. I *couldn't* be that person.

I had always prided myself on my independence. Years earlier, when I worked for Bank of Boston, I lived on Beacon Hill in a third-floor apartment with no elevator, and every morning I walked half a mile to my office in the financial district. Now I was supposed to get an electric wheelchair and an adapted van. Maria's words echoed in my head: *If you don't make any changes, someone will be feeding you in ten years.*

Inside our house, the list of things I would no longer be able to do was devastating: scrapbooking, jewelry making, painting, cooking, cleaning up. It felt like I would become a prisoner, trapped in a breaking body inside a disintegrating house—and unable to do anything about it.

~§§§~

I shared my struggles with Jennifer and Lisa a few days after I returned.

"The hardest part of this," I told them, "is that the more I do, the weaker I'll get. My decline will be based on how much or how little I do. My whole life has been about helping people and accomplishing things. How do I decide what to cut and what to keep doing? I don't even want to think about it. Let alone do it!"

Jennifer and Lisa listened and sympathized, giving me an outlet to say even the things I might hesitate to share.

At one point I told them, "Honestly, I'm upset at God about this. He made me a creative person and then suddenly took away my ability to create. It kills me to think of giving up my hobbies, especially scrapbooking."

And so my friends sat with me. We drank more tea, shared more stories, and prayed for each other. It felt good to have a safe place where I could be totally honest.

When I was a girl in the hospital ward, I had learned to cry in private and to present a strong face to my parents when they visited. Many nights my tears would soak the matted fur of my stuffed bunny. But when my parents sat beside my bed, I'd tell them funny stories about what had happened during the week. I never told them that a nurse had been mean to me or that I hated the food or that my legs felt like they were burning. I knew they loved me, and I didn't want them to worry that I was sad.

This sense of responsibility carried over, at least in part, to my adult life. But now, with Jennifer and Lisa, I felt free to share what was really bothering me. "The hardest part," I confessed, "is knowing I'll be a burden to people. I'd rather be dead than be a burden."

My friends sat in silence until Jennifer finally spoke. "You aren't a burden, and you never will be to those who love you. I'm going to pray that your strength will be like the flour and oil of the widow of Zarephath and it will never run out. You may not know how much energy you will have for the day, but God will give you all that you need."

Lisa nodded in agreement. But I lowered my head so my friends wouldn't see my horrified expression.

I knew the story of the widow of Zarephath in the Bible (1 Kings 17:7–16). She had only a few drops of oil and a handful of flour left when Elijah asked her for some bread. In fact, she was ready to die, knowing that they were the last morsels of food for her and her household. Still, she made bread for Elijah, and miraculously, she never ran out. She always woke to discover she had enough to make bread for her family and Elijah.

I knew what my beloved friends were promising me: that like the widow I could trust God to provide for me every day. But what they were describing was a life of uncertainty and dependence—and I hated both. I wasn't sure if I could handle that, let alone *pray* for that. Yet I appreciated their concern, their prayers, and their tears for me. We wept together.

As emotional as it was to tell Jennifer and Lisa about the clinic visit, I knew telling my parents would be worse.

My parents always pushed me to exercise and achieve as much as I could.

My dad often told me, "You're resilient, Vaneetha. You'll make it through." Mom often said she was thankful that my polio had done its damage all at once, in the beginning, so that each day afterward would be better than the day before. Now the opposite was true. Her dream for my life had always been that I'd be "normal." She encouraged me to walk as straight as I could and wear clothes that camouflaged my handicap.

When I shared the prognosis with them, Mom said she'd pray that the doctors would be baffled by my continued strength. "Vaneetha," she said, "you've *always* beaten the odds." I'd heard that countless times during my life, and so far it had been true. But the odds seemed longer now than they'd ever been before.

Each time I told someone about my diagnosis, I felt disconnected from the words leaving my mouth, as if I was describing what would happen to a stranger. I began to make dark jokes about it, hoping that entertaining people might push away the reality—or maybe I did it as a way to hide or deflect my fear.

Maxine and Jerry told me how sorry they were and that they were ready to help. I hoped they wouldn't think I was a burden on their son.

The girls seemed unaffected. "Daddy's gonna help more so Mommy can rest," Dave told them, and they seemed to accept that.

Jennifer made freezer meals so I wouldn't have to cook every night. My mom brought my favorite Indian meals over—shrimp curry, dhal with rice—and regularly took me grocery shopping. I learned to drive an electric shopping cart, but not before knocking over multiple displays of soup cans and watching in embarrassment as they clattered to the floor and rolled in all directions. Driving that cart was trickier than I thought.

I hired a friend to help organize closets, prep meals, and do basic household chores. I worried that with two young kids, Dave would become overwhelmed with all the extra work and see me as a burden.

I shared that concern with a married friend who had recently been hospitalized with bipolar disorder. Her mother-in-law addressed that same fear, saying, "You never know what God is doing in this. This might be the making of him."

I wanted to believe that for me as well.

⁓

I needed to begin following the directions Dr. Silver and her team had given me, but scrapbooking felt especially wrenching to give up.

I couldn't abandon Dave's family heritage album because I'd already poured hundreds of hours into it. So Dave patiently cropped pictures for me and proudly finished the album with me. But I knew I couldn't finish my family project, so I boxed up my research and put it in the attic.

I still took pictures of the girls, but I filed the photos in shoeboxes rather than scrapbooks.

One day I was helping Kristi get ready for a ballet recital. She was a rough-and-tumble little girl, but she'd agreed to take ballet to be with her big sister, Katie. "Hold still," I mumbled through lips pinching several bobby pins. I was attempting to pull back her short hair into a tight bun.

When I finally got all the pieces in, I noticed a ripple of hair on the top of Kristi's head that wasn't smoothed down. Kristi saw it too when she looked in the mirror. "Mommy! A bump!" she screamed.

She ran her hand over the top of her head, trying and failing to squish down the offending section of hair. She spun to face me. "You fix it!" she demanded, ripping out all the bobby pins. Her bun immediately unraveled.

I sighed and tried putting it up again, but my arms failed. I couldn't lift them, and when I tried to, I felt a searing pain.

"Why can't you help me?" she exclaimed. With her chubby arm she pushed the hairbrush onto my chest, but my arm, still hanging at my side, couldn't even grasp it.

Since Dave couldn't keep his own hair from sticking up, helping a four-year-old ballerina was out of the question. And I knew I would cry if I tried to explain the whole situation. "Go get Katie," I suggested. "Maybe she can help us."

"How come you can't do it?"

"Because my arms aren't working right now," I managed. The tears were *really* close. "Just get Katie."

Kristi sighed, then stomped off to find her big sister. I watched her pink leotard bounce through the doorway, and from the hallway I heard her yell, "I need my hair right, or I won't go!"

While accepting bad-hair days was one thing, accepting the menu changes was quite another. I was a foodie, and always made good dinners. Dave and I often had friends over, and I'd spend hours preparing the perfect meal. Then we'd sit around the table long after dinner was over, sharing stories and laughter.

But elaborate cooking wasted my energy, so I had to give it up. I stopped trying new recipes and eliminated old favorites. Instead, I began to cook basic fare: spaghetti with premade sauce, meatloaf, chicken with premade sauce, mac and cheese. Every meal involved a calculation: How much future strength was I robbing myself of to put food on the table for my family?

Dave began cooking, which I appreciated, but the girls categorically did not. He specialized in a dish I affectionately called tuna dump. The recipe was essentially as follows:

Ingredients
Canned tuna (3 cans)
Seashell pasta (1 package)
Velveeta cheese (1 block)
Cream soup (2 cans, any flavor)
Frozen or canned vegetables (any amount, any type)

Directions
Put all ingredients into a pot (in any order).
Bake at any temperature until molten.
Slop into bowls.
Enjoy!

The first time Dave served tuna dump, Kristi immediately asked, "Can I fast today?" Katie took a bite and promptly turned in her birthday coupon, which read: "Certificate good for not having to finish your dinner."

⸙

The electric wheelchair was the one change I couldn't gradually ease into. A wheelchair was binary: I was either in one or I was walking. And being in one meant I'd be viewed as disabled. I had spent my entire life fighting that label. But I couldn't ignore the math. Every minute I spent limping though Target or Macy's sapped energy from my finite battery.

I was forced to reframe how I viewed the wheelchair. I had to focus on what was good in my life and see the wheelchair as a blessing. Without it, I risked falling, wasting my energy, and being confined to the house more. The wheelchair offered me freedom. I had to change my perspective about using it—just as I had to change my perspective about everything. If I obsessed about what I'd lost or longed for or missed, I couldn't enjoy what I had. I needed to look forward and embrace the life I had, the life God had given me, even though I knew loss would be a constant.

Of course philosophizing didn't make things any easier. When Dave and I went Christmas shopping, looking for a sweater for Shalini's husband, I noticed the stares and curious looks. As we entered the store, the saleswoman looked at Dave and asked, "Is there anything I can help you find?"

I answered. "We're looking for a quarter-zip sweater for my brother-in-law. Do you have any of those?"

Continuing to look at Dave, she asked, "Is there any particular color or material you're looking for?"

"A wool blend would be great," I responded in a loud voice.

This time she looked down at me and said, "We just got a new shipment in with a merino blend." Then turning back to Dave, she said, "It's a little crowded in the store. The sweaters are in the back, and I'm not sure if her wheelchair will fit back there. I can bring them out to her."

Her? Her? I wanted to shout at her. "You can bring them out to *us!*" I answered.

Then she glanced down at me and said, "I'm so glad you're here. And I love your shoes."

My shoes? I laughed inside because we all knew my shoes—the kind the clinic had recommended—were truly ugly. She was simply doing what countless others would do: find one point of contact with me, like my shoes, and otherwise ignore me. Almost every time I went out in a wheelchair, people would address Dave *about* me, as if I couldn't speak for myself. I was no longer treated as an equal to people who were able-bodied, and I felt that humiliating loss of dignity.

But it was the small, seemingly insignificant losses that cut the deepest. Like the time I was trying to move a sculpture from one shelf to another and dropped it and it shattered. *I can't decorate anymore.* I hadn't even decorated much before, but I had once been *able* to if I wanted.

My mind flashed back to my childhood in the hospital ward, waiting for someone to bring me a bedpan. I could still feel the embarrassment and shame of being wiped, of being helpless. I shuddered knowing that one day I'd go back to that.

Was it possible to accept continual loss? To become used to the terror of constant decline? Or maybe the only possible reaction was to hate every single minute of it and rage against what was coming.

I began to read Joni Eareckson Tada, who became a quadriplegic at seventeen after a diving accident. As an artist and author of many books on suffering, she became my role model for living with loss and pain.

Joni wrote that her disability had deepened her passion for Jesus. I couldn't understand how, but I knew that the same God who had transformed Joni could transform me as well.

She often mentioned that the angels and demons are watching us to see how we respond to trials. Knowing her life could display God's worth to the unseen world inspired Joni to endure, to trust God, and even to choose joy when she was alone.

Joni's perspective helped me reframe my daily struggles that were largely hidden from others. I took comfort knowing God would never leave me and clung to this assurance from Isaiah 43:2:

> When you pass through the waters, I will be with you;
> and through the rivers, they shall not overwhelm you;
> when you walk through fire you shall not be burned,
> and the flame shall not consume you.

But even with these promises and Joni's example, despair and anger arrived in wave after wave.

God could have prevented this. Since he hadn't, did that mean he'd chosen this suffering for me? Why would he do that to me? Hadn't I been through enough? The questions felt unanswerable. Raw. I knew I needed God's help to go on. Yet I hesitated to cry out for help to the One who had seemingly *lowered* me into the pit, instead of lifting me out of it and setting my feet somewhere firm.

Just as in the months after Paul's death, lament became my language.

Morning after morning I woke to read and recopy the psalms of lament, claiming them for myself. Every word I shaped with my pen was depleting my body's energy, but writing by hand in my journal was too important to abandon. It was my one indulgence.

> Forsaken
> Broken
> Groaning
> No answers
> No rest
> No hope

I talked to God throughout the day, telling him everything that was hard, everything that felt crushing, everything I hated. I repeated the words of sorrow from Scripture until they became my vocabulary. As before, my brutal honesty pulled me toward God. And the closer I was drawn, the more my lament transformed into worship—and even trust.

Actually, it wasn't *transformed*. I learned that lament didn't need to be transformed—lament itself was an integral part of genuine trust and worship.

> I'd rather be dead than be a burden.

My fingers worked a pen across the page of my journal.

> Hearing others say their lives are harder because of me . . . it all seems too hard to imagine. It seems so unfair. But in your infinite wisdom, you chose this for me. You gave me the drive to push, to succeed, to help, and yet all along you knew this would happen. Show me what I can learn from this and help me glorify you through this. Help me to grieve honestly—but not as one without hope.

Sometimes it was hard to tell where my writing stopped and my prayer began. Sometimes I wrote things that I prayed would save my life.

My life is for your glory. Bring something beautiful out of it.

Chapter 15

DIRECTIONALLY CHALLENGED

Sometimes clichés are absolutely true. For a period of years, life *did* go by fast. Sometimes in a blur, sometimes just at a rapid clip, but never slowly. And despite being different from any other family we knew, we were also the same in too many ways to count—car pools, homework, vacations, all mixed in with bickering, figuring each other out, being selfish, and asking for forgiveness.

The girls were boisterous and spunky, and our home was fun and loud. We loved it that way. Dave and I were thriving as a couple and even started counseling other couples who were struggling in their marriages. Offering others what we had learned was rewarding.

Fortunately, some of the speeding through life happened while I was in the passenger seat—literally. I'd been directionally challenged my entire life, and post-polio gave me the excuse to drive less, letting Dave or a friend take the wheel.

Once when Jennifer was driving us on an errand using my handwritten directions, I told her, "Look for Exit 8."

"Which 8?" she asked. "8A or 8B?"

"I think we should take 8B."

Jennifer nodded and then smoothly turned off on 8A. We followed the rest of the directions closely and arrived without a problem.

"I'm so glad this turned out to be right and that you didn't hear me," I laughed, "because I said *8B*, not 8A."

Jennifer grinned. "Oh, I heard you. But since you have no sense of direction, I figured our best chance was to do the opposite of what you said." Parked in front of our destination, it was hard to argue with her logic.

My driving less and less—even with the *extremely* easy-to-turn adapted steering wheel in my minivan—coincided with a change in the girls' schooling. Katie and Kristi had both been attending a small private school, but with every passing year the cliques in Katie's class were becoming worse. As a result, she regularly came home from school in a miserable mood, and invariably she would take it out on us by arguing about inconsequential things, escalating into outright defiance. Dave and I knew something must have happened in class, but she would flatly refuse to talk about it.

Hoping to draw her out, I sat on Katie's bed and told her a story about when I was in fifth grade. It involved Shelley, the biggest and tallest girl in our class, who regularly stole cigarettes from her stepdad and smoked them by the train tracks after school.

One day, before class started, Shelley grabbed my left arm and shook it. "Look at her arm!" she hollered. "It *wiggles* when I shake it. There's nothing to it!" She lifted my left arm then let it go, so that it dropped to my side. Then she smirked and looked at the other kids who had gathered around. "Isn't that weird? I think it's funny."

No one said anything.

Then Shelley turned to me. "You don't mind me doing that do you? I mean, it doesn't make you cry or anything. If it does, you tell me and I'll stop. Okay? I think it's funny, that's all."

I bit my lip so hard it started bleeding, but I didn't say anything. I didn't want her to know how bad she had made me feel. The torture went on for months, but I was too embarrassed to tell anyone about it.

Katie listened to the whole story without reacting. "So . . . that's what happened to me," I concluded.

"Hmm," Katie said. I waited to see if any other information was forthcoming, but "hmm" turned out to be her whole response.

Even without being sure of Katie's situation at school, Dave and I decided to pull her out and teach her at home, at least for middle school. I was worried this would strain my arms, but Dave assured me that he'd help with anything I needed.

Kristi wanted to be homeschooled too. As always, she wanted to copy her big sister, but that wasn't her only motivation. She was a tomboy who insisted on wearing basketball shorts and T-shirts every day, something she couldn't do at her current private school. She also loved playing basketball with the boys—before school, at snack, at lunch, after school, then again in our driveway when she got home. So she was excited about the possibility of living in her athletic shorts and playing basketball all day.

With Dave's help, we set up our home office as a classroom. There was a computer desk with a PC the girls could share, my desk, a large round table where we could work, and bookshelves on two walls. We enrolled both girls in a nearby camp for homeschooled kids so they could play sports and have more social interaction.

Even with the perks of extra sleep, I knew homeschooling would be tough. Katie liked to question what I said—a *lot*—and often did the opposite of what I asked. I later learned this was normal behavior for teenagers, so Katie was just precocious for a ten-year-old. But since most of my friends had weirdly polite, obedient children who said "yes, ma'am" even to their mothers' nonverbal requests, I was never too far from feeling like a failure.

Because I couldn't figure out if the problem was me or Katie, I began to pray daily, on my face, asking God to change one or both of us. Not long afterward, when Dave and I were reading the Bible with the girls, I told them the story of how I had prayed when I was in high school, "God, if you are real, please show me," and how the next morning God had answered in an unmistakable way.

Katie rolled her eyes when she heard that.

But the next day she was a different person. She unloaded all the groceries when we got back from Kroger and asked if she could help make dinner. She organized the hall closet. She played with Kristi for hours without arguing. And when Dave came home from a business trip, she thanked him for working hard for us. I also noticed that when she had friends over, she asked them what they wanted to do instead of being bossy.

As Katie's new behavior continued into a second week, Jennifer and my mom asked what had happened, and I gave them both the same answer: "I have no idea!"

Three weeks later I had to know. "Katie, honey, your dad and I have noticed you're acting differently lately. What changed?"

She looked up from where she was reading on the couch. "I asked God the same question you did, to show me if he was real. And I asked him to help me be more cooperative."

"When did you ask that?"

"The night you told us about how you did the same thing."

I smiled, kissed the top of her head, and went into another room. I knew my enthusiasm would be a turnoff for her, so I tried to play it cool. But I couldn't stop grinning.

Katie had prayed the night of the eye roll. God had answered my prayers, and hers, exactly as we prayed them.

⸙

Our days settled into a rhythm of homeschooling, Dave's work, and evenings together as a family. My mom helped with homeschooling, introducing the girls to Shakespeare and quickly becoming their favorite teacher. This was good for all of us because my patience often ran short. For Mother's Day, Kristi made a MOMMY acrostic card, with Y for "yelling less and less." I took that as progress.

My fears about post-polio—excruciating pain, being fed by others, requiring a wheelchair full-time—had not yet materialized since my diagnosis four years earlier.

Dave and I led a church small group that had four other couples in it. We met twice a month over coffee, snacks, and dessert to pray for each other and discuss the previous Sunday's sermon.

Dave had left my dad's company in 2000 when it was sold and was now consulting with small start-ups. But he had recently started working remotely for a New York company that required him to spend two days away from home every other week. That meant our family was in the house together working during most days and talking or playing board games in the evenings. Katie and I always partnered, and Kristi, a daddy's girl, teamed up with Dave. The two of them hated to lose, and they usually didn't. But when Katie and I managed to win, we'd each start laughing uncontrollably by imitating their angry expressions, which, not surprisingly, rarely went over well with Dave and Kristi. They'd eventually get over it and challenge us to a rematch, insisting we play until they won. Those could be grueling nights. Still, it was a sweet season for our family.

Every summer we planned an extended vacation together. We were determined not to let my condition take away from our shared experiences, though we did adjust the activities we chose to do. While on vacation, Dave would leave his work at home and fully engage with us. One trip was to Hawaii, where we went snorkeling, and I got into the water with Dave's help. Later we drove to Hana for dinner and watched the sunset at an oceanside luau. On our last night I watched the girls coloring on placemats at a beautiful little restaurant overlooking the Pacific, and when all four of us burst into laughter together, turning every head in the restaurant, I wished the moment could last forever.

Our family was closer than ever, and even when Dave traveled for work, he included me whenever possible. When his new company had a national sales meeting at the Greenbrier resort hotel in West Virginia, he invited me to go with him. After check-in, Dave was pushing me down the long, carpeted hall toward our room when we saw Rich, an important client.

Dave shook Rich's hand and said, "It's great to see you. We're glad you can be here. I'd like to introduce you to my wife, Vaneetha."

Immediately I pushed up the footrests and stood, motioning Dave to move the wheelchair back. "It's so nice to meet you, Rich. Dave speaks highly of you," I said as I shook his hand. "I usually don't use this wheelchair, since I can walk without it, but this is such a big resort we thought I'd use it to get to our room."

Rich said that made perfect sense, since the hallway was about a mile long. The three of us stood talking for several minutes. Then Rich grabbed both my hands to say goodbye. "I've so enjoyed meeting you. You're a really special person."

I could tell Dave was pleased by that comment. As I got back into the wheelchair and we rolled down the hall, Dave said, "You always impress the people you meet. I'm really proud of you."

Rounding a corner, we saw a gift-shop window. Inside hung a large hammered-gold plate with the words "Proverbs 31" etched in the center, and around it were all the attributes of the Proverbs 31 woman, widely regarded as the ideal wife and mother.

"Hey, look at that, Dave," I commented. "You rarely see Christian decorations like that in hotel gift shops."

Dave walked into the store and came back right away. "Okay," he said, half laughing, "that plate costs a *thousand* dollars!"

"What?!"

"But listen, I want to buy it for the living room. I want everyone to know that you're even better than the Proverbs 31 woman."

I was quiet for a few seconds, touched by Dave's thoughtfulness.

Then, of course, I cracked a joke. "What kind of narcissist would display a *giant* gold plate at home as a tribute to their own godliness?"

We both laughed, but then I grew serious. "But, wow, I didn't expect that offer. We don't need to spend that money, but it means the world to me that you want to buy it."

Dave kissed me, and as we continued toward our room I felt lighter, happier than I'd imagined was possible.

In October 2008 Katie told us she wanted to be baptized.

By then Dave had been offered a big promotion, but the drawback was that he needed to be in New York full-time. I was willing to move, but Dave didn't want to uproot our family in case his new position didn't work out. He proposed commuting for six months—weekdays in a New York hotel, weekends with us—and then reevaluating. I was nervous we'd grow apart, but Dave assured me our marriage was too strong for that to happen. I was thankful he would be home on weekends for events like Katie's baptism.

Our church gathered at Falls Lake State Recreation Area where, in front of a few hundred people, Katie stood on the shore and talked about her faith. She spoke about how she'd asked God if he was real and God had answered. She told them she wanted to be baptized and make a public commitment and take communion at church as a full member. Everyone could see in her face and in the way she talked that God was real to her. God mattered. God had changed her.

Tom, our pastor, asked Dave if he wanted to help baptize Katie, and together they waded into the water.

"You'll go down in the water of baptism because you've been buried with Christ, and when you come up, you'll be raised with him to walk in a new life."

Katie held her nose, and Dave and Tom lowered her backward

into the lake. She emerged, spluttering but smiling, and hugged Dave, soaking his red polo shirt. Then she waded back to shore where one of her friends was waiting with a towel.

After the baptism, it was time for lunch. All of us heaped our Styrofoam plates with traditional Carolina barbecue, coleslaw, and hush puppies. For the next few hours, we laughed and talked to friends under the covered shelter while the girls played Frisbee on the beach. The four of us were among the last to leave.

As we gathered everything and walked to the car, Kristi grabbed Dave's hand and said, "I'm so glad you're here, Daddy. I love it when we're all together."

I smiled. I loved it too.

Chapter 16

SURPRISED AGAIN

We all missed Dave when he was gone during the week, but we grew used to it. The four of us looked forward to weekends together, and Dave and I talked on the phone for hours, so I felt we were close even when we were separated.

But ever so slowly we began to drift apart. Our phone conversations became five-minute informational updates before he had to go. And on weekends when he was home, Dave would play solitaire for hours on the computer. We also stopped leading our small group because of Dave's intermittent weekend travel, but we were still part of the group.

More and more Dave would be gone for two weeks straight because of weekend sales events, and even mentioned getting an apartment in New York instead of staying in a hotel. I told him New York wasn't our home—or his—unless we moved there together.

In early 2009 Dave and I went out to dinner to discuss how we were feeling. Our salads hadn't even arrived when he said, "I'm so unhappy in our marriage that sometimes I don't even want to come home. I feel like a stranger here."

Taken aback, I was silent for a few seconds. "It's hard for me too. Maybe you can cut back your travel and be home more often. I feel like a single parent."

"The thing is, I don't want to come back here more often. I feel more alive when I'm in New York. All the travel is getting to me, and

I want to find things to do up there. I think I want to start rowing crew or something like that."

"Rowing crew? Taking up a sport *there*? Where is that coming from?" He'd never mentioned rowing before in his life. "Then why don't we move? We were going to try this for six months and then see. So let's move!"

"I don't want to uproot the family yet. Let's wait and see what happens. Work has me under a ton of pressure right now," he said, agitated. "You wouldn't understand."

I tried to get Dave to tell me more about New York, but he became strangely silent. We finished the rest of our dinner and drove home with long gaps in conversation. I couldn't figure out what to say.

Back at home that night, I tried to piece together our conversation. *Why was Dave so unhappy? Why did he not want to come home? Why would he want to take up a brand-new sport? None of it made sense, unless . . .*

I impulsively asked Dave if he was seeing someone.

He hesitated, then said, "No, there isn't anyone else. I just feel numb."

His words relieved me, but our conversation had been so cryptic that I couldn't sleep. I felt too fragile to bring up the conversation again but asked if we could go to counseling. He wasn't interested.

Dave spent the rest of the weekend mostly in his home office, then left for New York on Sunday night. As he was leaving, he suggested I contact Tom, our pastor. I agreed.

Monday morning I called Tom and told him what had happened. He asked a few questions and then invited me to come to the church office. After I hung up, I looked for the birthday letter Dave had written to me in late December and stuffed it into my purse. The letter seemed affectionate, and I hoped it would show Tom that we weren't in an unsolvable crisis, and that maybe Dave was right and all the stress from work was getting to him.

When I sat down in Tom's office he said, "I'm so sorry that you guys are going through this. Tell me how things have been between you."

"Dave's been busy at work," I began, "but . . . I don't know. I brought a letter that Dave wrote for my birthday. It seems warm, don't you think?"

I unfolded the crinkled letter and smoothed it out for Tom. He skimmed it and commented, "It does sound affectionate at the beginning, especially when he says, 'My dearest Vaneetha.' But a lot of it could have been written by a friend and not a lover."

I'd been hoping Tom would confirm that Dave still loved me. Instead the pit in my stomach grew. I needed to hold on to something, anything, to assure myself that this was not a crisis. Suddenly, feeling foolish, I stuck the letter back in my purse and looked away.

Tom noticed my embarrassment. "Maybe the two of you should come in and talk. I'll reach out to Dave."

◎∰〜

"I'm seeing someone else," Dave said matter-of-factly, as if he were talking about the weather to a stranger.

It was Friday afternoon, and Dave had gone straight from the airport to meet with Tom before Kristi's evening basketball game. He'd just arrived home and asked if he could talk to me in the kitchen.

I grabbed the counter to stop myself from falling onto the hardwood floor. The ground beneath me seemed to be swaying uncontrollably. I lurched to a barstool and sat, waiting for my racing heart to calm down.

Dave looked down at me. "I'm so sorry, Van. Are you okay?"

I rarely used profanity but swearing seemed more appropriate than any response I could think of. Maybe if I'd had more breath in my body I would have. *Was I okay?*

"I know this is going to hurt you, but I never wanted to hurt you. Please believe me when I say that."

Maybe those words eased his conscience, but to me they were meaningless. I was having trouble breathing. Part of me wondered if I could actually suffocate from the pain. It felt like a real possibility.

Eventually I spoke. "How could you? After all we've been through, I never thought you'd do this to me again!" Then I added, "So who is she? And how long has this been going on?"

"I don't want to get into details now, but we'll talk about it at Tom and Carol's house. They've invited us over after the game," Dave said, then paused. "I really *am* sorry about this. Her name is Tiffany, and it's been going on for a while."

I felt my body wander into the living room and my muscles go slack as I collapsed on the floor. But I stood again. I couldn't think of a good excuse to give Kristi for missing her game, so I went into the bathroom and called Jennifer and asked her to meet us there. Then I steeled myself and reapplied my makeup.

Will people know I've been crying? I wondered as I stared in the mirror. I looked closer at my wrinkles. *Does Dave not think I'm attractive anymore?* There was no time for further reflection as Dave called me from the kitchen. Mechanically I got into the minivan, and Dave drove to the gym. I was thankful that Katie was at a friend's house and would meet us there and that I'd already dropped Kristi off with the team.

I sat in the front row because the bleacher stairs were almost impossible for me to navigate. Jennifer sat beside me. I didn't know where Dave was, and I didn't care.

"Her name is *Tiffany*," I hissed to Jennifer.

She sighed. "Oh, Vaneetha."

"And he said it's been—"

My words were interrupted by cheers. Kristi had just sunk a deep three-pointer. "You go, Kristi!" yelled Jennifer. As Kristi ran back up the court she looked over and saw the two of us. I smiled and waved.

"He said it's been going on for *a while*, Jennifer," I continued. "What does that even mean?"

She rubbed my back. "I don't know, Vaneetha. I'm so angry right now. I can't believe he's doing this to you." She paused, and then said, "I wonder what he's doing right now?" as she gestured with her head.

I looked. Dave was sitting a few rows back by himself, texting. I was pretty sure I knew who was on the other end of the message.

❦

"So, what have you two discussed so far?" Tom asked.

I gripped my coffee mug tightly. Tom's wife, Carol, sat beside me on a small couch. Dave and Tom sat in separate chairs.

I recapped what I knew. Dave talked about his feelings, saying he was confused about what to do and was sorry he had hurt me.

Tom talked about the nature of sin and how Dave would need to end things with Tiffany before he could move forward with God or with me, and how even that might not be enough. Dave promised he would try, but then confessed that part of him didn't want to break up with Tiffany.

"How often do you see each other?" I didn't want to know—not really, since once was too often—but I couldn't help asking.

"Well . . . we're actually living together," Dave said. "Instead of staying in a hotel, I got an apartment with her."

Tom, Carol, and I collectively inhaled. Then there was absolute silence for a few seconds as the three of us stared at one another and tried to process what Dave had said. All of us assumed this was a casual relationship or an impulsive fling, but the whole picture had just changed dramatically.

Nauseated, I struggled to push myself out of the chair. I walked toward the guest bathroom, dry heaving along the way. *This couldn't be my life. It just couldn't.*

"Vaneetha?" Carol had followed me.

I reached the bathroom door but didn't enter. Another dry heave. I put my right hand on the doorframe for support. Then I screamed at full volume, with every bit of rage and sadness and disbelief that was churning inside me. A long breath in, and then, "Why does God hate me!"

Dave and Tom heard it too. Who cared? I wanted them to hear. I wanted God to hear. Was God even listening? How could he have let this happen? Why was I always the one having to steel myself, calm myself, be the grown-up while Dave acted like a selfish child?

I returned to the living room. "Dave, I need to know. Do you love her?"

Dave nodded.

"How do you feel about me? Do you even love me anymore?"

He considered his answer. "Yes, I love you. But I love you like a sister."

❧

The old, familiar feeling of inadequacy enveloped me like a straitjacket.

My friend Christa kept the girls for the weekend. Dave hid in the office playing computer games. I stayed at the kitchen table.

When Dave left the office, he alternated between talking about how messed up he was and how distant I seemed. He remarked more than once that my body language and tone of voice was cold, and that it didn't help him want to come back to me.

I didn't expect empathy from him, or even sympathy, and I wasn't disappointed.

Dave flew back to New York Sunday evening, and Christa dropped the girls off Monday morning. I stayed in bed all week, wrapped in blankets. I told the girls I was sick, so they could homeschool themselves or hang out with friends. When they came into my room, I pretended to be asleep.

Sometimes I prayed and read my Bible. I cried a lot. I drank water but didn't eat.

My closest friends came to sit by my bed and put meals in the refrigerator for the girls. Tom called twice daily. He offered no false promises, just assured me that Jesus would never leave me.

Before leaving, Dave had agreed to end things with Tiffany that week, but on Thursday he called and told me he hadn't.

"Why not? You're coming home tomorrow night," I said. I didn't understand what he was telling me.

He clarified. "I haven't broken up with her yet because I love her and don't want to leave her."

Part of me died.

I hung up the phone and crawled back into bed.

The next morning I had to open the door for a plumber to fix the sink. I walked into Dave's office to get the checkbook and saw a handwritten letter covered in pink hearts. It was from Tiffany to Dave.

Don't read it, I thought.

I did anyway. Toward the end of the letter she mentioned the little chunks of chocolate he'd save for her from his last bite of ice cream when they were snuggling on the couch.

Tiffany had replaced me.

⁂

I forced myself to go to lunch with Sally, a friend and mentor. I told her I felt rejected and unwanted, as though I wasn't enough and never had been. I told her how Dave could only talk about himself and how broken he was and how hard everything had been for him. For *him*.

"Believe it or not, Dave's reaction is typical," she told me. "I've seen it before. Sin makes you stupid and selfish. People in affairs don't think about those they've hurt. They can't. Because if they did, they would be horrified. To keep going, they have to see other people as two-dimensional stick figures, like cartoons, with no feelings."

I asked her for advice because I no longer trusted my judgment.

She told me she wished she could tell me what to do, but she honestly didn't know.

When I finished crying, I ordered pad thai, and Sally asked for a cup of tea. She apologized, pointing to her forehead. "I'm sorry I'm not eating. I'm fasting, but I didn't want to cancel our lunch."

I looked and noticed the faint, dark smudge on her skin. I'd forgotten it was Ash Wednesday. It felt as if I'd forgotten everything important, everything good.

When the girls were asleep, I sat down in my office to write Dave an email. I was thankful that I could dictate the words using my voice recognition software, because I couldn't have done it otherwise. The stress of the past two weeks had made my muscles weaker than before. I settled into my chair and began speaking into the headset.

> I'm sure this letter will be jumbled and disorganized and stream of consciousness, because that is the only way I can get my thoughts together on this. Even as I write this I am crying.

My tears blurred the screen. *Get it together, or this is going to take all night*, I told myself.

> It's taken me a while to face how unloved I feel from everything that has happened. I kept trying to tell myself that you really do love me and that somehow you'll wake up and realize what you have done and are doing to me. That you want me back and you'll come running home and throw your arms around me and tell me that you never stopped loving me and that you're sorry for every way that you hurt me and that you'll make it up to me.

Even as I wrote, I wondered if this was just a crazy fantasy. What was real about us? Did I even know Dave or had I just made up who I thought he was?

You were my best friend, and I longed to share my days with you.

I thought about when Dave was away in New York or on a business trip to some faraway place. When he was gone, he was constantly on my mind. I prayed for the details of his day. I wondered how he was. I jotted down things I wanted to tell him. I couldn't wait for him to call at night—and felt devastated when he seemed distant.

I was crying again and had to constantly repeat my phrases because the software couldn't understand me. I cleared my throat and continued.

Sometimes I would hang up and cry after we talked because our conversation was so empty, and I felt lonelier after we talked than I had before we started.

Writing the email was forcing me to reevaluate everything about our relationship. Maybe my version of reality was just a fairy tale I'd made up.

I've come to question everything that I once thought was true about us. I believed that you loved me, that you liked spending time with me, that you wanted the best for me, that you were on my side, and that you would never intentionally hurt me.

I tried to stretch a cramp out of my arm, which was aching more and more. Dave used to rub out the knots, but there was no one to do that now. I reread the last sentence and realized that what I believed was irrelevant to Dave. No matter how many times he chose to play the "never meant to hurt you" card, I wouldn't believe it. Perhaps it was just callous indifference on his part, but that felt even worse. Couldn't he see that what he did would devastate me?

> I trusted you, but now I feel like a fool for trusting you. After all that we have been through, I didn't think you would have another affair.

I paused. I wasn't sure how vulnerable I wanted to be. He didn't deserve to know the depth of my pain, but I needed to say everything I felt. I knew I wouldn't be writing another heartfelt email like this, so I forged ahead.

> You have loved a lot of women, but I have only loved you. I trusted you to protect me, to cherish me, and to love me. When I was in high school, and very concerned about my body, I remember going to my doctor about having some type of plastic surgery. The doctor said that my scars and my body would be beautiful to someone because they represented all that I'd been through. I didn't believe him but hoped that would be true.

By the time I asked my doctor about plastic surgery, I'd had twenty-one operations on my legs. My best friend, Maggie, tried to convince me to hang out at the beach with our other high school friends, but I didn't want to.

"I feel ashamed when I look at my legs," I told her. "I feel ugly and out of place, like I don't belong with all of you and your perfect bodies. I want to *hide* my body, not let people see it."

Maggie told me there were things about her body she wanted to hide, and everyone she knew felt the same way about their bodies. She added that no one cared about my scarred legs but me. I believed her and ended up going to the beach with the group. But now I wondered if her words were really true.

I continued with the email.

After the first affair, I felt the doctors were wrong and that I really didn't measure up. But after several years, I started to really believe that you loved every part of me and it didn't matter how scarred and imperfect my body was. I have to tell you that this affair has shattered any illusions I ever had about my body. But there's nothing I can do to change my body. This is me. It is all that I have.

I stared at the screen. I considered deleting the last paragraph. I felt so exposed writing it. But it was the truth, and I wanted him to face how deeply he had hurt me. But what was next? Just this clarity:

I am face-to-face with the way things are.

By the time I finished composing the email, it was almost 2:00 a.m. There was no way I was going to force myself to reread the whole thing. My eyes were so tired—*I* was so tired—I wasn't even sure if I could. I simply reread the final part.

I gave you my hopes and dreams and I feel that you didn't value them, but rather discarded them to look for something better. I wasn't good enough.

It was true. I clicked Send.

Chapter 17

REACTIONS

I asked Dave to move out.

He agreed, albeit reluctantly, and found a place nearby to rent. We agreed that before he left we needed to tell the girls.

I dreaded the conversation. Kristi and Katie were ten and thirteen, and I knew they would be devastated. But I was glad I wouldn't need to keep the secret from them anymore. Both had noticed my coldness toward Dave and asked why I was being so mean to their dad. At least now they would know the reason.

I wanted Dave to tell the girls himself so he could feel the weight of his choices. That night we rented a movie, *Kung Fu Panda*, and ordered pizza. Before we put in the DVD, Dave took the girls into another room to talk while I waited in the bedroom, praying constantly.

Then I heard Katie run sobbing into the guest room and then slam the door. Kristi knocked softly on my door a minute later.

"Are you in there, Mommy? Can I come in?"

"Sure, come on in, sweetheart. How are you doing?" I asked, trying not to let her see my tears.

"I'm okay. But how are you, Mommy? Are you okay?"

"Yeah, I'm okay too, sweetheart," I said. I hugged her tight and then asked, "How is Katie doing?"

Kristi shrugged. "I dunno. She ran into the guest room, so I came to check on you."

"Thank you, sweetheart. I'll go check on Katie, and then we can watch the movie if you want to."

Kristi nodded and left.

I found Katie huddled in the corner of the guest room, crying. It looked like it had snowed wadded-up Kleenex all around her. I sat on the edge of the bed and waited for a minute. "Do you want to talk about this, princess?"

Katie shook her head, but then asked, "I didn't know any of this. Why didn't you tell me before? What's going to happen to us?"

"Oh, Katie, I wish I had answers. I don't know what's going to happen. But I do know God will take care of us. I didn't tell you earlier because I was trying to figure out what was happening myself, and your dad hadn't decided what he was going to do. But I haven't known very long either."

Katie tossed another Kleenex on the floor.

"So what really happened with Dad? He didn't tell us much. Can you tell me?"

What exactly had Dave said? I learned from Katie that he presented minimal information, making it sound like I was the one provoking our separation. He told them I had asked him to move out of the house because he was seeing someone else. When Katie asked if we were getting divorced, he said he didn't know what was going to happen in the future, and that all he knew was that I had asked him to move out.

He told them I asked him to move out? Why didn't he tell them I wanted him to stay but that he couldn't have Tiffany and us? Wasn't that the whole issue?

I hesitated to tell Katie too much. I was torn between giving her the details Dave had omitted and letting her find out from her father. I felt he needed to be the one to explain—these were his choices, not mine. And I didn't want to potentially turn the girls against him by giving my version of the story that they'd have to weigh against his. The truth would come out eventually.

I settled on saying, "For the details, you can ask your dad. It's his story to tell."

Katie was quiet for a minute. "So you can't tell me anything? I have to ask Dad myself?"

"I'm sorry, Katie. I know this is hard, and I hate this for you. But I don't want to make this any harder than it is, and if I tell you things that your dad hasn't said, it will make things more confusing for you."

Eventually Katie and I cleaned up the tissues and went together to the kitchen. The pizza was lukewarm. As Katie and I grabbed slices, I noticed Kristi was already on the couch with the DVD paused on the first scene.

Dave was on the couch as well.

Why I didn't make him go somewhere else, I don't know. Maybe I was still too afraid to assert myself. I wanted to cry or laugh but couldn't do either. The four of us watched the entire movie in surreal silence.

I didn't cry again until a few days later. I was sitting at the kitchen table, watching in silence as Dave carried a box of clothes and his toiletries to his car in the garage. *Why isn't he taking everything?* I wondered. But we weren't speaking much, so I didn't say a word. I heard his car start, and then I heard the garage door closing as he drove away from our home, from our marriage, from me.

I wept. And then it was done.

⚞⚟

Jennifer invited me over for lunch with Lisa, saying we could eat and pray. The stress had taken away my appetite, and I'd lost ten pounds, pulling my weight down below a hundred pounds. Jennifer's table was loaded with beautiful grilled panini sandwiches with tomatoes and mozzarella, a leafy green salad, a pasta salad, and fresh fruit.

"This looks amazing," I said as I sat down. "Thank you so much, but I still can't eat. Maybe I'll have a little green salad."

Jennifer looked at me, and then she set some pasta salad onto my plate. "I understand you're not hungry, but I made this for you. I know that, like me, you love food, so if you eat a little, it might make you hungry again. I also made a chocolate cake for you to take home to the girls."

I knew I couldn't win, so I reluctantly picked up a fork and took a bite. The pasta salad was delicious, so I kept eating. Jennifer had been right—and I was grateful to have a friend who knew when to tell me what to do.

Between bites I said, "I'm really struggling with what people will think of me. Will they think I lied to them about having a good marriage? I thought we did, but now I just feel like a fool. And if Dave stays with Tiffany and we get divorced, my ministry will be over."

"What do you mean over?" Lisa said, setting down her sandwich. "It's not like you've done anything wrong. Why would *your* ministry be over? You can still teach Bible study and mentor people."

"I think it'll be over because people act like divorced women aren't spiritually mature. Some even feel that divorced people shouldn't teach or even lead a small-group Bible study, no matter why they got divorced. It's kind of like having a scarlet A taped to your chest. Everyone who's divorced gets lumped into one category."

"I hear you, Vaneetha," Lisa said. "And I understand *some* people might not let you teach. But God is bigger than all of that. He will use this for good. So don't worry about your ministry. God will take care of that. Let's commit to pray about it."

"Could you guys also pray that I won't be bitter? I've talked to divorced people who immediately want to tell everyone how they've been wronged, and I feel tempted to head in that direction already. Pray that I'll have restraint and won't get bitter."

"You honestly don't seem bitter," Jennifer said. "But you know your heart better than anyone else."

Did I really know my own heart? Or was I hiding behind God talk because I didn't know how I felt or how I was supposed to feel?

Lisa interrupted my thoughts. "What else can we pray for?"

"Just the day-to-day details. I need wisdom on raising the girls and figuring out what to tell them and how to help them. They feel like I'm keeping secrets from them, which in a way I am because I don't want to tell them everything. They don't know about the first affair or that Dave is living with Tiffany or all the callous things he said. And, practically, I need to start doing things like paying the bills, which I haven't done in almost twenty years. I know it's not hard, but it's overwhelming to think about."

Eventually we finished talking and praying. Jennifer and Lisa hugged me, and Jennifer sent me home with her world-famous chocolate cake. I knew the girls would enjoy it because food was still a comfort to them.

They weren't home when I walked in, so I set the cake on the counter, cleaned up the kitchen, and looked at the calendar for the week. Our church small group was gathering the next night. Dave and I had missed the last meeting, and I was supposed to bring dessert to this one.

I felt my cheeks getting hot. No one in our group knew that Dave had moved out or that he was living with Tiffany in New York—and Dave and I were the former group leaders!

I'd once told the group, "We had a rough start to our marriage, but I love being married now. Through our struggles we learned that the secret of a great marriage is to talk about everything."

Now I wished I could swallow those words.

Impossible scenarios began to spin through my head, a cascade of events that would save my reputation. *Maybe Dave will leave*

Tiffany. He will repent and meet with our pastor. He'll win me back, patch things up with the girls, and move back home. Change could even start tomorrow, and no one in our Bible study group would even need to know about it until after the fact, when everything is happy again.

Intentionally shutting down any follow-up thoughts, I hid the cake in the garage fridge. That night, while the girls were watching TV, I told them I needed to run an errand. I drove to the home of the couple hosting the following evening. I smiled as I dropped off the cake, saying I was sorry that we couldn't make it, but Dave was out of town and it had been a long week for me.

I walked back to the minivan with the lie burning in my mouth. What I'd said was true, but only technically. *You can't even face the truth yourself, let alone tell other people about it.*

I drove home thinking about the girls. They would have happily devoured the cake, but I had cared more about how I looked than about how they were feeling.

That seemed like a recipe for trouble.

ℰℱℱ

Only a handful of friends knew what had happened—and of course Shalini. But I wasn't sure how to tell my parents.

I was afraid the news would crush them, especially my mother, who was already worried about how I was conserving my strength. And I knew they would want to know what had happened, but I didn't have the emotional energy to recount the details. Everything was still too raw. Shalini offered to tell them for me and flew into Raleigh. When I picked her up from the airport, she told me to take her directly to our parents' house and drop her off.

An hour later she called. She said Mom had been shocked when she opened the door. "Shalini! What are you doing here?"

Shalini jumped right in. "Mom, Dad, Dave left Vaneetha, and I wanted you to hear it from me in person."

The three of them sat in the living room while Shalini told them the entire story.

Dad was disappointed in Dave, especially because they had worked together and he respected him, but he had sensed that something was wrong for a while. "Tell Vaneetha we'll be here for her, whatever she needs. She just needs to ask. We'll do anything."

My mom said, "Oh, my poor girl. How is she? How will she make it on her own? What should we do?"

Shalini said she'd answered every one of Mom's questions.

I called my parents that afternoon, and they offered to help with whatever I needed. In the following days and weeks, they regularly kept the girls, and my mom often brought me comfort food. My dad called and offered to help with several home repairs that had been on Dave's list.

"Thank you, Dad," I told him. "But I remember how you once 'fixed' the garbage disposal. At this point I don't think we can afford the repairman who will inevitably come to fix your work!"

He laughed, and I could picture his eyes wrinkling as he smiled. "Okay, Vaneetha, okay. But listen, you need to be resilient. You've been through a lot in your life, and you can get through this too. I have faith in you, and I know that God will take care of you."

Dave came to Raleigh most weekends to spend time with the girls. After a while, though, Katie wrote him a letter saying she didn't want to see him. She wrote, "It feels like you are choosing Tiffany over me, and that hurts too much. You say you love me, but the fact that you are with Tiffany and have left us shows me that she means more to you than we do."

After that, Dave still kept coming on weekends, but he only saw Kristi. And life—now a very different life for all of us—went on.

⟡

When Dave left, I'd been reading Psalm 119, and it seemed long and repetitive. The psalmist went on and on, recounting the benefits of God's Word. But could it really do all it promised? Was the Bible actually going to help me? I'd trusted God to take care of me, and I wanted to believe the Bible when it said,

> I shall walk in a wide place,
>> for I have sought your precepts. . . .
>> and shall not be put to shame. (vv. 45–46)

But the road I was walking was twisted and dangerously narrow, and being put to shame felt like a daily occurrence.

I didn't really *doubt* God—not as I had after Paul's death. I knew intellectually that what was happening was for my good, but I couldn't see how it could actually *be* good. It felt awful and looked awful from every angle.

Dave's leaving brought an unshakable sense of worthlessness and shame. Shame that my Christian marriage had fallen apart. Shame that my husband had left me for someone else. Shame that I had proclaimed how good our marriage was, only to have my words turn against me.

Hadn't I suffered enough? I felt it was my turn to live a comparatively carefree life. But here I was with a broken marriage, struggling children, and a failing body. What was the use of faithfulness, and what would that faithfulness mean to others? My life felt like a jigsaw puzzle with every piece loose on the tabletop, and someone had flipped every piece upside down and thrown away the box. In my heart I still believed God could make something beautiful from my life, but I had no idea how or when I would see that.

Difficult as it was, continuing to teach the women's Bible study with my friend Florence helped keep me grounded. And even though Florence was one of a handful of people who knew what was happening in my life, simply being around people who loved God encouraged me—particularly because we were studying 1 Peter, a letter to churches that were being persecuted. It urged its recipients to stand strong, even in the face of suffering and opposition.

As a group we were memorizing 1 Peter 2:9–25, so each week I had a reason to focus on a different verse in depth. I would repeat the words throughout the day, asking God to make them real to me. I was struggling to apply these verses to my everyday life when Dave's parents arrived for Katie's fourteenth birthday at the end of April. They too had been devastated by Dave's actions, and I was looking forward to their usual support and help. They never missed either of the girls' birthdays, and I was thankful that they were willing to keep up that tradition.

Soon after they arrived, Jerry said he wanted to speak to me privately. When the moment came, I sat on the couch, but Jerry remained standing. He began to pace back and forth, faster and faster, then suddenly spun and began to hurl words—accusations—at me.

He detailed what I'd done wrong.

He outlined what I could fix.

He stated what my many shortcomings were and how much of this situation was my fault.

It felt as if his verbal assaults were pushing me deeper and deeper into the couch, and I was being weighed down by his wrath.

Before he could finish, I left and went straight to my bedroom, followed seconds later by Katie. She'd overheard part of the conversation and wanted to defend me to her grandfather. But I was afraid it would make things worse. So she just sat on my bed, stroking my arm, telling me that I had been a great wife and was a great mother and that she would vouch for me to anyone.

When I woke the next morning my mind instantly snapped to Jerry's words from the previous night. I thought about them as I was getting dressed, replaying them until I was livid. Then the words of

1 Peter 2:19 came to mind: "For this is a gracious thing, when, mindful of God, one endures sorrows while suffering unjustly."

I repeated that verse in my head as I greeted Jerry and Maxine, cooked breakfast, and chatted with them. I repeated it a hundred times, a thousand times, until I found myself standing on the front porch with Katie and Kristi, waving goodbye as Jerry and Maxine drove away.

Maybe for the last time.

Chapter 18

ACCEPTING WHAT IS

I sat at the kitchen table, staring at a stack of bills—just another downside of our family accountant moving out.

I'd already filled the minivan with gas for the week, shopped for groceries with my mom, and withdrawn cash from the ATM. Now I was struggling to make sense of a credit-card bill. Dave and I still used a joint checking account, so I was free to spend whatever I needed. The girls and I would be fine, at least financially.

But one amount on the bill jumped out at me: $2,499. It was from a jewelry store in New York. I put on my detective hat and found the number for the store.

"Hello, this is Matthias at DaVinci Family Jewelers. How can I help you today?"

"I noticed a charge on my credit-card statement, and I wanted to verify it. Can you tell me about a charge made a month ago?" I gave Matthias the amount and date, and he said to hold for a minute while he looked into it.

"Hello again," he said, coming back on the line. "Don't you remember that day? You came in together and picked out that stunning ring with the three emeralds and four diamonds, twisted together in a scroll design. You both loved it."

"Thanks," I mumbled, then hung up. I picked up my water glass and threw it hard against the edge of the sink, shattering it.

How in the world could any part of me *still* want to get back together with that man?

I could tell that some part of Dave wanted me back—or rather, he wanted the safety of his old life back. There was only so much I could manage in the way of empathy for him. But my guess was that he felt pulled in two directions, and rather than commit fully to Tiffany, he wanted to keep his options open. That was the point in my empathy where I usually felt the urge to look into gun permits, or at least sell his contact information to telemarketers.

Dave and I occasionally spoke with our former counselor, Bill, to make sure we could communicate civilly about necessary information. At those meetings Dave would say that he hadn't wanted to hurt me and still didn't, but then he would say also that whatever was happening between him and Tiffany was their business, not mine, and that I seemed cold and unwelcoming to him.

Of course I'm cold and unwelcoming now, you jerk, I thought, though I didn't voice it. The whole situation was honestly crazy making. Divorce would have been so much simpler in some ways, but I wasn't ready to give up on our marriage yet—or at least not on God's ability to redeem it.

Dave and I used to love hanging out together, more than most couples I knew. It had taken him a while to leave the fog after the first affair, but when he finally did, he had become a totally different person, and that person and I had been happy for years. At the same time, I didn't want to be duped or give in to wishful thinking. I knew our only hope was if God changed him, but I didn't know if God was going to do that.

So I came up with three conditions, both for my sanity and for absolute clarity with Dave. I could honestly say that *if* he met them, I would consider reconciliation. I knew that if God could raise the dead, he could certainly mend our marriage—again.

I outlined my conditions to Dave in an email and in person. I told him he needed to leave Tiffany completely and have no contact with her for an extended time. I told him he needed to repent truly, and that I'd seen it thirteen years before, so I *knew* what real brokenness looked like. I'd seen the fruit, at least for the years before he met Tiffany. And I told him he needed to *win* me back, not just settle for being back with me. Then I gave him an image I knew he'd understand. "I can't be broccoli, Dave. I need to be ice cream this time."

From the way his face hardened, I could tell he understood perfectly. He deflected on the first two points. Fine. That was what I expected. On the third point?

"For the record," he said, "I *like* broccoli. It's good for you. You can live on broccoli, but you can't live on ice cream. It's full of sugar and empty calories, and it's bad for your health. It's better to stay away from ice cream, so if I were you, I'd rather be broccoli than ice cream."

The stark clarity was helpful, if also devastating.

I reached for a tissue. Crying made me feel more vulnerable, but I needed to be absolutely certain about where we stood. So I asked, "If you found me so physically unattractive that I could never be ice cream, then why did you ask me to marry you, knowing you would always be drawn to other women?"

"I feel you're being overly sensitive and twisting my words out of context so you can throw them at me later," he sighed. "I'll probably regret saying this, but to be honest, I proposed because I knew you'd be good for me. And you have been. You were a great wife and the best friend I'd ever had. But you've got to have known that we never had that spark. I'm not sure what you want me to say. I can't make up feelings I never had. So don't expect me to win you back with wine and roses."

I didn't. And I never would. I was sure we were finished forever.

✦

Certain things I was good at, and certain things I wasn't. Painting was in the first category, and navigating in the second. Cooking in the first, homeschooling in the second. Making people laugh in the first, making unpopular decisions with the girls in the second.

There were some things, however, I truly excelled at, like at a world-class level. One of those was taking painful words and making them disappear. As soon as I heard them, I'd push them away and bury them as deeply inside myself as I could. So that's exactly what I did with Dave's words. As I dug a pit for them, a few other long-buried phrases whispered to me.

Cripple!

When I was in school rather than the hospital, I was self-conscious about everything. People made fun of both my limp and my mother, who wore Indian clothes, so I started asking Shalini to walk me home instead of her.

One day I decided to surprise my mother by walking home by myself. After all the kids had left the classroom, I went out from a side door so no one would accidentally knock me down. I was paying so much attention to walking straight that I didn't notice the boys until one of them threw a small rock at me. When I looked over at them, they began pelting me with small stones.

One of them yelled, "Cripple!" to a round of laughter. Another boy walked toward me, swaying from side to side to imitate my limp. I was terrified. When he reached me, he pushed my shoulders, and I fell to the ground. Then they ran away, leaving me crying in the gravel.

There was no one around to help me up, so I crawled to a nearby rock and pushed myself to my feet. Everything hurt as I walked home. I didn't tell my mother because I knew it would upset her. Instead, I pushed the experience down and tried not to think about it.

They feel sorry for you.

In high school my friend Maggie secretly submitted my name for the Winter Festival Queen ballot at the Sadie Hawkins Christmas dance. On the day of the election, I was working after school on the layout for the newspaper when a guy on the paper staff popped his head in the newsroom. "Hey, I want you to know that I voted for you today because I think you are pretty and nice," he said casually. "I mean, I know a lot of people are voting for you because they feel sorry for you, but that's not why I did."

I pushed his words away and focused on the layout, since I didn't think there was any chance I could win anyway. I was Indian and handicapped. Who would vote for me? The night of the dance, the DJ stopped the music to announce the winner. I walked to the front, feeling wildly out of place next to the other nominees with their perfect bodies, perfect makeup, and perfect hair. I scanned the faces in the crowd, wondering how many people felt sorry for me. When the DJ announced I was the new Winter Festival Queen, Maggie clapped wildly, but I didn't know how I felt. What was an award if it was given out of pity?

I can't date you because of your disability.

In Boston a guy named Patrick was a little too eager in his flirting for my taste. One day he asked me out to dinner, saying he wanted to talk about something. All week I dreaded that dinner because I knew he wanted to start dating.

At the cute neighborhood diner, Patrick sat opposite me. He took a deep breath and said, "There's actually something specific I want to talk to you about." I was mentally rehearsing how I'd let him down politely when he continued, "I know we're both kind of interested in each other, and we flirt from time to time, but I want you to know before this goes any further that I can't date you because of your disability."

A mixture of rage and shame filled me. Though I'd always walked with a pronounced limp, my disability didn't stand out otherwise. I never mentioned how tired I was or let people see how weak my shoulders were. I kept up with my friends in everything but sports.

So Patrick was saying that he was too embarrassed to be seen walking beside me as my boyfriend. His words stung.

Why am I pulling up all these hurtful comments from decades before? Whatever the reason, I shoved Dave's words down with the others, deeper and deeper, until they were gone.

I was afraid to express my anger and hurt, unsure where that would lead. And I felt obligated to be a good example for the girls. They needed me to be strong as we struggled to find our new identity as a family of three.

⁂

Shalini agreed. She came for a visit, and after two days of observing the chaos and bickering, she said, "I think you need to establish new traditions. You can't put your life on hold, waiting for Dave to come back and rebuild everything."

"I'm not exactly waiting for him," I said. "I gave him a three-part ultimatum."

My sister raised her eyebrows.

I ticked off the points with the fingers of my right hand. "One, no Tiffany, ever again. Two, show me you're really sorry and prove that you've changed. Three, woo me."

"*Woo* you?" Shalini laughed. "I'm sorry. I'm not making fun of you. I just—"

"I said 'woo,' and I meant it!" I said, joining her laughter. "It's fine. But look, I need to be the princess here, okay?"

"No, I get it," Shalini agreed. "And you deserve every bit of wooing in the world, but . . ."

"But you don't think he'll do it," I finished.

She looked at me. "Do you?"

"Probably not, at least not on his own initiative. But God could change that, right?"

"True. But it's not good for the girls or for you to wait on that, right?"

I nodded.

"The three of you need to figure out your *new* new normal."

"I don't have the energy, physical or mental, to do very much."

"I know you don't. But you need to change your family time. The four of you were like the legs on a chair, but now that one leg is gone it's unsafe to sit on it."

"Yeah, everything does feel unstable right now. But I don't know how or what to change."

"You guys are now like a three-legged stool. You need to find *new* ways of doing things together rather than trying to patch what you had."

So Shalini and I sat down at the table and listed all the things the girls and I could do. Have friends over. Go to friends' houses, even if we had to *strongly* hint for an invitation. Watch new TV shows and movies. Discover new restaurants. Buy games we'd never played with Dave. Go on vacations with just the three of us. We wrote out a list of friends to spend more time with.

When we had exhausted our ideas, Shalini said, "What else can I do here? Should we box up the rest of Dave's stuff from your closet? I noticed there's a ton of stuff still there. He has his own place here in Raleigh, so maybe he should come and get it."

When I didn't answer right away, she hesitated. "Vaneetha, why are they here anyway?"

"That's a good question," I admitted. "I'm not sure if I'm a wimp and too afraid of confrontation to *make* him take his things . . ."

Shalini nodded her head as though she understood my struggle.

"Or," I continued, "if I want to be a martyr and have everyone praise me for my graciousness. Or maybe something in between."

Shalini nodded again. "I get that doubting your own motives can be crazy making, but have you thought about asking him to take his stuff to his new place?" Her tone made it sound like she was asking me if I'd thought about breathing every day.

"Yeah, I have," I answered. "He said he'd rather keep things here, but he'd take them out if I wanted him to. I could tell my asking irritated him, so I didn't want to push it. But maybe I should."

I heard it when I said it. The codependency. The fear. The loss of self-respect. Why was I trying to placate Dave? How and when had I changed from a strong, self-confident person into someone who was too weak to stand up for herself? Why was I feeling guilty about any of this? That wasn't who I wanted to be—who God was calling me to be. Sisters sometimes see you better than you can see yourself.

"Yes, you should," she said, standing. "So let's go. We're boxing everything up. Meet me in your closet."

Before I could answer, she left to find boxes.

What followed was a frenzy of packing. Shalini started with an armful of shirts that she hastily stuffed into a box.

"Maybe we should fold—" I began.

"*Fold* them?" she practically shouted. She used her fist to shove the shirts deeper, wrinkling them even more in the process. "He's lucky I'm not going to leave all these cardboard boxes outside in the rain, which is what I *want* to do!"

Both of us burst into laughter.

"Listen, Vaneetha," she said. "We're doing this for you, not him."

When she finished taking Dave's things away, my large walk-in closet looked stark. Staring at the bare shelves and rods reminded me of how empty my life felt. Metal coat hangers from the dry cleaner were scattered on all the bars. Cobwebs clung to the back of the shelves. Empty drawers stuck out, revealing nothing inside. One of the light bulbs was burned out in the back, making the space even dimmer.

"This, Shal," I said, gesturing with my right hand. "This is what I'm afraid of. Look at everything. It's empty. How can I walk in here and be reminded of how bare my life is, when it used to be so full?"

"I know," Shalini said, as we both stared at the closet. "But now we can decorate the space for you. Your closet is huge! We can put a table and chair and even a bulletin board in here. It could be your prayer closet. Let me find things to use, and I'll show you what I mean."

My sister crisscrossed the house, grabbing scarves, Willow Tree figurines, framed Scripture verses, photos, and small pieces of artwork. She would put a few things up on a shelf, stand back, and see what was missing—a splash of color, or something taller—then run through the house again looking for it.

Two hours later we admired our handiwork. "Wow. I had no idea it could look like this. You were totally right. It's perfect."

Shalini shook her head. "It's not quite right. Not yet. But we're almost there. Come on, I'm taking you to Michaels."

I had to laugh at my manic sister. I hadn't been to that store in years. Not since my post-polio diagnosis had ended my scrapbooking and Dave had helped me crop my pictures and finish his family's heritage album. He had been so proud of it—and of me. Somehow that didn't matter anymore. This trip wasn't about him.

On our drive Shalini cranked up WRTP, my favorite local radio station, and we started dancing to the music. People who saw us through the windows must have thought something amazing had happened.

I got into the electric cart at the store as we started our hunt. I hadn't rolled down half an aisle when my eyes locked on a printed canvas. Shalini stopped beside me as we eyed the words of Proverbs 31:25–26:

> She is clothed with strength and dignity,
>   and she laughs without fear of the future.
> When she speaks, her words are wise,
>   and she gives instructions with kindness. (NLT)

My mind flashed back to the Proverbs 31 plaque in the gift shop at the Greenbrier. Dave had called me the Proverbs 31 woman, only better.

"Do you want that?" Shalini asked.

"No," I said. Then, with certainty, "No, not at all! It just reminded me of something."

Shalini crouched in front of me, and I told her the backstory. "I keep wondering when Dave stopped loving me. Did he love me then?"

Shalini leaned forward and took my hand.

"I keep reliving the past few years," I continued, "wondering what was real. It feels strange to look at my life through a different lens. Betrayal rewrites your memories."

"So . . . a *different* aisle," Shalini joked, and I laughed back.

Two aisles over I impulsively chose a notebook half filled with watercolor paper and half with plain paper. When I felt its weight in my hand, I knew it would be important. Somehow I knew it would be part of whatever God had planned for me in that closet.

We left Michaels and headed to Office Depot, where I found a French memo board, a bulletin board, and a chair for the long folding table Shalini had placed in the closet. Then we came home and put everything up. I stared in amazement. The space had been transformed. I would never have believed it was possible.

Everything happened so fast. One minute I was rambling to Shalini, and the next she was hanging the final bulletin board. My old Dave-and-Vaneetha's closet, with its empty shelves and painful memories, had become my new, beautiful prayer closet.

As we gathered my Bible, journal, and pens from my bedroom, where I'd read the Bible in the morning, and arranged them on the table, I knew I'd love this new space. I wondered if it would feel like a daily prayer retreat. Would I meet God here? Would he hear my prayers?

Would he organize this life that was in shambles?

Chapter 19

TRYING TO LOOK GOOD

Being a single parent felt almost worse than being in an accident. In fact, it felt like a daily collision in slow motion. In my watercolor notebook I painted a woman rowing a boat, alone, in the midst of a storm. She was looking up at a sky covered in black clouds.

When Kristi saw the painting, she asked where she and her sister were and insisted I add them. I inserted the tops of their heads, barely visible, as if they were huddled on the floor of the boat. In some ways it was nice to have all three of us in the picture, but even together, we were still in the middle of the storm.

I wouldn't have put it that way to any of my friends or the girls, of course. And I knew millions of other parents were struggling with the same everyday issues I was, but that didn't make it any easier. Defining our new life together was a constant challenge for two reasons. The girls and I were each individually processing our pain, sometimes in vastly different ways, which made our three-way relationship unpredictable. That, combined with my lack of energy and physical stamina, made each day the wrong kind of adventure.

There was a third factor too: Dave. I was still praying that I would not become bitter and thankfully had avoided criticizing Dave in front of the girls. I began to wonder, though, if my silence was harming them. If I was unwilling to be vulnerable about my own struggles— mostly because Dave's painful betrayal was the primary cause—what example was I setting for my daughters?

I took Kristi on a date to Chick-fil-A so we could talk one-on-one. When we settled into our booth, I took a sip of lemonade and asked, "So, sweetheart, how are you doing? I can't imagine how hard all of this is for you."

"I guess I'm doing okay," she started as she picked up a waffle fry and dipped it in ketchup. "I want to get mad, but I know that I shouldn't."

"What do you mean you shouldn't get mad?" I asked. "Of course you can get mad about the situation."

Kristi looked up. "Dad did all this stuff to you too, and you never seem angry or upset. You're trying to forgive him, and so I need to do that too."

I leaned back against the seat, surprised by her answer. Part of me was proud that she thought I wasn't angry and wanted to imitate my handling of the situation. But the other part of me was shocked that I'd hidden my anger that well. I wasn't sure how to talk about my own feelings of betrayal and rejection without being overcome with emotion. So I didn't. Instead I stuffed my anger down, afraid to let it out because I couldn't predict where it would take me.

I had a reputation for trusting God through hard things, so I wanted to respond perfectly, whatever that looked like. To keep up appearances I had repressed any emotion that seemed inappropriate and focused on what I was supposed to do and feel. I was trying to take the high road by presenting a calm exterior to my children. But what if that wasn't the best path for them? What if they needed more authenticity from me?

I wished someone could tell me what to do, but none of my close friends were single parents. When I asked how to find the balance between being honest and telling the girls too much, all they could offer was that they hoped I'd figure things out.

It was the same with discipline and enforcing consequences. My friends would warn that if I didn't get my girls under control, they would be headed for disaster like many other kids from broken homes. A friend would often start to describe how she and her husband would . . . and then stop, realizing her story made no sense in my context. Two parents could hold the line, but one parent—especially if the one parent was *me*—could be mown over in a second.

After debating what to say to Kristi, I finally confessed, "I *am* angry and upset, and I'm not handling this perfectly. But you're right that God does call us to forgive, and he'll help us do that in time."

Kristi nodded and picked up another waffle fry.

The high road seemed like the only place I was capable of walking. What I wished I'd told Kristi was that sometimes my anger felt so hot it was like a fire inside me. Or that I hadn't even considered forgiving Dave yet and that I despised Tiffany. Or that sometimes I wished I'd never started talking to Dave that day in the Stanford courtyard.

But I didn't say any of that. I just picked up my sandwich and took another bite and then took another sip of my lemonade. I was so used to denying my own feelings that I didn't know how or what to tell Kristi. It was easier and safer to say nothing. Since I had chosen this path of deflection, albeit unconsciously, we finished our meal with sporadic small talk and long pauses.

Holding the line with the girls felt necessary yet almost impossible to do. Chaos sapped my energy, so I fantasized about order and consistency and predictability inside our home. I wanted routine to be the stable foundation. Despite my dreams, I was a single mom with post-polio syndrome trying to raise two girls, ages ten and fourteen. And life was anything but stable.

Once, a friend from church came over to fix our computer, and a series of little incidents—Katie not being polite to him, him implying

I didn't know how to parent well, me feeling embarrassed—led to a blowup between Katie and me after he left.

"Why do you *always* do that?" Katie shouted. "When people are over here, you get *so* mad if we don't do what you say. It's like you only care about what other people think of us and make rules because they're what other people think you should do. Why can't we just do what's right for *us*?"

I protested, but I knew she was right. I cared more about looking good than what was good for them. The next morning I was startled to read that Jesus warned the Pharisees, "Woe to you . . . hypocrites! For you clean the outside of the cup and the plate, but inside they are full of greed and self-indulgence" (Matt. 23:25).

He was describing me. I was less concerned about what was inside my daughters' hearts—their motivations, their thoughts, their fears— and more focused on the outside. Focused on what I could see and, more importantly, what everyone *else* could see. Their world had been upended just as mine had, bringing with it emotions too painful for adolescents to fully understand. *What if their only outlet to express these unnamed feelings was to act out?* While I had flashes of insight and compassion for them, in the middle of conflict I was more focused on my goal of perfect obedience and less concerned with what was behind the disobedience.

Katie especially continued to test the limits, both of my discipline and my patience. I knew what she was doing—trying to figure out where her guardrails were after the upheaval of Dave leaving—but knowing that didn't make it easier to handle. She wanted to wear a bikini, but I wanted her to wear a one-piece. She wanted to text late at night, but I wanted her phone on the counter at 10:00 p.m. She wanted to socialize before she'd finished her homework, but I wanted it finished first. Though our frustrations kept changing, the feeling was constant.

Once, Katie returned from a shopping trip with her friends, carrying a plastic bag with a pair of white shorts. As soon as she pulled them out to show me, I said, "Those are way too short. You need to take them back."

"Mom, these are *fine*. Everyone wears these, except for old people." Katie looked down and started texting.

"Put your phone down. We're talking."

But she kept texting. "Chill out, Mom. I need to finish this one thing."

That "one thing" was one thing too many for me. Something snapped inside. "Give me your phone right now!" I yelled. "And if you don't hand it to me immediately, I won't give it back to you for the rest of the day!"

All I could think about was maintaining control. I'd just drawn a *very* clear line. Now I wondered if I had the strength to defend it.

Katie kept texting nonchalantly, then finally she looked up, apparently finished with her one thing. "Are you serious right now?" she laughed. "Aren't you being a little extreme?"

That did *not* defuse my anger, even if I had been a bit irrational in the first place. Infuriated by her dismissal, I tried to grab the phone, but she pulled it away as she stepped back.

Helplessness washed over me. We both knew that Katie was faster and stronger than I was, but that had never been an issue. I suddenly realized that verbal threats had been my sole form of discipline, and now even those weren't working.

Katie must have noticed something in my face or body. She grunted in frustration then tossed her phone to me. Relieved that I managed to catch it with my right hand, I slid it into the pocket of my jeans.

I could have said countless things in the next moment to deescalate the situation. Like telling Katie that, while finishing her text was a little thing, her attitude was what bothered me. Or that I'd been overly aggressive when I saw her shorts, and I'd like to try the conversation again. Or that since we were both upset, we should wait to talk about it after we'd both cooled off. I could have asked her questions, listened to her heart, relinquished my desire for control—but instead I only tightened my grip.

We were both battling in this power struggle, and I was doggedly determined to win. So it didn't matter what was the wisest or most productive thing to do. Truthfully, I had no idea what it would have been anyway. I was so scared of losing control and becoming a pushover that I'd lost all perspective.

"Now you can't have the phone for at least a week. *And* you're grounded tonight."

Katie accepted the loss of her phone for about an hour and then found me in the kitchen. "Mom, I've learned my lesson, so can I have my phone back?"

"No, this time you can't. I said you wouldn't get it back for a week and I'm sticking to it. I've been too easy on your blatant defiance."

Katie stormed off and skipped dinner. Kristi and I ate leftovers, mostly in silence.

Several hours later, when I was almost asleep, Katie came into my bedroom. After apologizing for how late it was, she politely asked for her phone back. I refused. She tried reasoning with me, and I wanted to stay calm, but before long we were arguing angrily. She began opening all the drawers in my bedroom and rummaging through the contents.

"I can find it, you know," she yelled. "And when I do, how will you keep me from taking it?"

She didn't find it—I'd gotten a lot of practice hiding her cell phone well—but she was right. If she had found the phone, I would have been powerless to stop her.

Finally she gave up and screamed, "I hate you! I really do. I can't wait to leave here and go to college and never come home. You have the worst rules. No wonder Dad left you!" She ran out of the room, then out of the house, slamming the front door behind her.

I waited and prayed, hoping she'd come back soon. When she'd been gone two hours, I called Jennifer to come help me look for her.

We found her at 2:30 a.m. on the back deck, curled into a ball and sleeping on one of the deck chairs. Without speaking we helped her to her room, and she crawled into bed. I closed her bedroom door and walked back to my room as Jennifer left. This crisis was averted. But for how long, and how many more could we take?

⁓

Kristi didn't want her sister to enjoy *all* of my wonderful parenting.

Her explosions of anger became even more frequent than Katie's, and she'd often stay outside shooting baskets for hours. From the window I could see her dribbling and shooting the ball, often flinging it against the side of the house in a rage.

I was happy when Kristi was out there. At least that meant she wasn't taking out her frustrations on me, as she did when she came inside. When inside, hot anger and outright defiance marked most of her days. Kristi often baited me, yelling in my face, almost trying to make me cry. But I couldn't let her win. I'd grab my keys to go for a drive so I wouldn't cry in front of her.

At that point Kristi would beg me not to leave. Seeing her sobbing in the doorway would tug at my heart, but by then I'd had enough. I would ignore her pleas and drive away, heading to a nearby grocery store parking lot. I would sit in the car, crying, while trying to clear my thoughts. I felt guilty about leaving but was worried that if I stayed, I would explode under the pressure. There was nowhere to cool off inside the house, especially because Kristi would pound on my locked door when I tried to be alone.

After twenty minutes in the parking lot, I'd come home, and we'd resume whatever we had been doing, neither of us apologizing. It was a destructive, unhealthy pattern, but I couldn't seem to break it—until the morning Kristi showed me a journal entry she'd written while I was away.

I wanted to say I was sorry, but words would not come out. I didn't want Mom to be mad at me, but I didn't want to say I was sorry if I really wasn't. . . . Times are tough with Dad, and I feel bad for Mom. I feel like God is telling me, "Kristi, it is okay to be mad at your dad for what he did to you." I can't believe Dad would do that. I really lost trust not only in him but everybody. I trusted in him so much. I just want things to be back to normal. A family of four. My life will never be the same.

After reading it, my heart softened toward both girls. I'd tried to shield them from pain, but that wasn't possible now. They were already *in* pain. And I realized my pattern of squelching my emotions— sometimes not even acknowledging them to myself—wouldn't help the girls heal. It was magnifying the problem.

A few days after reading Kristi's journal entry, I rediscovered the Serenity Prayer:

God, grant me the serenity to accept the things I cannot change,
the courage to change the things I can,
and the wisdom to know the difference.

It clicked. Instead of trying to fix *everything*, as if the burden was on me to make sure all our lives had a happy ending, I needed to focus on what I *could* control and let go of the rest.

I already knew I couldn't fix everything, of course. That was evident by all the things I was making a mess of. But I experienced a welcome freedom in recognizing the things that weren't mine to change.

Once I saw them, I could release them to God and find peace, even though our lives would never be the same.

Life had changed for Dave's parents as well. They used to visit at least three or four times a year to see their only grandchildren. Not anymore.

I still talked to Maxine on the phone, and she'd always update me on Jerry. She'd talk about his involvement in their parish, where he led a men's discipleship group. She once told me he was getting up early every morning to read the Bible and pray for an hour or more. She said, "Van, I want you to know that your faith has had a big impact on Jerry, bigger than anyone else's."

I knew she meant well, and I was touched, but I was still very angry with Jerry. Hearing how he was trying to put *his* life back together after causing a huge crack in *my* life wasn't exactly comforting.

Maxine and Jerry usually visited us in the summer, but this year I decided that Katie and Kristi would visit them. The girls and I would fly into Detroit, and then I'd go visit Shalini, who now lived a few hours away in Grand Rapids. At Maxine's gentle insistence, I reluctantly agreed to stay one night at their place. They would then drive me halfway to Grand Rapids to meet Shalini, who would drive me the rest of the way.

Maxine and Jerry met us at the airport, and we made small talk on the short trip to their house. As we pulled into the driveway, Jerry turned to me and asked, "Van, can we talk for a minute?"

My stomach immediately knotted, but what could I do? Avoid him entirely inside his own house? "Okay," I mumbled.

The girls went inside with Maxine. I climbed out of the car and stood facing Jerry. The sun was setting, leaving a hazy pink sky. Jerry crossed his arms, then quickly uncrossed them and stuck his hands into his pockets.

"I'm sorry, Van. I don't know why I said what I did then. I was asking God for wisdom, but I think I listened to the wrong channel and heard from Satan. What I said wasn't right. It was *awful*, really. And I'm sorry I hurt you. Would you forgive me?" After looking directly at me, he averted his gaze, staring off at the sky.

His humility shocked me. Without a second thought I reached up to hug him. "Oh, Jerry, absolutely. Thank you for saying that. It means more than you know."

"Thanks, Van. I knew you would. I mean that. I've been praying so much about this conversation, and I had friends praying too." We hugged again, and he added, "Our friends can't believe Maxine and I still see you. But I'm so glad we do."

I nodded my agreement. I didn't know what would happen between Dave and me, but my relationship with his parents no longer depended on him. It was something new, and God was present in it.

Jerry and I looked at the sky a few moments longer, then turned to go inside and join Maxine and the girls. We walked through the open garage door, and when we reached the steps that led into the house, Jerry grabbed my hand to help me up.

⊘∮∮∾

I was thankful my relationship with Dave's parents had been restored that summer. I later learned that Jerry's hurtful conversation in Raleigh was intended to help. He had wanted Dave and me to each own the problem completely so we could each take full responsibility to resolve it.

Unexpectedly, Dave's parents and I grew even closer after the conflict, which meant they would join us for Christmas. It would be our first Christmas without Dave, and I hoped having them with us would make it feel more normal for the girls.

With that question out of the way, I decided to add a fun little diversion to the mix, and the week after Thanksgiving I bought a miniature poodle. While I didn't know anything about puppies, I'd studied ways to help kids process trauma, and having a dog was at the top of the list. Our new family member was the color of mocha, which is exactly what we named him, though the girls affectionately called him Mochie. Both girls immediately loved Mocha, who offered them unconditional love and affection.

One morning, a few weeks after Mocha joined us, I peeked my head into Kristi's room and discovered her bed was empty. Rather than panicking, I cracked the door to Katie's room and looked inside. Kristi was sleeping in Katie's bed, and so was Mocha. It was a puddle of flannel and fur and nonverbal love that I knew would do more to heal them than almost anything else. Being a family of four again—with a four-legged member—was really wonderful.

Through it all I was trying to live the Serenity Prayer, to figure out what I needed to accept and what I needed to change. Some days it was crystal clear, and other days I had no idea. But somehow we were making it work.

One night just before Christmas, I was running late for a potluck. As I pulled my casserole from the oven, it slipped off the rack. Chicken and cheese overflowed into the oven and onto the floor. I saved the glass dish from hitting the hardwood, but I had nothing else to take to the dinner. I couldn't show up empty-handed, so of course I did the only thing that made sense.

I carefully set the dish on top of the stove, then used a large, shallow spoon to scoop some of the casserole from the floor and inside the oven and back into the dish. And then I topped the whole thing with breadcrumbs. *Voila!*

The girls saw me and were naturally horrified, but they promised not to tell anyone at the potluck if they could eat whatever they wanted there. As for me, I enjoyed two helpings, and I only plucked one dark hair off my plate—though I wasn't positive whether it was mine or Mocha's.

Chapter 20

CRAZY LOVE

At one of Kristi's seemingly infinite basketball practices, I was reading Francis Chan's *Crazy Love*, and I came across a quote that stunned me.

I closed the book and looked around the gym. I wiped my cheeks and reread the quote to make sure. It was poetic and beautiful, yes, but also sharply insightful about human nature.

And then, minutes later, as I thought more about the quote, I became angry.

It poked a nerve. I had thought the quote about love and forgiveness was a great observation for other people's lives. For world peace perhaps. But not for my situation—certainly not for my life. When I thought about applying it, I immediately felt defensive. I put the book down and concentrated on watching Kristi practice. Her three-point shot was getting even better.

When Kristi and I got home, I intentionally left the book in the car. I didn't want to read it anymore. But I still couldn't get the quote out of my head, because it was making me think of Tiffany, whom I blamed for all our trouble. I never wanted to meet her, except maybe at her funeral.

Despite that, I felt strangely drawn to get the book out of the car and reread the quote. It was a bit like the way I can't *not* look at an accident as I drive past. I couldn't put my finger on exactly what was bothering me or what I was supposed to do with it. Hebrews 12:15

came to mind—"See to it that no one fails to obtain the grace of God; that no 'root of bitterness' springs up and causes trouble"—and I realized there was probably only one way to cut this root of bitterness out of my life.

I asked God, *Why is this quote so important? What do you want me to see in this?*

The thought of writing Tiffany a letter came to me, and I pushed it away immediately. It seemed crazy. What would I say?

Dear Tiffany,
You've ruined my life to this point, and probably for good. I hate you, though I might reconsider if you left my husband right after reading this letter. No, actually, I'd still hate you.
                              Sincerely,
                              Vaneetha

That sounded like a pretty great letter. But for some reason the thought of writing a different one kept pushing its way back into my mind. While preparing dinner that night, I turned the music up louder, trying to distract myself. Selah was singing "Unredeemed," and I had the album on repeat. It described the ashes of my life and the redemption I was longing for.

Somewhere between boiling the water for the pasta and leaning forward to cut some tomatoes, I started to wonder if God was prompting me. So I started praying. I had a lot of practice by that point in telling God exactly what I was thinking.

Maybe this is your idea, Lord, but I still don't want to do it. If you want to tell Tiffany something, go ahead. I certainly have nothing good to say to her. Give someone else that job, or else come back to me in a decade. Like a decade after she and Dave break up and you restore our marriage. Or a decade after I divorce Dave and marry Prince Charming.

That night I slid into bed and pulled up the sheets, looking as I always did at the empty space beside me. But I couldn't sleep. Just the idea of writing Tiffany a letter felt like an elephant sitting on my chest. It felt deeply unfair for God to ask me to even *consider* writing to her. But as the hours dragged on and on, I realized that was exactly what was happening.

I walked to my computer and began to write. This was crazy. What was I supposed to say? I prayed that God would give me the words; after all, it felt like it was his idea. I didn't pray that flippantly, but truly, because the only words I had for Tiffany were of condemnation, laced with sarcasm and vindictiveness, and I was sure those weren't the sort that God wanted me to use. So after praying, I wrote:

> I must confess, I never thought I'd write this letter to you. I wanted to hate you, but somehow, I could not.
>
> . . .
>
> I have been asking God that you would truly experience abundant life.
>
> . . .
>
> The cross changes everything. We exchange our sin, our shame, our mistakes and regrets for his righteousness and grace and peace.
>
> . . .
>
> You may wonder what my agenda is. I don't have any hidden agenda, but simply offer this letter to you in obedience to a life-giving, relentless God to whom I owe everything.

By 4:00 a.m., when I finished, my attitude had changed and a sense of peace had settled over me. I exhaled. For months I'd been in turmoil, but simply writing the letter had freed me. The next day I bought Tiffany a CD with the song "Unredeemed" and slid it into the envelope along with the letter. After I dropped it off at the post office, I felt both relieved and curious, wondering what would happen.

$\sim$

A week later Shalini called. "Have you heard back yet? What did Tiffany say?"

"Dave said she received it and told him to thank me. He asked if I wanted a response, and I said I didn't need one. I'm not sure what to make of it."

Shalini was silent for a few seconds. "I guess she probably didn't know what to say. Are you sorry you sent it?"

"No, but it's making me reevaluate my motives. They're so hard to untangle in my mind. I wonder if part of me wrote it so she would see that I'm a really nice person and would feel guilty that she's with Dave and maybe even end their relationship. But then part of me knows I wrote it out of obedience to God, so I don't know exactly what I'm expecting."

"Yeah, I get that. After you sent it, I know you were waiting for her reaction. But now that you have it, how do you feel?"

"I don't know. It's funny. After sending the letter, I've actually started praying for Tiffany. And not just praying she'll get hit by a car!"

Shalini laughed.

"Seriously, though, it made me less mad at her. I still want her and Dave to break up, but I don't hate her anymore. I know it takes two people to have an affair, but in my mind, it was her fault. I wanted to hate her, and I constantly thought about what she'd done to me. I felt like a prisoner in my anger, rehearsing all the horrible things I wanted to say to her or the horrible things I wanted to happen to her. It's the weirdest thing, but I'm not doing that anymore. When I start to get mad, I try to pray for her instead. I'm beginning to feel that the letter wasn't primarily to change her. This may sound crazy, but I think writing that letter was to change me."

"That doesn't sound crazy at all," Shalini said. "In fact, it sounds like the way God works. You sound different. Healthy, actually. It's wild how a single quote had such a profound impact on you. What was it anyway? I don't think you ever told me."

"Let me read it to you," I said, and went to get the book from my office. I returned and immediately flipped to the dog-eared page with the quote by Fredrick Buechner:

The love for equals is a human thing—of friend for friend, brother for brother. It is to love what is loving and lovely. The world smiles. The love for the less fortunate is a beautiful thing—the love for those who suffer, for those who are poor, the sick, the failures, the unlovely. This is compassion, and it touches the heart of the world. The love for the more fortunate is a rare thing—to love those who succeed where we fail, to rejoice without envy with those who rejoice, the love of the poor for the rich, of the black man for the white man. The world is always bewildered by its saints. And then there is the love for the enemy—love for the one who does not love you but mocks, threatens, and inflicts pain. The tortured's love for the torturer. This is God's love. It conquers the world.[4]

Chapter 21

ESCALATION

While my disintegrating marriage was always in the back of my mind, my girls were in the forefront. Parenting was exhausting and took all my time and energy.

In April, more than a year after Dave had left, Jennifer called and asked to get together. The only time I had was while I was out on errands, so she met me in a parking lot. I felt happy when I saw her minivan pull up beside mine. It meant a friend to talk to, even for a few minutes, instead of a teenager or a high-strung poodle.

Jennifer slid into the passenger seat of my van and handed me a steaming vanilla latte.

"Ooh, thanks," I said as I pulled out the stopper and took a sip. "I haven't had a treat like this in a long time."

"That's kind of why I wanted to talk to you," Jennifer began. "I think you need to slow down and take some things out of your life. What you're doing is not sustainable or smart, especially with your post-polio. You need to take care of yourself. You count too."

I took another sip and looked over at her. "I know you're right, but I've got two girls to take care of. What can I cut out? Everything falls on me as a single parent."

"Well, there *are* things you can change if you want to. You've been homeschooling since Dave left, which is amazing. But why don't you put them in school in the fall?"

"Honestly, I'd love to, but I don't know how they'd react. They love their homeschool group, and they've already had so much change."

"I think they'd be fine in school. It wouldn't start until August, so they'd have time to get used to the idea. And you can put your kids where mine are. They know lots of kids there already."

I ticked off a series of objections, but Jennifer countered each one. Finally, I said, "Okay, I'll think about it. Katie will be in tenth grade and Kristi in seventh this fall, which isn't great timing, but I guess it never will be. Honestly, thinking about putting them in school feels like a huge burden would be lifted off me."

"That's what I think too," Jennifer said as she looked at her watch. "Actually, I need to go now to pick my kids up at school. Maybe next year we'll be doing that together." She got out of my van and waved from hers as she pulled out of the parking lot.

The night before school started that August, Katie and I had a long talk about high school and what to expect. She was excited about going back to school, but Kristi had been angry ever since I raised the idea. Being forced to stop homeschooling was another loss that she was powerless to change.

When Katie and I finished chatting, I went into the kitchen and saw Kristi getting a glass of water. When she turned around, I gasped. Her eyebrows were missing.

"Mom? What's wrong?"

"I can fix your eyebrows in the morning," I finally said.

Kristi ran to the bathroom and shrieked. Then she stormed into her room, slammed the door, and started sobbing. When I knocked, she said, "Go away! This is all your fault. You're making me go to a stupid school, and now I'm going to look even weirder! I never want to talk to you again."

Eventually she let me in and said she'd been randomly picking at her eyebrow hairs while watching TV. She had no idea why. We talked for a while, and then she got into my bed and slept with me. The next morning, I drew in her eyebrows with a pencil, and after school we went to a beauty salon for a semipermanent tattoo.

I did have more energy with the girls in school, but I used most of it dealing with Kristi's escalating anger. Seventh grade was miserable for her. She often ate lunch in a bathroom stall and was never invited to anyone's home. And church, which had been a place of refuge, had changed for her as well. Several girls in the youth group cornered Kristi and asked her personal questions about our family. Dave's actions had become public, and Kristi didn't know anyone else who came from a single-parent home. Other kids struggled to relate to what she was experiencing, and most adults struggled not to be condescending. It wasn't surprising that her anger boiled over. She had a lot to be angry about.

One evening Kristi asked if we could go out to dinner. I was working at my desk and responded, "Not tonight. I'm exhausted and don't want to go out. We're having leftovers."

"I hate leftovers," Kristi said. "Why can't we ever go out? Dad takes us out. Besides, dinner last night was gross, and I don't want to eat it again."

I looked up and said, "Even if I was considering going out, which I wasn't, I would definitely not go after that comment."

Kristi rolled her eyes. "Why don't you ever make anything good anyway? We never have anything good to eat in the house, and you keep making the same disgusting meals."

That struck a tender spot. I knew my cooking was simple and boring, mostly so I wouldn't overuse my arms. Besides, when I'd ask the girls what they wanted me to make or buy, they'd often ignore me or shrug their shoulders. Feeling vulnerable and unappreciated, I exploded, "Go to your room right now, you ungrateful little brat!"

Kristi was as surprised by the fury of my response as I was. She stood staring at me, wide-eyed. Then she walked over and, with one swoop of her arm, swept everything off my desk. Pens and pencils, paper clips and Post-It notes, mail and stacks of paper—all of it went flying.

Anger poured out of me. "I can't stand you!" I shouted. "Pick that up right now!"

Kristi smirked as she towered over me. She leaned down until she was a few inches from my face and I could feel her warm breath. "You want me to pick that up? Why don't you go ahead and make me?" She waited about ten seconds, her eyes flashing with anger, and then she pulled back. "That's what I thought. You can't make me do anything." She walked away, laughing.

I sat at my desk, stunned and helpless.

That night I lay in bed, angry at Kristi and ashamed of what my life had been reduced to. I wasn't the same person anymore, and neither was she. We were all doing and saying things that we never would have imagined years earlier. I had no idea how to parent.

Why do you hate me? I asked God. *Why don't you fix this? Isn't it enough that my marriage is destroyed and my body is falling apart? Now you're letting my children walk all over me? Don't you even care? How long are you going to put me through this? Every day is harder than the day before, and you could change it all if you wanted to.*

I sat up and grabbed my Bible, opening to Psalm 13 and reading it aloud:

> How long, LORD? Will you forget me forever?
>   How long will you hide your face from me?
> How long must I wrestle with my thoughts
>   and day after day have sorrow in my heart? (vv. 1–2 NIV)

I was thankful I still had friends who could help me process the pain that often enveloped me. One morning I was attempting to tell several friends about the girls' defiance and my feelings of rejection, but the words wouldn't come. All I could do was cry, and my friends cried with me in silence.

Finally, after a long time, one friend spoke. "When I think of you and pray for you, I keep seeing this image. It's of the disciples and Jesus' mother, Mary, weeping at the foot of the cross. They are huddled together, trying to comfort each other. Trying to make sense of all that has happened. But it just doesn't make sense. The sky is black. All hope looks lost. Their dreams have died. It seems that nothing good will ever come from this. To them this day, Good Friday, is the darkest day they've ever known. But there is one thing they do not know. Easter is coming."

Easter is coming. I clung to those words of comfort.

I never imagined what it must've been like for Jesus' friends on Good Friday at the foot of the cross. They'd put their hope and faith in the man they were now watching die. And with his death, their dreams must have died also. On that Friday they would have questioned everything they had believed about him. Nothing would have made sense. Their only certainty would have been that their plans were ruined and their future seemed hopeless. Everything must have looked black.

That's how I felt. I couldn't see how God could bring any good out of my situation. But as I entered into that Good Friday scene, I realized my story wasn't over yet either. My suffering was temporary. One day it would be over.

Maybe relief was around the corner. Or maybe it would take a while. But Easter *was* coming. I had to hang on to that.

Chapter 22

TWO STEPS FORWARD

S ince Easter was coming, I wanted to start looking at life through a new lens, paying attention to the good things that happened.

One day the girls went with me to get a new set of orthotics. My previous ones had been made soon after my visit to the polio clinic seven years ago and had worn down, making my feet ache. I had put off getting nonessential things for myself, but this was becoming essential.

The pedorthist, Robert, met us in the waiting room. He introduced himself and motioned to the girls to come with us to the small casting room. He brought in chairs for the girls, and then sat on the rolling stool opposite me. "So, just pull off your socks and shoes. You're going to put your feet in these squishy molds, and then I'll help you stand up."

"Seriously, Mom," Katie teased, "you're going to take your socks and shoes off? You didn't prepare us for this kind of trauma!"

Unlacing my shoes, I joked back. "Maybe you guys want to go back to the waiting room where you'll be safer? There's no telling how scarring it'll be if you see my feet."

"I'm fine *seeing* your feet," Kristi joined in. "It's the *smell* I'm worried about. I mean, you've got cute little toes."

"Cute? My toes are disgusting!" I said as I pulled off my socks and stared at my feet. I hated them, just as I always had. They were small and wide, with a bunion and surgical scars. They were why I never wore sandals. Now I was embarrassed that the pedorthist was going to see them in front of the girls. I curled my toes under, trying to hide them.

Robert picked up my right foot, put it in the soft mold, and helped me stand. "Girls, you know what I see when I look at your mother's feet?"

"Something no one wants to see?" Katie teased.

Robert smiled, allowing her to joke. But then he grew more serious. "When I look at your mother's feet, I see courage."

The girls were listening intently as he continued. "I know you're proud of your mother. She's a brave woman, and her feet show it. Those feet have walked through a lot."

Both girls nodded at him and then smiled proudly at me. I hadn't seen that in a long time.

I held on to moments like that and replayed them when I grew discouraged. But I didn't always need to do that, because goodness would sometimes break out unexpectedly in our lives.

One typical morning on the way to school—typical because Kristi had been impossible to wake up, neither of the girls had made their lunch, I couldn't find the keys, and Mocha had been sick on the kitchen floor—I turned the car radio to K-LOVE. Usually the girls picked the music in the van, but that day I needed something to help me relax.

"Do we *have* to listen to Christian music?" Katie asked, reaching to change the dial. "You can listen to whatever you want on your way back."

"That's very generous of you," I said, half joking. "But I can listen to whatever I want whenever I want, including now."

Katie groaned and I continued. "Seriously, though, you guys always pick the morning music. I need to hear something encouraging today."

Katie groaned again and Kristi joined her. I saw some exaggerated eye rolling in the rearview mirror.

After one song, the DJ began to interview singer Natalie Grant. After she talked about her latest release and her family life, the interviewer asked what her most requested song was. She said it was "Held," and she went on to talk about the songwriter and the story behind the song. I smiled as I remembered how my dear friend Christa, who had brought me meals and a listening ear just after we lost Paul, had been inspired by our conversations to write that song. "Held" had been an overnight success. It was nominated for Song of the Year at the Dove Awards, and Christa had won Songwriter of the Year.

Christa had called me when she first received Natalie's song demo, and I'd rushed over to her house. The second I pulled up in her driveway, she ran out the front door, jumped into the passenger seat of my minivan, and pushed the CD in. We sat there surrounded by the song as Natalie's powerful voice belted out the story of my precious Paul and the truth of how God had met us in our loss. Christa and I sat frozen, tears pouring down both of our faces, as we listened. This. *This* was what it meant to be held.

And now here we were, all these years later, reliving those memories. One of Katie's friends texted her during the interview, telling her that someone on the radio was talking about us. When the brief interview ended, Kristi said, "I'm kind of glad we listened to that. Sometimes it feels like no one cares about us. But hearing that on the way to school made me feel that God still does."

I was thinking the same thing.

❦

Now back in school, Katie got involved in everything from drama to basketball to volunteering. She preferred staying busy to staying at home. She earned the gold presidential service award, given for performing over two hundred and fifty hours of service, each year of high school. Kristi wasn't quite as motivated. When I asked her if she was interested in doing any community service, she said she'd volunteered for ten minutes at the concession stand and that was enough service for the year—she didn't believe in spreading herself too thin.

At home, though, I felt that both the girls expected to be served. While I wanted to make their lives as easy as possible, my body was continuing to break down. The girls hardly ever commented or seemed to notice, which made me feel unappreciated.

I had cut back on cooking years earlier, more to conserve my energy than because I was unable to do it. But now, after just a few minutes of doing simple tasks like cutting, stirring, or opening jars, my arm would give way. It would hang motionless by my side, often with a burning pain. But if the girls happened to come into the kitchen then, they'd still nonchalantly ask when we were having dinner, seemingly oblivious to my struggles.

Or so I thought.

One evening Kristi complained of a bad stomachache, so I sat on her bed, stroking her back before she went to sleep. We talked and prayed, and then I recited Psalm 91. I had memorized the psalm in our women's Bible study years earlier, and after hearing me repeat it countless times, she had memorized it as well.

That night she murmured, "It seems like you've done all the right things, but nothing is going well for you. Your body hurts all the time. I can tell. Every time you say from that psalm, 'Because you have made the Lord your dwelling place—the Most High, who is my refuge—no evil shall be allowed to befall you, no plague come near your tent' [vv. 9–10], I wonder why that doesn't apply to us. Lots of awful things have happened to us, especially to you. Why did God let that happen?"

I paused before I responded. I wanted to be honest. "That's a great question, sweetheart. I honestly don't know the answer. I don't understand why all these hard things keep happening, and sometimes I wonder why God doesn't just fix it. But I have to trust that he is doing something bigger than we can see, and one day we'll see it."

After a moment of stroking her back in the dark, I asked, "Remember that song, 'Blessings,' that we listened to the other day? It asks if the trials in our lives could be God's mercies in disguise." I pulled out my phone and softly played the song for her as she drifted off to sleep. I ended by whispering, "Maybe that's the way we both need to look at all this."

After Kristi fell asleep, I went to bed. In the morning I went into Katie's room to wake her up for school. She was always easier to get out of bed. I flipped on the light and called out, "Katie, it's time to get up."

She yawned and tried to open her eyes. "It's already morning? I'm exhausted. I was up all night. Can you turn the light off?"

"Really? What were you up doing all night?"

"Kristi threw up, and it got all over her sheets and the floor. I cleaned it up and changed the sheets. Then she did it again, and I had to clean it up again. She went back to sleep, but then she woke up and asked if she could get in bed with me. I was too tired to say no."

For the first time I noticed the shape of Kristi's body, huddled under the blankets in Katie's bed.

"Why didn't you wake me up? I'm so sorry you had to do all that yourself."

"I knew you were tired and that your body hurt yesterday. And I know you hate cleaning up vomit more than anything, so I wanted to do that for you. But I left all the gross sheets and rags in a plastic bag, so you need to put those in the laundry."

"Thank you, princess. You have no idea how much that means to me." My voice cracked. Then I added, "You were really thoughtful."

"You're welcome, Mom. So can I sleep in a little longer, and can you turn off the light? Kristi is probably not going to school, and maybe I can go in a little late?"

"Sure, sweetheart. I love you," I said, pulling the door shut and walking into the kitchen. I was starting to suspect that *I* was the one who was oblivious to what was really going on at home. I promised myself I would focus more on celebrating what the girls were doing right.

I also promised myself to look for what I'd been doing well, to celebrate the times that I'd done something right rather than dwelling on all I'd been doing wrong.

One night Kristi called me to the dining room table. Through tears she said her art teacher told her she would fail if she didn't complete her assignment to copy "The Great Wave off Kanagawa," the work of the famous Japanese artist Hokusai. She had always been a straight-A student, except in art, which I knew could overwhelm her.

"I don't know how to do this, Mom!" she admitted, gesturing at a picture that had been drawn, erased, and drawn again so many times that the paper threatened to rip.

Drawing was one area I could help her with, so we got a clean sheet of paper, and I created the very basic outline of the waves before passing the paper back to her. Using my artistic abilities, even for a small project, felt amazing.

"Drawing is about paying attention, Kristi," I said, pointing out a few of the print's features. "Look carefully. Study the whole picture. Notice where everything is in proportion to everything else. Filling in details is great, but always start with the big picture."

We worked side by side for over an hour. I'd never really seen Hokusai's woodblock prints before, and I enjoyed imitating his work. As Kristi was finishing up, outlining the final wave tip in black marker, I said, "You can learn a lot by imitating a master artist."

Kristi kept outlining and said, "It's fun now, but I hated it at first." She paused, then added without looking up, "I want you to know that you are my Hokusai. You are the person I learn from, the person I watch and want to imitate."

That comment melted away years of pain.

Having the girls in school helped me conserve physical energy during the day and brought other voices into the girls' daily lives. That meant I had more time for friends, but with friends came more advice than I expected or even wanted. Everyone had an opinion on what I should do, and they were eager to share it with me.

One friend said I needed to focus on healthy eating by making nutritious meals from scratch. But another friend reminded me I was overusing my arms and should pick up fast food more often.

Someone said I should make the girls go to youth group and Sunday school because they needed support. But someone else insisted I shouldn't force conversations about faith because it would turn them away from God.

A woman at church was adamant that I needed to follow through on discipline with immediate consequences. But my mother called to let me know I was being too hard on my children.

Dave had a rental place in town and was flying down every weekend to see the girls. My friends thought I shouldn't be so nice to him when he picked them up. But Dave thought I was too critical of him.

One friend said I shouldn't get divorced, or at least I shouldn't be the one to file. She believed I made a covenant I was obligated to keep. But other friends thought I should have filed for divorce already because Dave had broken the covenant. They said I needed to move on.

A teacher said I should teach Kristi better study and organization habits so she wouldn't keep turning assignments in late. But Kristi's counselor told me to let her miss her deadlines and face the consequences.

"Start standing up for yourself more, Vaneetha!"

"Putting others first, in humility, is the best witness, Vaneetha."

Katie said I micromanaged her life.

Kristi said I expected too much from her.

The polio clinic told me—not in so many words—that I was crazy for not using a wheelchair full-time, but the girls were embarrassed when I showed up to their school events in a wheelchair.

It would have been nice to be able to tune out all the voices and decide things for myself, but that wasn't in my DNA. I'd learned early on that pleasing people was the safest option.

꧁꧂

Nurse Lane was one of the first to teach me that, back when I was seven years old, and in a body cast from the chest down.

I'd been living on a ward for almost nine months straight at what was then called the Shriners Hospital for Crippled Children in Montreal. Because my parents visited only on weekends, the nurses handled my day-to-day needs. Most of them were nice, but Nurse Lane terrified me. She was even mean to the other nurses.

One morning I woke up feeling awful. I didn't want breakfast and didn't even want to be propped up. Nurse Lane brought my plate anyway—eggs dripping with water; cold, burnt toast; and brown bananas—and set it beside my bed.

When she came back to pick up the trays, she asked, "Aren't you going to finish your breakfast?"

"I'm done. It looks yucky."

"You've hardly touched your food," she said, sliding the plate closer to me. "Take a few bites."

"I don't want it," I said, reaching out and pushing the plate farther away. "I don't feel good."

She paused, then picked up the plate and slammed it back down. "You need to take a few bites *now*, before we clean up breakfast. If you don't, you won't get lunch."

The ward was totally quiet. Everyone was staring at us, and I could feel my ears burning. I didn't mean to upset her, but now *I* was upset, and she couldn't force me to eat. "I don't want lunch anyway," I said.

Nurse Lane's face turned red. She grabbed my breakfast and left the room.

Baths started after breakfast. Every day the nurses would bring a large silver bowl filled with steaming hot water and hand me a warm, sudsy washcloth to scrub my face. Then they would wash my arms and my toes. My cast was sweaty and itchy, and I loved the feel of the warm water on my skin. Then the nurses would roll me over on my side to wash my back and change my sheets. It was always my favorite part of the day.

That morning, though, everyone else on the ward was given a bath except me. When I noticed the nurses starting to clean up for lunch, I whispered to the nurse standing near me, "Can I have my bath now? I've waited all morning."

Nurse Lane walked over at that moment and said, "It's too late. You said you didn't feel well, so I thought you wouldn't want your bath. We're getting ready for lunch right now, so there's no time."

I tried hard not to cry. When lunch trays came out, I pretended I was asleep. No one checked on me all afternoon, and I didn't ask to be propped up to see the TV in the corner. I just lay there, making up stories in my mind.

That evening the nurses brought the dinner trays and I was served last: watery vegetable beef soup with stale crackers. When it was time for bed, Nurse Lane helped me get ready in silence. She pushed a bedpan under my bottom and wiped me. "Maybe you'll feel better tomorrow," she said, "and you can get a bath. After you eat your breakfast, of course."

I nodded. I realized I could never beat her. What I wanted didn't matter. What I felt didn't matter. All I needed to do—all I *could* do, really—was eat my food, listen to the nurses, and pretend to be happy. If I did that, everyone would treat me better.

Nurse Lane was a very effective teacher.

Despite the mixed advice I was receiving, our church was a life-giving place for me. Friends from church prayed for us, offered practical help, and listened to me vent.

Tom and Carol had us over for dinner often, and we played games with their family for hours. We hotly debated whether Tom or I was better at Bananagrams, but he conveniently lost the scoring records. Even though church had been hard for Kristi, she still loved Tom and even asked him to make her birthday dinner at their house.

Tom gathered a group to brainstorm how they could best care for me. Florence, my Bible study coleader, organized regular prayer meetings at my home. Florence and Lisa took turns driving the girls to piano lessons in Durham, almost forty-five minutes away, so I could stay home. Ray, Mike, and my cousin Phil helped around the house, fixing computer problems and overflowing washing machines. When Ray came over with several boxes of light bulbs from Home Depot, I was relieved that he would be replacing the ceiling bulbs, which seemed to burn out constantly.

"How many people with post-polio does it take to change a light bulb?" I joked.

Ray raised an eyebrow, sure he didn't want to answer that question.

"Zero, since it's an impossible task," I said. "Which is why I'm so glad you're here."

He laughed politely and got to work. At least I'd made myself laugh.

Michele offered to keep the girls overnight whenever I needed help, which made it easier to ask. And whenever I asked, she agreed without hesitating, so I never felt like a bother. Numerous people would say, "Let me know if you need anything," but I never called because I wasn't sure what type of help they meant. Michele's offer, in its specificity, was a relief for me. She also often texted me in the morning to let me know she was praying. Once her text came at exactly the right moment: "Praying. Praying. Praying. On my face. Every day."

My parents also prayed daily for me, and my mom would call every morning to ask, "How can I pray for you today?" I knew I could count on them for anything I needed. And when I needed advice, I'd call Shalini, whose sister-superpower was being able to listen to me for hours and still offer wise counsel.

Jennifer asked friends to write encouraging cards or letters for my birthday one year, and she put them all in a scrapbook. I read and reread those letters, wearing the binding thin from turning the pages so often. Texts, practical help, prayers—all made me realize I was not alone in this.

But while the support from my friends and family was invaluable and life-giving, I still missed working through my grief artistically as I had in the past. I started asking God to bring me another way to process my feelings. He had taken away my ability to create art, I reasoned, so he should give me something to replace it.

That same week, three friends separately asked if I'd thought about writing my story.

When the first person suggested it, I laughed and said I hadn't.

When the second person said it, I explained that I wasn't a writer.

When the third person mentioned it, I listened.

I went home and asked God to make it clear if he really wanted me to write. The next morning I walked to the mailbox and pulled out a flyer that read: "Do you want to write your life?" It advertised a continuing-education class at the University of North Carolina that focused on teaching adults to write their stories. I walked inside and called to sign up.

With the professor's encouragement, I began writing about my childhood years in the hospital. For our final session he asked us to bring in a piece that we'd like help on from our classmates. He also mentioned that he wanted us to read it aloud to the entire class. Regrettably, I didn't hear that part of the assignment. Had I known, I would have picked my best, most poignant scene, then nonchalantly acted as if it was my worst writing. Instead I picked a horribly awkward section that I hoped could be salvaged by a brilliant writing partner.

One by one the students read their pieces. Each time the class clapped and then chimed in with praise. When my turn came, I comforted myself, thinking, *Don't worry. You're your own worst critic.*

Apparently not.

I finished, and there was total silence. Finally, someone offered, "I, uh, read some of her other stuff, and, um, she writes better than this."

More silence. A minute or two went by and people began to shuffle their feet and make small noises. The professor mercifully ended my critique, saying, "Maybe you should eliminate the scene altogether. I don't think it's working."

Despite the embarrassment, taking the class and trying something new made me strangely optimistic. Before the class, I hadn't written anything besides business memos and letters. This new way of expressing myself creatively and processing my pain showed me that God could open up unexpected and wonderful doors in my life.

At the same time, I still wondered where my life was going. Living in limbo was hard for all of us, and our feelings were up and down. One day we'd be open to the future, and the next day we'd feel trapped in the past.

Dave and I weren't together, and we hadn't slept in the same house since the day he moved out. But we also weren't divorced. Neither of us had filed. I wanted to be sure that God wasn't going to do a miracle before I did something permanent. I knew God *could* restore our impossibly broken marriage. That was completely consistent with his character and ability. Yet I was slowly realizing that God might have another plan for me, that maybe there were other ways to honor God than a repaired marriage.

No matter what happened, I knew I needed to cling to God himself and not a particular outcome.

Chapter 23

THREE STEPS BACK

B eing trapped in limbo between a painful past and an uncertain future wore on Katie, Kristi, and me. We had good days and even amazing days, but that didn't mean bad days couldn't come roaring back.

On one of those days, Katie was in the living room, visibly upset. She motioned to me to join her on the couch, and I plopped down beside her. She said, "I overheard Sarah and Kaitlin talking about me a few days ago. They were blowing up something I had said. When they realized I'd heard them, they apologized and said they didn't mean it. But I don't believe them, and I don't want to forgive them. They've tried to talk to me, and they keep apologizing, but I'm done with them. I just keep thinking about what they said."

I knew they were important to Katie, and I hated to see her throw away their friendship. At the same time, she needed empathy, not life lessons. But I wanted to offer both. "Oh Katie, I hate that you had to go through that. I've been hurt by friends, too, and I've endlessly replayed everything they did wrong, stacking their offenses on top of each other. But then I end up feeling worse, getting madder and madder at the people who hurt me. I've lost plenty of friendships that way."

Katie was leaning in now, listening closely. "So you know how that feels. I just can't figure out who to trust anymore."

"I totally get how hard it is to trust anyone right now. It's hard for me too. But you might want to give these girls another chance by forgiving them. For me, I start by releasing my anger to God and asking him to help me forgive. Then I deliberately remember the good things the other person has done, even making a list if I have to. When I do that, I become more open to restoring the relationship. And even if it's not restored, I feel freer, less bitter. God can help you do that."

"You don't get it, Mom! I don't want to be their friend anymore. And I'm not sure what I think about faith. It hasn't done anything for Dad or for you. Your life sucks and so does mine."

"Yeah, it kind of does," I agreed. "But we'll get through it together. I'm trying to trust God even though nothing looks the way I want it to. I really do believe that one day we'll see that God has been using all of this for our good."

"Is that all you can say to me? Trust God?" Katie said, clenching her fists. "God isn't going to use this for good. I wish you were like other moms, who give their kids practical advice on things. That you were cool like them and didn't bring everything back to the Bible. All you do is talk about God."

I had pushed too hard. I wondered if I should back off and say something a cool mom would, but I had no clue what that would be. I wasn't up to date on popular culture like her friends' moms seemed to be, though I'd been trying to enter her world in small ways, like watching *American Idol* with her at night.

But I wasn't bringing "everything back to the Bible" to ram it down her throat or backhandedly try to shame her. I was talking about God because God was honestly the only way I was making it. God speaking to me through Scripture and prayer. God being present as I went about my day. God comforting me when I felt alone and scared. God was changing me, and he was the only reason I was still standing. I was just trying to tell her what I'd been discovering in my walk with God.

"I hate what's happened. I wish I could fix it all for you, Katie, but I can't. The only real hope I can offer you is Jesus."

She jumped up from the couch, grabbed the tissue box she'd been using, and threw it at me. "Just stop talking to me about God, would you? I don't want anything to do with your God!" Then she stormed out of the room, down the hall, and slammed her bedroom door.

Stunned, I stayed on the couch, alternating between praying and simply staring into space. I was learning to live with ambiguity and uncertainty, accepting the way things were. Each day was just one frame of a long movie, and the situation could change quickly. I reminded myself that I needed to take my own advice and trust God with this.

Still, seeing my oldest daughter turn her back on God felt like a body blow.

≈

One thing that Shalini had suggested that the girls and I do together was visit friends for dinner, which became our favorite thing to do. After my conversation with Katie, I was grateful to have friends who supported and loved us, especially when our lives were a mess.

Jennifer often had us over for dinner, making both elaborate and simple meals. "We aren't having anything fancy tonight," she said, as we walked into her house one evening. The girls ran off to hang out with her kids, and I sat in the kitchen, watching Jennifer pull out tomatoes, cucumbers, and other vegetables from her weekly produce box. She effortlessly made homemade croutons, a fresh salad, and a simple pasta dish. All of us loved it.

A few weeks later I decided to re-create Jennifer's meal for the girls. I bought fresh bread, cubed it, and toasted it with garlic and olive oil. While the croutons were in the oven, I chopped the tomatoes and basil for the pasta. My arms and hands tired as I chopped, but I pushed forward. Kristi had to leave for a basketball game before long, so I rested for just a little while before resuming preparations.

"Hey, what are we going to eat?" Kristi called from the living room. "I'm starving, and remember I have to leave in thirty minutes."

"Yes, I remember. It'll be ready soon." I wish I'd asked the girls for help, but as usual, I'd chosen to do it all myself. The timer buzzed for the croutons, and as I slid the tray from the oven, my legs gave way from exhaustion and I fell. Croutons flew into the air, and my shoulder hit the cutting board on my way down, flinging the chopped vegetables onto the floor.

Both the girls came running in to see what had happened. "Oh, Mom," Katie said.

Together they helped me to my feet, and then I was standing, looking down at a kitchen floor covered in what was supposed to be a successful dinner. Discouraged, I ranted to myself, *Why do I even bother to cook? Why do I expect anything I do to turn out well?*

It felt like an image of my life. For every step forward, somehow I managed to take three steps back.

⟳ℰℱℱ~

The next day, as I always did, I got up, put on my robe, and went to my walk-in prayer closet. I didn't feel spiritual. I certainly didn't feel excited or passionate about spending time with God. I mouthed the only prayer I could muster: "God, help me."

I'd drawn closer to God through my pain, but today my time with him felt more like an obligation. I didn't want my devotions to be fueled by duty, but sometimes even duty could lead to something better. Habit was important, so I continued to do what I knew would help me without waiting for a warm, fuzzy feeling. I knew that in spending this time with God, even just out of obedience, I was inviting him to change me.

I opened my journal and began writing down a few things I was grateful for, even though I didn't feel particularly grateful. The frustrations of the night before were still fresh. I thought for a minute and wrote:

1. The girls were sympathetic when I fell.
2. They both helped me clean up.

I frowned, thinking, *What else is there to be thankful for?* Just then Mocha poked his little head in the door and ran over to me, tail wagging. I wrote:

3. Mocha, who just brightened my day.

I put my pen down and reflected on the previous day. *What made me happy? When was I most upset and why? When did I feel God's presence, and when was I most distant from him?* I thought of the few moments that had been good, and I pondered why the fall had so devastated me. *What is at the core of my frustrations? Are there lies I've been telling myself?* Just answering those simple questions was helpful.

Then I prayed the familiar words from Psalm 119:18,

> Open my eyes that I may see
> wonderful things in your law. (NIV)

I didn't want to mindlessly read without understanding, so I needed to ask for God's wisdom and help.

I grabbed my pens and opened the Bible to the place where I'd left off the previous day. I was reading 2 Corinthians 4, and several verses jumped out at me. I immediately copied one into my journal in red ink: "So we do not lose heart. Though our outer self is wasting away, our inner self is being renewed day by day" (v. 16). God was definitely speaking to me in that verse. In black pen I furiously wrote about how I felt physically and how I'd been losing heart because of it. But as this verse reminded me, I needed to remember that, though my body was wasting away, God was renewing my spirit every day, including today, so I needn't fall into despair. I read on:

> For this light momentary affliction is preparing for us an eternal weight of glory beyond all comparison, as we look not to the things that are seen but to the things that are unseen. For the things that are seen are transient, but the things that are unseen are eternal. (vv. 17–18)

These were God's words to me. My suffering was temporary, and it was preparing me for heaven, where there would be incomparable glory, far greater than my pain.

I closed my eyes and thanked God that he had shown me exactly what I needed. Then I confessed my impatience and shortsightedness and asked him to keep me from losing heart. I asked him to change things in my life and in the lives of people I loved.

Increasingly, prayer became a lifeline for me. In prayer I came face-to-face with the reality that *I* couldn't change things but that the God of the universe could. Everything was possible, not because of my own scheming and efforts, but because of God's limitless wisdom and power. I could pray boldly and expect miracles.

"Thank you," I whispered, "that you give life to the dead and call into existence the things that do not exist."

I knew my requests wouldn't always be answered as I envisioned or wanted. But I also knew that even when God didn't deliver me or give me what I'd asked, he would sustain me and give me what was best—the very best for me.

Grateful for God's presence and love, I opened my eyes and prepared for the day.

Chapter 24

A DIFFERENT STORY

Though I found hope in the Bible and prayer, it didn't always last throughout the day. I still struggled with holding my everyday life together, especially when it came to parenting.

One day Kristi and I were arguing about something insignificant. She was stubbornly defiant, mocking my words. I was stubbornly righteous, determined that she listen. We went back and forth, as we had so many times before. Then, from deep down inside, a volcano of anger began to boil toward the surface. I was drinking a glass of ice water, and as I looked at Kristi smirking at me, I lost control. In a rage I tossed the water at Kristi, soaking her face and shirt.

She was speechless for a second and then started screaming obscenities at me.

"Shut up!" I screamed back at her. "You know what? I can't wait for you to go to college. It will be less than six years until you're gone. I hate your disrespect, and I hate being around you. Everything about you drives me crazy!"

I looked and sounded like a raving, vindictive lunatic because that's exactly what I was in that moment. Kristi's eyes welled up with tears. She spun around and ran to her room, leaving drops of water across the kitchen floor. I watched her go.

I stood there for a minute, processing what I had done and, even worse, what I had said. I slowly walked to Kristi's door and stood outside, knocking every ten minutes until she let me in. Then I sat on the end of her bed.

I tried to apologize, but she interrupted me. "I can't believe you said those things to me," she said. "I know I was being defiant, but you're my *mom*. You knew that what you said would hurt me."

"Kristi, I'm so ashamed of what I said and did. It was horrible and inexcusable. I should never have said those things, and I don't mean them. You're right, in the moment I *was* trying to hurt you. But I'll cry when you go to college because I'll miss you tons. And I will never be able to forget what I said to you just now. Will you forgive me?"

She nodded and reached over to hug me. We talked for a while longer, and then I left her room.

What was wrong with me? The girls' defiance had been intensifying for months, but my responses had been too. I was *so* loved by God—I knew I was—so why was I acting this way? Why was my anger choking out everything else?

My main focus had been on how I could fix the girls, but I should have been concentrating on fixing my own attitude.

I tried not to lose heart.

⟳

I needed a different perspective because I was too close to the situation to see it clearly. So I went to see my counselor, Paula, and recapped the last few months. She agreed that throwing water on Kristi in anger wasn't the best idea, but she also reassured me, saying, "We all have those moments. I'm glad you apologized. That's what she'll remember."

"I feel like a failure in parenting," I told her. "I keep focusing on the wrong things, and I'm turning my kids away from God."

"First of all, you're not a failure. You're there for your daughters, you listen to them, you teach them the Bible, you help them see the difference between right and wrong, you correct them when they need it, and you keep loving them through it all. None of that sounds like failure to me."

"I just wonder where they're headed. And I keep replaying what I've done wrong and how I could have steered them differently."

"That's where I think you need to let go. You've done what you can, but how they turn out is *not* up to you. Too often people think of their kids as products and assume their job is to make them perfect. But children are their own people. You can train them, but you can't control them. And you aren't responsible to fix everything you think isn't right. Think of how annoying that would get!"

"You're right," I chuckled. "But I guess I see them as a reflection of me, so I want them to look good. Especially when I'm around parents with perfect children."

"Let me assure you, no one's kids are perfect. As a counselor, I know." Then she added, "From all you've said, I think your girls look up to you. I'm guessing they admire you and take your advice more than you think."

"Maybe you're right. I talked to Katie a few weeks ago about forgiving her friends but chose the wrong moment to do it. She got mad at me, but then later she took my advice and thanked me."

Paula smiled as she leaned back in her chair. "I'm not surprised. Don't let their anger and defiance derail you and make you doubt your parenting. It's directed *at* you because you're safe. But it's not *about* you. Kids often feel powerless in the face of separation or divorce, and acting out gives them a temporary sense of power. So talking about the source of their anger might help." She paused, then said knowingly, "And maybe it's okay to admit you're angry, too, Vaneetha. It's okay to be angry."

I realized that once again I'd been suppressing my anger, pushing it down so no one could see it, including me. Of course I was angry, but I had to admit it first. And just like the girls, I had to make sure my anger was directed appropriately and not aimed at the people who felt safe.

We talked further, and I began to see more clearly. I realized that I could provide support and counsel but shouldn't take it personally when the girls made mistakes. Those mistakes might even be their best teachers. I could warn them about the dangers and be supportive when they needed me, but I couldn't shield them from pain or bad choices by saying the right things. They'd eventually learn and choose a different path when they were ready.

<hr />

I couldn't *entirely* give up talking to the girls about their behavior, though. And when I did discuss it with them, I'd usually hear, "Not another life lesson," accompanied by a heavy sigh.

One night at bedtime I was shocked that Katie didn't groan or interrupt me while I gave her a short pep talk on kindness. It was a poignant, stirring, and insightful little talk, in my humble opinion, and I thought Katie's silence meant she was taking in every word.

Until I noticed she was asleep.

A few weeks later, though, I read one of Katie's school essays, entitled "My Mom Is the Strongest Person I Know."

My mom's influence enables me to find joy in situations that seem joyless and hope in situations that seem hopeless. She helps me see the positive side of everything, even when life looks bleak. As a result, I have a bright outlook on life, though I could have become bitter when my father left our family. Most people would describe me as a happy person, which is directly attributable to my mother's influence. She has taught me to focus on what I have rather than what I'm lacking, which is an invaluable asset.

I printed an extra copy of the essay and stuck it in my journal for encouragement later.

Shalini encouraged me as well. "You're a great mother," she told me on one of our frequent phone calls. "I promise that one day the girls will look back and be grateful for who you are and what you taught them. Besides, how your kids turn out isn't necessarily a reflection of your parenting. They are their own people, and they make their own choices."

"It's funny you said that, because I just heard the same thing from Paula. And Katie wrote a really sweet essay about me."

"Then maybe you should start believing it, don't you think?" We both laughed, and then she continued, "Secondly, despite what it looks like, you were, and still are, actually, a great wife. You were faithful to Dave and prayed diligently for him. Even now, you're not bitter or vindictive, which is incredible. And you've shown me how to trust God when life falls apart. Your faith has buoyed mine, and I know it's doing that for others.

"I see you living out James 1 in that the testing of your faith is producing steadfastness, and God is changing you right before my eyes. You're a different person now. A better person. You're leaning into God and it's breathtaking, Vaneetha. So don't ever think that your suffering is being wasted or that what has happened to you isn't being used to show people how great God is. Because that would be a flat-out lie."

That was what I'd needed to hear. God was using my suffering for something good. It was the kind of eternal perspective that helped me hang on to hope.

Chapter 25

NOT ABOUT ME

Dave and I had talked several times about whether we'd ever get back together. But I honestly didn't know what I wanted or what would be best—for the girls, for me, even for Dave. I did know that if our marriage was restored, it would be a miraculous testament to God's transforming power.

In late 2010, I opened an email from Dave.

> I have destroyed a once-blessed family with my selfishness, self-centeredness, and pursuit of my own satisfaction. When I look back, I cannot fathom what I have done. The guilt and pain at the destruction and pain I have caused others—those who mean the most to me in the world—is at times unbearable. It is as if I was blind and hard as stone, not able to perceive the pain and destruction I was causing. And now I look back and see it clearly—in horror.

That sounded wonderful, the start of what I'd been waiting for. I didn't know if it was real repentance—that would take time to discern—but it sounded like the start of genuine change.

But soon after sending that email, Dave told me Tiffany was pregnant. Even more surprisingly, if that were possible, he said he wanted to come back to our family. He would provide for Tiffany and their child, but he wanted us—me and the girls—back.

I couldn't imagine how that would work. All I could picture was a bizarre sitcom with all of us ending up in the same house, trading corny punchlines about the similarities of parenting infants and teenagers. I shivered at the thought. Dave's proposal sounded insane.

I tried to consider it more calmly. Dave said he had changed, but my well of trust for his words was almost bone dry. Remorse and regret are not the same as repentance, and I wanted to know which this was. I had said I was open to reconciliation, but was I really?

I realized I was, but only if I *knew* God was asking me to reconcile. Otherwise, how could I be?

I knew Dave's offer would mean security in the short term. With my increasing physical weakness, I was afraid of being alone—and aging—with no one to care for me. I also still believed that a restored family would be best for the girls. We'd had some truly good years. But I wondered if the damage was irreparable.

Still, since I knew that God could do *anything*, I told Dave I'd consider it, but with the same three conditions I'd set forth from the beginning, two years prior. He would need to make a clean break with Tiffany, show evidence of true repentance, and win me back because he wanted and loved me as a wife and woman, not as a sister.

Honestly, I wondered if restoration still made sense. Wouldn't that devastate Tiffany and their child the same way Dave had devastated the girls and me? My prayer life went into overdrive.

Discouraged by his past failed attempts, Dave said he needed my help to give him the strength to do them. What that meant in practice was that he couldn't—or wouldn't—cut off contact with Tiffany unless *I* committed to restore our marriage and take him back. He'd flipped my conditions back on me, reversing them. With no evidence that he wanted to woo me, and with no fruit of repentance, he wanted me to promise to restore contact with him, all before he even met my first condition. I couldn't do that.

From the beginning of our separation, Tom had emphasized that real repentance bore fruit. Dave was undeniably sorry for what he had done, and he was kinder to me, but I felt he was negotiating with me about our future *before* actually changing. I'd read that repentance meant choosing to turn completely away from sin, moving in the opposite direction by intentionally and consistently choosing to trust God and act in ways that were pleasing to him.

I could forgive Dave and reconcile with him as friends with no hostility, but I couldn't restore our relationship back to husband and wife without seeing fruit. I refused to give Dave what he said he needed.

Via email I tried to describe my feelings using the analogy of Leah and Rachel in the book of Genesis. Jacob was tricked by his future father-in-law into marrying the less attractive older daughter, Leah, though he loved the more beautiful younger daughter, Rachel. Leah bore Jacob his first four children, and God blessed her—her fourth son, Judah, was in the line of Christ—but she never had Jacob's heart. I told Dave that I felt like Leah, who was unloved, rejected, and unattractive. She never captured her husband's attention. He never *wanted* her.

Dave wrote back to say that Leah was respected, blessed by God, and even noble. To him, being Leah wasn't ultimately a bad outcome.

Not a spiritually bad outcome, no. But on a human level, even Leah wouldn't have chosen to be unwanted. And I couldn't either.

I realized that Dave and I had vastly different ideas of what a good marriage should look like. He wanted us to be partners who worked well together. I wanted to be loved, cherished, desired.

In my time alone with God I had come across Song of Solomon 2:10–11:

> Arise, my love, my beautiful one,
> > and come away,
> for behold, the winter is past;
> > the rain is over and gone.

I had printed it out and tacked it to my bulletin board. I felt that somehow that verse would be significant for me. Paula had the same sense when I told her about it.

I wondered whether I'd always been Leah to Dave, the wife of obligation and duty. I hadn't considered that before. That didn't mean we hadn't been happy. We honestly had been very happy for many years.

I didn't understand how it all pieced together. But I knew that now, Tiffany was Dave's Rachel. And I could not and would not be Leah again.

During that time our pastor, Tom, approached me after church. He told me that I had the full backing of the elder board, including him, if I wanted to file for divorce. But he also said that they'd be there for me, helping in any way they could, if I wanted to wait. He trusted my judgment and discernment.

Driving to Paula's office one afternoon, I asked God to show me what I needed to see about Dave. What had I missed? I was somewhere on Six Forks Road near the Chick-fil-A, waiting at a stoplight, when the words *It's not about you* came into my mind, almost as clearly as if someone was speaking.

I smiled and kept driving.

Paula thought it was a breakthrough. For months she'd been saying that Dave's rejection was God's rescue and for my protection. She didn't want me to keep waiting for Dave to pursue me or to assume that it was the only good outcome possible.

I couldn't change Dave. I could only change myself. And I didn't need to change myself for him. That was his battle, not mine. This revelation freed me from so many things.

Somehow I'd been convinced that since God had the ability

to restore my marriage—which was a good, biblical truth—God was obligated to do it. That line of thinking was no different from people who were convinced that God was obligated to bring physical healing when asked. Both involved confusing God's *power* with his *promises*. The fact that God *could* do something didn't mean he *would* or *should*.

For so long I had believed that the problems in our marriage were rooted in what I was lacking. I blamed my scarred body, my limp, my lack of arm strength. I blamed myself for failing to find just the right words, do exactly the right things, and pray the perfect prayers. But when God assured me it wasn't about me, I felt liberated. God had created and chosen me. I didn't need anyone else's validation. My life could glorify God through either the restoration of my marriage or the dissolution of it.

I'd learned to be a pleaser in the hospital ward when I was forced to play by other people's rules and subordinate my needs for their convenience. I was helpless on my own. It was there that I first pretended I was fine for my parents, even as I soaked my pillow with tears every night. Nurse Lane taught me that if I rocked the boat, defied people, or stood up for myself, I'd regret it. The bullies in grade school supported that lie, reinforcing my conviction that my disability made me less than them and that my only value lay in playing the Tiny Tim role, cheerful and self-sacrificing for their benefit. People praised me when I was brave and uncomplaining, so I did everything I could to hide my pain, push away my needs, and present a positive attitude.

I had lived that way for decades, sacrificing my feelings and desires for others, trying to live up to their expectations. I wanted everyone to think I'd made the right choices. I needed to look good and be admired.

After Dave left, my well-hidden craving for approval became starkly apparent. I lived my life according to a poll of popular opinion. I craved approval so much that I tried to follow everyone's suggestions.

And even after all that had happened with Dave, I still wanted his approval so badly that I wouldn't stand up for myself.

So many people in my life thought I was a saint. To be honest, I had thought so too. Didn't they know how much pain I had put up with? Didn't they know how often I subordinated my own needs and desires? Didn't they know how much I had sacrificed or been made to suffer?

But no longer. Finally I embraced the truth about myself. I was flawed and broken, wanting appreciation and approval to my detriment, but I didn't need to make decisions based on what other people thought. What I thought counted too.

And I wasn't going to twist myself into a pretzel anymore to fit Dave's reality. I would trust myself. More importantly, I would trust God.

⁓

With this radically new perspective, I told Dave I could not accept his offer. I would not settle for being Leah again. While I saw that Dave was trying to do the right thing, I needed delight and desire to be part of his motivation, not just duty. Not only would I feel perpetually unwanted, but our marriage would be constantly at risk, leaving me continually wondering if I'd be discarded for someone else.

Dave reiterated that he needed my help to move forward. I responded that I was too wounded to help him. I would instead pray for him and wait for God to change him.

Discouraged, Dave moved back in with Tiffany, and, several months later, he filed for divorce.

My lawyer was sure we'd have a bitter divorce battle. "Most people start off graciously," she said, "but then end up fighting over every dime."

At the outset of the divorce proceedings Dave had said, "Tell me what you want, and I'll give it to you. I trust you. I know you'll be fair to me."

To my lawyer's astonishment—but not at all to mine—Dave made good on his word. He was more than generous, agreeing to everything I proposed. Even better, he continued to stay involved in the girls' lives, rooting for them at their basketball games, flying in to see them almost every weekend, calling and texting them regularly, providing for all their financial needs, and doing everything he could to be a good father to them.

Once the divorce was final, Dave and Tiffany married. They had a second child, another beautiful, healthy boy.

I was grateful that we could end our marriage as friends.

⁂

Soon after, I headed to St. Francis Springs, a retreat center nestled in the woods several hours' drive from my house. After Dave left, it had become my place to recharge, to hear God's voice, to understand myself. It was here that my healing began.

I discovered that it was only in the silence and solitude, marked by being absent from people, that I could be present to God. It was in those moments that critical outside voices—and the voices inside—could be sufficiently stilled so I could hear God clearly.

It wasn't a place to be productive, or at least not the kind by which I used to measure myself. A stack of books, my Bible study, helpful articles—none of that was the point. Surrounded by quiet and by beauty—in the small prayer chapel, in the myriad trees outside and the warm, polished wood inside—I understood it wasn't a place to *accomplish* things. It wasn't a place for earthshaking revelation. It was a place to simply be still, to be present with myself and with God.

With no other noises and voices, I could hear my own thoughts more clearly and find the shape of my own heart. And I could hear

God. My Bible and journal and silence, with no agenda, were all that I needed. I relaxed, exhaled, breathed in deeply, and waited.

Scripture says that God does not hide himself, and that if we listen, we can hear a voice behind us saying, "This is the way, walk in it" (Isa. 30:21).

I was thankful for this intimacy with God, which had grown deeper as my life grew more troubling. In my darkest days God had spoken to me, just as he had spoken to the Israelites in the fire from a mountain wrapped in darkness, cloud, and gloom.

For years I'd been hearing that voice at St. Francis Springs. It prepared me to walk without fear, knowing God was with me.

"Speak, Lord," I whispered with a smile, "for your servant is listening" (1 Sam. 3:9 NIV).

Chapter 26

REDEMPTION

Several weeks after the divorce was finalized, I invited a young couple from church, Blair and Lauren, for dinner. Blair's parents had ended their marriage years earlier, and at dinner he talked openly about how much he'd struggled with it. Very few of the girls' friends, or mine, had weathered divorce—or at least no one had mentioned it—so we found it helpful to talk to someone who understood. Katie was out with friends, but Kristi and I listened intently.

"I don't know how you feel about what happened with your dad," Blair told Kristi, "but when my parents separated, it rocked my world. All of us kids were hurt in different ways. My sister had it the worst because she was still living at home."

Kristi's eyes were glued to Blair. Noticing her reaction, I asked him, "Would you mind telling us what happened? If it's not too painful or personal?"

It turned out it was both painful *and* personal, but he chose to share his story anyway.

"I still remember the night when my mom's new boyfriend was in a car accident and was transported to a nearby hospital," he said. We all stopped eating and focused on him. "My mom was really worried about him and asked me to go in and see how he was, which was tough for me because I'd never met him before. I didn't want to do that, but my mom was a mess, so I went into his room."

Blair paused and took a sip of water as he thought about how—or if—he was going to say the next words. "To be honest, when I went into his room, I thought, *I could probably pull out all these machines and tubes so he will die, and no one will even know.* I was tempted for a second. I hated him. In my mind he had ruined our lives."

He paused and closed his eyes as if reliving that moment. "I prayed, and God gave me the strength to be kind to him. God did a great work in my heart toward him, which has continued to this day. But believe me, at first it wasn't easy."

As soon as Blair finished talking, Kristi blurted out, "I hate Tiffany. I really hate her."

We all turned to look at Kristi. It was one of the most revealing statements she'd made in years. She'd been in shutdown mode, burying most of her thoughts and feelings from the rest of us—I knew exactly who had taught her that trick—and it hadn't been good for either of us.

After dinner, Kristi wanted to show Blair and Lauren the house. When Kristi opened the door to show them the guest room, she impulsively blurted out, "You should live here with us. Could you do that?"

Blair said, "Kristi, thanks so much for asking us, but we're pretty good right now in our own apartment. If we change our mind, though, we'll definitely let you know."

A few months later, Blair called unexpectedly. "I'm not sure quite how to ask this, but something has changed with Lauren's job and also with our apartment. We're moving to Texas in December, and we need a place to stay for four months. Please, *please* feel free to say no, but if Kristi's offer is still open, we'd love to use your guest room and pay you rent."

Two weeks later they knocked on the front door, Blair with their suitcases and Lauren holding their nine-month-old, Abel. Right away the five of us—six if Abel was awake—became like a family unit. We would recap our days over dinner, clean the kitchen together, then play games and talk for hours.

I was astonished by what Lauren and Blair, who were still in their twenties, could get away with saying to the girls. When Katie and Kristi whined about something, Blair loved to imitate Veruca Salt from the movie *Charlie and the Chocolate Factory*, saying, "Daddy, I want a golden ticket *now*." All of us would laugh, and the girls would get the point without feeling criticized or lectured.

Over the next several months, Kristi spent hours every week with Blair and Lauren, talking about her fears, the divorce, her faith, and school. Blair would play basketball with her in the driveway, and often she'd open up about her life. Meanwhile my friends and I continued to pray hard for Kristi, asking for God's protection and deliverance.

And Kristi changed. Slowly, slowly, but she changed. I saw her smile again. I noticed her reading the Bible, at first secretly in her room, and then openly as she talked about what she read. She made a group of good friends and flourished in school.

By her senior year, Kristi was a strong student, a thoughtful friend, and the homecoming queen. Even better, she and I read books together, laughed together, and prayed about everything together. The transformation was astonishing—and beautiful. Kristi ended one of her many letters to me saying,

Thank you for never giving up. You haven't given up on God. You haven't given up on joy. You haven't given up on being a great mom. Basically, I'm so thankful that I have a mom like you. Thank you for teaching me what it means to love mercy. Thank you for never being satisfied in your walk with Christ, for never growing complacent in your relationship with him. I love you!

God had been working all the time, all those years, even when I couldn't see it. Kristi was offered a full scholarship to play basketball at an NCAA Division I college, but instead she chose to play for Wheaton College, a Christian liberal arts college that was a Division III school.

One of the moms from the team told me that her daughter loved Kristi, who her daughter said was the funniest person she knew. "Kristi has really changed my daughter's life. I don't think she'll ever realize the impact she's had on my daughter, both in basketball and in her faith."

Katie's journey back to faith, after telling me she wanted nothing to do with *my* God anymore, was gradual as well. It involved Christian mentors, faithful friends, and a Bible study she loved attending. I treasured the way she described her faith journey in a testimony she gave in college:

> Honestly my faith became shaky at times. I questioned God for allowing these things to happen and continue to happen to my family, and I questioned whether or not I believed he was real. But God pursued me and would not let me run far during those times. . . . He showed me he would walk through all times in life with me—including those times I did not understand why they were happening.
>
> God has been faithful through it all. . . . God calls me his daughter and says that I am completely loved by him. It still is crazy for me to think that the God of the universe loves me and desires to have a personal relationship with me.

Though I had completely blown it as a parent too many times to count, God held on to both girls. I was so grateful that their faith and faithfulness were up to God, not me.

⟊⟊

God continued to work in me through all my mistakes and missteps.

A few months after my divorce, a friend invited me to a Generous Giving conference and I excitedly agreed, not because I was feeling generous but because I needed a break. Dave and I had been financially generous, but now I felt more like a miser, protecting my finances, my strength, and even my time. I wanted to conserve, and even hoard. I felt like I had nothing to give.

When my friend and I entered the hotel ballroom, a sense of joy permeated the room. Many people shared stories of loss and struggle, yet they all seemed noticeably radiant.

At a breakout session, I met a woman who had gone through a painful divorce. I cried as I heard her story, but she grabbed my hand and said, "Oh, please know that God has given me far more than he's taken away. But I am grateful that I haven't experienced *all three* D's."

I squeezed her hand back. "I love your attitude. I'm emotional because I recently went through a divorce as well. But what are the three D's?"

"Oh, that's an expression. The three D's are divorce, disability, and death. Those change your world."

I sat back, startled. I had experienced each of them, though I'd never heard them described like that. Just then, the host announced a short break, so the woman and I got up and walked out together. In the lobby, we were met by a cameraman who was asking people to describe the most amazing gift, besides salvation, they had ever received. "Suffering," I said without thinking. But I had no idea what that meant.

Back in Raleigh days later, three words kept swirling around in my head: generosity, suffering, and joy. How did they fit together? Was suffering really a gift I needed to steward? While I didn't want any of the three D's, I sensed that having gone through them was somehow a gift I needed to offer others generously. But how?

I still felt I had nothing to give, but a line from one of Christa's songs kept coming back to me: "Serving another when our table is empty."[5] How does anyone do that?

The answer slowly emerged. I thought about the ways I could comfort others as God comforted me. I could listen to people in their grief, and I could share mine. A year later I started a blog called *Dance in the Rain*,[6] named after a Vivian Greene quote that I loved: "Life isn't about waiting for the storm to pass . . . it's about learning to dance in the rain."[7]

As people responded to my blog, I understood why the generous are joyful. Giving away what God has entrusted to us, helping others on their journey, and not hoarding but holding everything with an open hand felt incredible. It was like the living water that flowed out of the temple in Ezekiel, bringing life to whatever it touched. While I missed painting, helping others find God in their suffering was infinitely more life-giving. Though the Lord had taken away my ability to create graphic art, he had given me something better in its place.

Around that time, I noticed those three words from the conference converge in 2 Corinthians 8:2: "For in a severe test of affliction, their abundance of joy and their extreme poverty have overflowed in a wealth of generosity." It was true. Being generous in suffering, when you feel that you have nothing to give, is the surest way to unexpected joy.

God brought me unexpected joy through generosity in other ways as well. A friend was helping me clean out some cabinets when she found the "You Are Special" plate I'd painted years earlier. She set it on the counter, and we looked at it. It featured a birthday cake and stars, along with the words "Congratulations!" and "You are special," with Dave's last name—still my last name—written along the bottom.

Send it to Dave and Tiffany, I thought. The impulse was immediate.

At first I dismissed the idea as crazy. I'd painted that plate for *our* family. We had used it for special occasions like birthdays or to celebrate when the girls had done something out of the ordinary. It was also precious because I had painted it soon after Paul died. Since I knew I wouldn't be able to do any more plate painting, I wondered if I should save it. But the idea to send it to Dave and Tiffany kept coming back to me. So I did.

I prayed as I wrapped it that God would use it somehow for Dave's new family. He had two little boys who would be having birthdays and celebrations of their own. If I remarried I'd have a new last name, and our girls would probably take their husbands' names. But Dave's boys would be able to enjoy the plate and even pass it on to future generations. As I mailed the plate, I felt genuine joy, which took me by surprise.

Tiffany sent me a thank-you note—our first ever communication—saying they were excited to start using the plate. Later, when Katie and Kristi went to visit Dave and Tiffany, they told me their little brothers had put the "You Are Special" plate at Kristi's place setting just to make her smile. Dave's family regularly used it to make people feel special.

Dave frequently thanked me for the ways I handled our separation and divorce and for not turning the girls against him in anger. He once emailed me saying, "Just wanted to share with you that God has been glorified by both your overt extension of forgiveness to me as well as the way you handled the girls through things between us. Many others would have handled things differently, and my relationship with the girls today would likely look very different as a result. Thank you again."

Forgiveness had changed me. It had changed all of us.

I was also grateful that I had experienced full forgiveness and love in my relationship with Maxine and Jerry, who still visited regularly. During one visit, Maxine handed me a neatly folded creme-and-rainbow quilt—the most beautiful handmade quilt I'd ever seen. Quilting was her hobby, and over the years she'd given us some lovely quilts. But this one was *spectacular*.

"It's my favorite," she said, as we laid it out on the table to look at it. Her fingers lovingly straightened one edge. "It's the prettiest quilt I've ever made. And I want you to have it. I don't know how long I'm going to live, and I wanted to make sure you got this. You'll always be my daughter."

We embraced, crying. They were like second parents to me, and now, more than ever, I loved and respected them deeply.

I realized our bond was like Maxine's quilt—made beautiful by cutting apart whole fabric and stitching the fragments together again. We had all chosen this new relationship, piecing it together in a unique way, which is what made it remarkable.

Chapter 27

BRAVE NEW WORLD

The fall of her senior year in high school, Katie invited me out to Sola, our favorite local coffee shop, to talk. My treat, of course.

As she sipped her latte, Katie asked, "So, Mom, now that you're divorced, have you thought about dating?"

I almost spit out my latte. "Dating? Are you kidding? There's nobody around here to date. And I'm not sure if I'm ready to start dating anyway. Why are you even asking this?"

"Don't freak out, Mom," she said, smiling. "But I've been thinking a lot about it. I know you loved being married, so I think you'd be happy being *remarried*."

"Maybe I would, Katie, but I'm not sure if I'm ready." I took a sip of my drink. "Plus, how would I even meet someone? I don't know any single men, and I definitely don't want to go looking for them!"

"I get that, but things have changed since you were younger." Katie picked up her phone from the table and waved it at me. "You could meet someone online."

"Online? That sounds creepy. I don't want to meet some psychopath I don't know anything about."

"Psychopath? Okay, you might be a *little* paranoid." Katie laughed. "It's actually pretty safe. You have good judgment, so you wouldn't meet anyone you weren't sure about. Why don't you try one of the Christian dating sites?"

"I'm not sure about that, Katie," I said. "But I'll think about it. I just don't know anyone who's done it."

"Well, maybe you need to be the first. Just pray about it. It might be a great way to meet someone."

⁓

Soon after my coffee date with Katie, I went to see my counselor, Paula. At her recommendation I'd taken a twelve-week DivorceCare course held at area churches. It involved weekly meetings featuring videos and small-group discussions, along with daily homework. I'd finished the course and wanted to let her know how helpful and healing it had been. I also wanted to fill her in on my conversation with Katie.

"It's funny," I told her, "but since Katie mentioned dating, that's all I think about!"

"It's crazy how our minds work. So, do you *want* to start dating?"

"I think I do. I liked being married, and I'd love to find someone else to share my life with."

"There's a 'but' coming, isn't there?"

"You know me too well." I laughed, then grew more serious. "But I wonder if anyone would be interested in dating someone with a disability. I've been insecure about the way I walk my entire life, and now I'm even more conscious of it. Also, I have no idea how bad the post-polio is going to get, or how soon. I don't know if anyone would want to date me with the disability I have now, let alone the possibility of eventual quadriplegia."

"You've thought about it a lot, I see. I'm sure there are men out there who would be fine with your disability because it's not all that you are. You have a lot to offer, Vaneetha. But have you thought about exactly why you want to get remarried? What need would it fill? Would friendships, male and female, fill that need, or do you think only a husband would?"

"It won't surprise you to hear I've been thinking about that too," I said, half smiling. "I do think friendships could fill that void. It's not like I feel incomplete without a man. And I'm enjoying the time to rediscover myself . . . what I want, who I am, what makes me happy. For so long I never knew that."

Paula raised her eyebrows.

"Yeah, yeah," I admitted. "*But* I'd love to spend my life with someone, wake up in the morning with them, laugh with them, and be there for them. I don't think I *need* to remarry. If I'm single the rest of my life, that's okay. I certainly wouldn't want to rush into it, because being married to the wrong person would be a lot worse than being alone."

"I'm glad you see it that way," Paula said as she leaned back. "Lots of people end up in my office who wanted a husband or wife because they were lonely and married the first person who loosely fit the bill. Meaning, breathing and interested in them!"

We both laughed, and she continued, "Soon they're miserable and wish they'd waited. You need to know that you're vulnerable right now, so take it slow. Trust God in this process."

That was good advice for all of life, and I was determined to heed it.

⁂

I called Shalini. "So what do you think about online dating?" I asked. "I'm worried that I'm going to meet someone who's weird or has a lot of baggage. I do *not* want baggage."

"I get what you mean, but Vaneetha?"

"Yeah?"

"You're not exactly carry-on luggage yourself."

"Very funny, Shalini. Hi-lar-i-ous. But seriously, what should I do? Do you think there's anything wrong with trying it?"

"No, actually, I don't. Listen, a lot depends on how you approach it and how you present yourself."

I added "wisdom about online dating sites" to my prayer list and scoped out a few Christian dating sites. The rules of dating had *definitely* changed since I'd last been on a date in the previous millennium. And I definitely needed advice from the girls—at least on how to take selfies.

I asked Tom for advice too, half hoping he'd tell me the idea was crazy. But he encouraged me to try it. He thought that if I checked in with him and other friends regularly and introduced him to people before I got serious with them, then it sounded fine.

With so much confirmation, I gathered my courage and walked into the brave new world of online dating.

I met a man for coffee, and we started talking about books. He mentioned that he had just recently read *Fifty Shades of Grey* and wondered if I'd read it. I suddenly remembered I had another appointment.

One guy suggested we meet for dinner at Hooters. "For the wings," he said.

An Anglican priest showed up to Panera to meet me wearing full clerical garb. At the counter he asked loudly, "What's the *most* organic thing you have here?"

Finally I started emailing back and forth with a divorced man who seemed sincere and thoughtful, and we talked a lot about faith. But just before we were supposed to meet in person, he ghosted me—a term I learned from my girls. I didn't hear anything, until his wife asked me not to contact him. She'd just discovered our emails on his computer and said they were going to counseling.

Cats were just a *little* too important to another man I briefly dated. He had a cat sitter every day when he was at work, and that same cat sitter, he told me proudly, was at his house during our date, just in case Mr. Magoo needed something. I didn't tell him about Mocha.

A message arrived from someone who told me he was a

"sweat-loving man." I thought of a few questions in response. Was his affinity for his *own* perspiration, or was he looking for a mate with active sweat glands? Or perhaps he was a *sweet*-loving man. Or was he simply a sweet *and* loving man who saw spelling as a low priority?

One Thursday night at the local Chili's, my date flipped my menu over to the back before I could open it. "You're gonna need to order off this two-for-twenty-dollars special."

Though I enjoyed entertaining my friends with my dating stories, I was getting discouraged. I'd connected with a few guys I liked, but they backed off after we met, or after I mentioned my disability in an email or over the phone. I hadn't even gotten to the post-polio part!

That was their right, of course. But their reactions triggered feelings I thought I'd left behind. Each time old wounds threatened to reopen, I had to remind myself that I was enough without the approval of some guy who had clicked on my dating profile. In fact, I was fearfully and wonderfully made by the God of the universe, and I didn't need to apologize for my disability.

God could bring me someone at the right time, but I was done with random dating.

⌇

When I logged on to one of my accounts to deactivate my subscription, I got a notification that someone I'd been matched with months earlier had new activity. A man named Joel was busy uploading new pictures of himself. Lots of them. Multiple times.

Amused, I thought to myself, *Joel must be a narcissist. Maybe I should take a look at his profile to see these all-important photos he's adding.*

His profile surprised me. His answer to the first question—"What are you passionate about?"—wasn't generic like those of most guys on the site. They all self-identified as strong Christians, but generally answered the question with something resembling, "God, family, country, but not necessarily in that order."

Joel had written: "I am passionate about Jesus Christ, because there is nothing else to be passionate about."

That got my attention—but so did his looks. Dark hair, which I liked. Five-foot-ten, which was a perfect match to my five-foot-two. And a beard, which I normally didn't like, but his looked distinguished. In one of his photos he was wearing a hard hat and looked like he'd just finished chopping wood. *Good for you for adding updated pictures*, I thought.

In his profile he talked about his late wife, who had died of cancer, and his two adult daughters. I found that we both loved to read, and we'd even read two of the same books recently.

Maybe I wasn't *quite* ready to deactivate my subscription.

Joel was notified that I'd looked at his profile and sent me a "smile." I immediately responded, and we exchanged emails. Soon our daily emails became every-few-hours emails. I felt a rush of emotion whenever my inbox chimed, and I caught myself refreshing it entirely too often.

I had coffee with my mentor, Sally, and told her all about Joel. "I'm about to tell him about my post-polio syndrome," I said. "But I'm nervous about what he'll think."

"Vaneetha," she gently chided, "you don't think he's already googled you and read all your stuff online? You're not exactly hard to locate with that first name. Your ministry has expanded so much in recent years, and now that you're regularly featured on well-known sites like Desiring God, you'd be easy to find online."

She had a point.

When I got home from coffee, I discovered that Sally was right. My afternoon email from Joel said he'd searched my name and found my writing. He wanted to be up-front about it in case I had concerns. Embarrassed that I hadn't yet told him about my post-polio, I asked Joel what he thought about it and hit Send, bracing for another rejection.

I didn't even need to refresh my inbox. Joel immediately replied to say that it wasn't a problem. He'd looked up post-polio and knew what he'd be getting into if we decided to date. He said my disability wasn't a factor to him.

Over the course of the next week or so, Joel and I exchanged more than twenty thousand words by email—deep discussions, family news, and jokes that made me laugh hysterically. There weren't any red flags, at least not yet, so I thought it might be safe to let my guard down.

It was time for a phone call.

The first time I heard Joel's voice, my heart skipped a beat or three. It was deep and warm and comforting. I instantly felt reassured. He sounded exactly the way I'd envisioned the man on the other end of the emails would sound.

In the middle of that two-and-a-half-hour conversation about everything and nothing, I asked, "So why did you upload so many pictures, anyway? I got so many notifications about new photos that I clicked on your profile. I thought you were a *narcissist*."

Joel laughed. "I'm so glad you looked at my profile, because then I looked at yours. But to answer your question, as a nuclear engineer, I'm precise. I'd initially uploaded pictures of myself in various settings, and they appeared in a different order than I wanted. So I took them all down and uploaded them again, but each time they appeared in the wrong order. Even the tech support couldn't fix it. It's funny, because at the time I was really annoyed. But it's the reason I met you."

"That's kind of a metaphor for life, isn't it? Sometimes the things that annoy us, that we wish were different, turn out to be the best things for us."

"I hadn't thought of it that way, but you're right," Joel said.

The weekend after I talked to Joel on the phone, I was in Chicago for one of Kristi's basketball tournaments. Shalini drove from Grand Rapids to pick me up at the airport, and on the way to the tournament I talked nonstop about Joel, often even as I was texting him.

"I can tell when it's Joel texting you and not one of the girls or one of your girlfriends," Shalini commented.

"What's that?" I asked, not paying attention because I was texting Joel.

"I said, I can tell when it's Joel, because—"

"Sorry!" I interrupted her, looking up from my phone. "That was Joel, and I wanted to answer his text. What were you saying?"

"Nothing," Shalini said. "I was just going to let you know that you're glowing."

⟨⟨⟨⟩⟩⟩

Joel offered to drive to Raleigh from his home in Knoxville, Tennessee, so we could meet in person. But first he insisted I call some references.

"I want you to feel safe and to feel certain about who I am, Vaneetha," he told me. "Clearly I can pretend to be anyone I want over the internet or phone, so I'm giving you the names of three people who can vouch for me. The references are all from Pittsburgh, where Barb and I lived for twenty-three years. People there know me better, because I've only been in Knoxville for five years. I moved here to sort of make a fresh start. So my first reference is my pastor, and you can check out the church online to verify it's legitimate. Another is my late wife's closest friend. And the last is one of my friends. You need to call them all before I'll visit."

I felt awkward about calling strangers, but Joel was adamant. The next day I called Patty, his late wife's best friend, and explained who I was. Immediately she said, "Oh, Vaneetha, Joel told me all about you. I want you to know how highly my husband and I think of Joel. He was tender and attentive as he cared for Barb through her cancer. He was at her side the whole time to care for her every need. And he even maintained a fun sense of humor with her through it. He's the real deal and is a great father to Ashley and Emily. I can't say enough about him."

I hadn't been worried, but somehow now I felt a huge sense of relief. "Patty, thank you for telling me about Joel. I'm so glad he insisted I call you. It's nice to know he is who I thought he was and that all he said was true."

"It's probably more than true. Joel is modest and serves others without drawing attention to himself. Most people have no idea how much he does for people. He dated a few other women, but none of them were exactly right for him. Barb passed away seven years ago, but Joel wanted to wait for God's choice for him." She hesitated and then said, "Joel mentioned your polio, and I want you to know that he has counted the cost."

Her comment startled me at first. I paused and then asked, "That's good to hear. But what exactly did Joel say about that?"

"He didn't say much, but he told me you had polio and now have post-polio and that would involve some care. Knowing Joel, he's researched it thoroughly. Whatever you need, I know Joel will joyfully do it. I'm not sure if you guys talked about that directly, but I wanted you to know."

I hung up and leaned back in the chair, exhaling deeply. Joel sounded like the real deal. After all those years of bullying and loss, looking for acceptance and feeling less than, I finally felt accepted for who I was by a man without needing to hide anything.

But I didn't want to get ahead of myself.

Chapter 28

WINTER IS PAST

Joel drove from Knoxville to Raleigh for the weekend and booked a room at a nearby hotel.

The second day of his visit, we went to a play in the afternoon and then returned to my place to make dinner together. I handled the seared scallops and roasted asparagus, and Joel made Parmesan risotto. We laughed and joked in the kitchen while we cooked—and I noticed that Joel was a man who knew the difference between a chef's knife and a santoku knife.

We were due at Tom and Carol's for dessert and coffee afterward so they could meet Joel. Unfortunately the risotto took a little longer to soften, as it's known to do sometimes, and I realized we'd be cutting it close. I let Joel know our dinner wouldn't be as leisurely as I'd wanted and then walked to the dining room to set the table.

I was bringing some candlesticks in when Joel said, "No, I don't think we'll do candles now. We don't have time for that."

I'd been planning a candlelight dinner—a *romantic* candlelight dinner—but instead we ate under the bright overhead lights.

But the candles wouldn't have taken any longer, I thought. He didn't owe me any romance, and I was okay with just being friends, but I couldn't deny that I'd wanted the candles. After Joel's comment, I wondered if he was only interested in friendship.

The previous night, when Joel arrived, we'd gone out for dinner. I must have checked and rechecked my outfit five times as I got ready—and checked my makeup an equal number of times. Wanting to look casual but dressy at the same time, I settled on white jeans, a dark blue silk shirt, and gray flats, shoes I only wore for special occasions.

When Joel rang the bell and I opened the door, I knew I'd gotten it just right. He was wearing a casual sport coat, a button-down shirt, dark jeans, and brown leather shoes—and he looked good. We both smiled, said awkward hellos that overlapped each other's, and exchanged an awkward hug.

Dinner the first night was great. But he'd been less talkative than he usually was on the phone. The next morning we met a group of my friends for coffee at Sola, and everyone liked him. We both liked the play we saw in the afternoon, but I hadn't noticed a spark on his part. So maybe I was putting too much weight on the lack of candles at dinner . . . or maybe I wasn't.

We didn't make it back from Tom and Carol's until later that night, and Joel walked me to the door. "I'm really tired," he said. "I might just go to church tomorrow and leave right afterward rather than staying for lunch. It's a long drive home."

I closed the door softly behind him after we said our goodbyes. I was pretty sure he wasn't interested.

The next morning it was raining on our way into church, and Joel held an umbrella for me as we walked from the car. While he used the restroom, an acquaintance in the foyer asked me, "Was that your chauffeur?"

Tom's sermon about sex, based on Proverbs 5, was wildly uncomfortable. Of all the sermons in Proverbs, of course this one had to land on the weekend of Joel's visit. Joel did stay for lunch, but we definitely did not discuss Tom's message. And then Joel surprised me by coming over to my place and talking for several hours. Then, before he left, he took my hand in his and said he couldn't remember having a better time. He played with my hand for a minute, gently stroking his thumb across my skin as we talked. My stomach was doing flip-flops.

"I want to see you again, Vaneetha, as soon as possible."

I told him that I had a writers' conference in Charlotte, halfway between Raleigh and Knoxville, the following week, and Joel promised he would meet me there.

When he left to drive back to Knoxville, I felt pretty sure he *was* interested after all.

~ ❦ ~

All week I was excited about seeing Joel again, and the writers' conference had become incidental in my mind. Desiring God had asked me to write a book for them about suffering, but since my relationship with Joel was already taking up so much of my time and energy, I asked them if we could postpone the project.

Joel made reservations at a romantic Italian restaurant in Charlotte on a Saturday night—and there were candles, which I took as a good sign. The next morning over coffee, he impulsively invited me to visit his family with him in Kansas, and I enthusiastically agreed.

Before that trip I flew to Knoxville to visit Joel. I met his daughter Emily and her fiancé, and Joel invited friends from his small group over for an afternoon dessert and coffee so I could meet the people I'd heard so much about. After they left, the two of us had dinner at his house. During a lull in the conversation, I noticed Joel staring at me, so I asked what he was thinking.

He hesitated, then said, "Actually I was thinking about kissing you."

"So . . ." I smiled, "why don't you?"

He leaned over and kissed me, and I kissed him back.

The next day he said, "I only want to say 'I love you' to one more woman, ever."

I didn't reply, and the conversation moved on to other things, until half an hour later he said, "I want you to know . . . I love you, Vaneetha."

I didn't have to think about it. I looked at him and said, "I love you too, Joel."

⁓⁂⁓

Both of us understood what that conversation meant, but we didn't talk about details until we visited Joel's family in Independence, Kansas.

Our three-hour drive from the airport to rural southeast Kansas, where Joel's widowed dad lived, was amazing and intense. We talked about our previous marriages. About our dreams. About music and movies, friends and faith. We even discussed what we wanted included in our wedding. I brought up post-polio because I needed to make sure Joel understood what it meant for me—and what it would mean for anyone I married.

"Vaneetha," he said, "I've researched this, the post-polio, the quadriplegia, everything. It doesn't bother me. It's not what this is about. As long as one of us is able to do things, we'll be fine. And if both of us are disabled, we could get helpers. I love you. I love your mind, your faith, your sense of humor, your beauty. It's not about what you can or can't do. It's about *you*."

Our visit with Joel's dad was so much fun, and several of his siblings and their spouses came by as well. During the days the guys chopped wood and cleared the property, while Joel's dad sat outside with me. He told me stories about Joel and even shared his testimony. We ate dinner together every night and laughed constantly. Before we left, Joel's sister, Jan, pulled me aside and said she hoped I'd join their family. She hadn't seen her brother laugh or look this happy in many years.

⁓⁂⁓

We began talking about marriage in October 2014 and planned a late February date the following year. We wanted to wait until after the wedding of Joel's younger daughter, Emily, in January 2015. Joel offered a ladder and ample gas money to Emily and her fiancé so they could elope in style—partly to save them from stress, but mostly so we could get married earlier. But they just laughed. They thought he was kidding.

Meanwhile, life continued on. We decided to spend Thanksgiving in Grand Rapids with Shalini and her family. The girls and I flew up together, and Joel met us there. After an amazing Thanksgiving dinner, courtesy of my wonder-cook sister, all of us stayed around the candlelit table, talking and laughing and playing games.

When we played charades, Katie and Kristi couldn't stop laughing at me as I employed my legendarily bad pantomime skills. None of the other adults were much better, and all the kids were highly amused. I decided to concentrate on something I was better at: eating Shalini's pumpkin pie.

Then, in the space of about five seconds, everyone left the table except Joel and me.

"Hey," he said, "I wanted to talk to you about something in that marriage book we're reading together. And, ah, I think we should go into your room," he continued, "and use your copy."

When we entered my room, Joel pretended to grab the book, but then he turned around with a navy velvet box opened to display a ring. He got down on one knee and said softly, "Vaneetha, I love you so much. Will you marry me?"

I threw my arms around his neck and said, "Yes! I'd love to marry you!" Then I pulled back and looked at the ring. It was gorgeous. It was the most beautiful engagement ring I had ever seen. Even in the bedroom light, the stones were so perfect they looked liquid.

I looked at Joel and said, "I can't believe we're finally getting married, *officially*."

"I can't believe it either," he said. "And I can't wait."

Chapter 29

THE WAY YOU WALK

As the wedding raced toward us, Joel made sure I never doubted his delight and passion for me. He was determined to keep pursuing me, keep wooing me, keep reinforcing how much he loved me. The constant flow of sweet letters and packages, combined with regular deliveries of orchids, sunflowers, and tulips, underscored that.

It wasn't all flowers and cards, either. Once Joel told me, "Finding you is like . . . finding a vintage Porsche 911 in a lot full of used Yugos."

We talked every night after Joel finished work, the phone cradled in his neck while he ironed his shirt for the next day. Then he'd pour a glass of wine and sit down at his kitchen table, all while chatting with me. Though I couldn't paint much anymore, I used a phone headset to talk so I could work on a watercolor for Joel. When I later sent it to him, he was speechless when he opened it—which he did when I was on the phone—and finally said it was one of the most beautiful paintings he had ever seen.

At Joel's suggestion, we began the same Bible reading plan so we could share what we were learning, either over the phone or in person. We saw each other often on weekends as Joel regularly wore out I-40, the highway between Raleigh and Knoxville. When he visited, he stayed with my parents. My father appreciated Joel's care for me, his sharp intellect, and what my dad referred to as his "sartorial elegance." My mom thought Joel was so perfect for me that she wondered if I'd verified his birth certificate in case God had whipped him up out of thin air just for my benefit.

We held our rehearsal dinner at Bay 7, an old warehouse converted into an elegant gathering space, in a hip part of Durham. About one hundred and fifty of our friends and relatives gathered with us on the polished hardwood, lit by row after row of sparkling white lights that hung from the rafters and by candles on every table. Outside, the city grew dark and cold, but inside we glowed with love and laughter.

Family and friends spoke after dinner, expressing how thrilled they were that Joel and I had found each other. A friend described my transformation since meeting Joel, saying, "She's this giggly, lovestruck girl." And Katie ended her toast by saying, "Joel, I'm so excited for you to join our family. You make my mom so happy."

For our first dance Joel and I chose "Come Away with Me" by Norah Jones. Joel had sent me her CD early on, and both of us had grown to love it during our courtship. Everyone gathered around us, the lights dimmed, and Joel took my hand and led me onto the dance floor as the song began to play. He held me close, and I let the moment wash over me. I felt so loved, so cherished, as if every moment I spent with Joel was rewriting another lie from my past.

The song ended, and then it was time for us to greet our guests and for others to dance the night away—or at least until 10:00 p.m., which was plenty late for me. We needed to get some rest so we'd be ready for our wedding day.

❦

I opened my eyes the next morning. It was finally here. As I lay in bed remembering the events of the last few days, Shalini knocked softly on my bedroom door.

"Come on in, Shal. I was just lying here thinking."

She walked to the window and opened the blinds. "Did you see? It's beautiful outside. The perfect day for a wedding."

I sat up and looked. "You're right. But it's been a crazy week, hasn't it? Who would've guessed that we'd have nine inches of snow on the ground, a massive ice storm, and all of North Carolina under a state of emergency?"

Shalini laughed as she sat on the edge of the bed. "Yeah, I'm so glad we were able to get your wedding dress right before the store closed, because otherwise you might be walking down the aisle in your nightgown." She glanced over at me in my frayed pajama top. "But definitely not that!"

We both laughed as she continued, "Seriously, though, two days ago, when Bay 7 wasn't sure they'd be open for the rehearsal, and your friends had to clear the ice-covered church parking lot, and we finally found one lone copy center across town to print off the wedding programs, we wouldn't have believed that today could be so sunny and gorgeous."

"You're right. It's strange," I said. "A few days ago it seemed as if everything was falling apart and nothing was going the way I'd planned. But now it seems like everything's perfect."

"It does. But even if we didn't get the wedding dress or the programs, and even if no one could come and everything was closed, it still would've been perfect, because you get to marry Joel," she said wisely.

I nodded, and we continued talking and savoring our time together—until Katie and Kristi walked into the bedroom and interrupted our reminiscing.

"So, when are we supposed to leave again?" Kristi asked. "I thought you said we needed to leave ten minutes from now, and I'm *pretty* sure you threatened us with bodily harm if we were late."

Shalini and I looked at our watches and jumped up. Time had gotten away from us. Minutes later we were all in the car and headed to the church, where we'd meet Ashley and Emily, Joel's daughters, to get ready.

We met in a large upstairs room at the church with a long mirror and lots of chairs. Several of my friends came to hang out with us, and we shared stories while I had my hair and makeup done. Kristi, in usual form, kept us laughing hysterically as she parodied all that was happening.

Then Jim, Joel's brother and best man, knocked on the door to deliver a letter and a small gift from Joel. Shalini had done the same for me. As I opened my letter I inhaled sharply, stunned. Joel's letter to me ended exactly as my letter to him had—on the same Bible verse. Then, as I unwrapped Joel's gift, I was shocked to see that the verse engraved on the crystal plaque he'd given me read: "Arise, my love, my beautiful one, and come away." It was from Song of Solomon 2:10. The same passage I had pinned on my bulletin board years earlier as a promise from God to me. At the time I didn't fully understand its meaning. But now, at least in part, I did.

Before we knew it, it was time to line up outside the sanctuary. The bridesmaids walked down in order—Emily, then Ashley, then Kristi, then Katie, and finally Shalini. I wanted to peek around and see Joel's face, but I couldn't risk being seen. Then the church doors closed, and I could hear Tom speaking to Joel. When he said the words, "Joel, behold your bride," the double doors swung open.

I heard the opening notes of Jeremiah Clarke's "Trumpet Voluntary" and looked at my father, who was standing beside me. He held out his arm and I took it. Then we began to walk together—something I had wanted more than anything else as a child. As we stepped onto the carpeted aisle, I was overwhelmed. I scanned the faces of the people I loved, people who had walked through the toughest years with me, all grinning like they couldn't stop.

There were Ann and Jim, who winked when I walked by, sitting near Lisa and a row behind Sally. I looked up front and saw Christa, who was going to sing, and Jennifer, who was about to read Scripture. They had been with me through so many seasons. Then I saw Lauren and Blair, who flew in from Texas, sitting with Carol and other church friends, including Florence, Michele, and Ray. I was indebted to them all for their practical care. I noticed Paula and Bill, who didn't know each other, though both had been integral to my journey.

As I kept walking, I glimpsed high school and college friends who came from all over the country. I wanted to take it all in, for the moment to last forever. It was holy and sacred and wonderful all at the same time.

Then I glanced at the other side and saw Joel's friends, looking equally joyful. I noticed his friends from his small group and his work in Knoxville, all of whom had been so welcoming to me. I saw several families from Pittsburgh, including Patty, who had first told me what an amazing man Joel was. People had flown in from all over the country on Joel's side as well, including his family from Kansas.

My father and I neared the front, and I saw my mother, beaming. This day was the answer to so many of her prayers. And then there was Joel, standing before me, his eyes shining. We both smiled, tears in our eyes, as he took my hand from my father's, and we faced Tom together.

The ceremony went by quickly. Friends read Scripture, and Tom gave a short message that included stories about us and our courtship and the kindness of God in bringing us together. Then we exchanged our vows and rings, and Christa sang "The Day Before You." Finally, Tom pronounced us husband and wife, and Joel leaned down to kiss me.

We walked out, smiling uncontrollably, passing our family and friends once again. I was limping, as usual, but it didn't bother me. Not today and not ever again.

I remembered my conversation with Joel months earlier, when I'd confessed to him my embarrassment about the way I walked. We'd been talking about the wedding and my hesitation about having everyone watch me walk down the aisle because of my limp.

Joel had looked directly at me and said, "I wish you could see yourself the way I see you, sweetheart. You're beautiful in every way."

Then he'd taken my hand, as he was holding it now, and said, "I love the way you walk, Vaneetha. I've loved it from the beginning."

Chapter 30

LOOKING BACK, WALKING FORWARD

It is an ordinary Thursday morning, and I'm sitting in my prayer room at 6:20 a.m. It's on the street side of the house that Joel and I designed together several years ago, and my window looks out on several camellia bushes, our front lawn, and the tall pine trees that line our street.

The sun won't be up for another half hour, so I have my desk light on. A candle is burning too, which I light every morning. I open my Bible to Psalm 66:

> "All the earth worships you
>   and sings praises to you;
>   they sing praises to your name."
> Come and see what God has done:
>   he is awesome in his deeds toward the children of man.
>   (vv. 4–5)

God's Word, as it so often does, mirrors my heart and opens it. As I start to write in my journal, I hear Joel walking softly toward me from the kitchen, with Mocha pitter-pattering behind him across the hardwood floor. Mocha, in his old age, has adopted Joel, much to Joel's delight—except when Kristi is around, that is.

"Good morning," Joel says. "Happy almost-five-year anniversary."

I spin slowly to face him in my low-resistance office chair. We smile.

He sets a steaming mug of coffee on my desk, and beside it an insulated straw-lid tumbler filled with ice water. I can no longer carry the tumbler, so Joel makes sure there is always one within reach.

I take my coffee with Splenda—despite Shalini's protests about chemicals—and enough cream to turn it the color of caramel. Joel drinks his coffee black. We're members of a coffee-of-the-month club, Katie and Kristi's Christmas gift to Joel, and while the chocolate and floral notes of Guatemalan beans are our favorite, this month's mellow Brazilian beans are still delicious. Every morning Joel uses a gram scale to grind exactly the right amount of beans.

I glance at the coffee mug. The level is low enough that it would be a stretch to call the mug full. He sees me look and says, "I know, I know, I took a few sips on the way."

"Babe," I say, "you're allowed to like Splenda and cream. You can even put it in your *own* coffee!"

"I prefer it black," he says with a twinkle in his eyes, "and I *also* like to take a sip of yours sometimes."

I smile and look down to see which fun socks Joel has on today. This pair is teal and covered in orange-and-yellow parrots. He once told me that for a nuclear engineer like him, silly socks are the equivalent of purple hair and a nose ring.

"I'll see you later?" I ask.

"I'm already looking forward to it," he says.

He and Mocha leave. Joel will finish his morning quiet time while I finish mine, and then we'll meet for a second cup of coffee before he goes into his home office to work and I do the same.

I turn back to my journal so I can think and pray about my life.

My wedding to Joel didn't tie my life up in a neat bow, as if I were the princess in some happily-ever-after fairy tale. Happily ever after definitely is coming, but that's reserved for heaven.

I'm incredibly happy to be with Joel, yes, but my happiness now doesn't mean it was "worth" getting divorced. That rift will always be a part of my story, and my daughters' stories. The supposedly tidy and beautiful bow of my life was untied, and I know that in time, even the very fabric of my life will unravel.

It has now been seventeen years since Shalini and I left the clinic with my post-polio diagnosis; seventeen years since they told me I would need a wheelchair full-time and that if I didn't cut out everything immediately, someone would be feeding me in ten years. I'm still defying the gloomy predictions—I don't use a wheelchair in the house, and I'm not being fed yet, which is good because I'm a foodie. I'll eat almost any delicious food, but I want each bite to be just so. The right amount and the right combination of flavors—the perfect ratio of spicy chicken to brown rice to homemade chipotle sauce.

Yet the trajectory of my physical decline means I will almost certainly need to give up feeding myself one day. On my own I can no longer make it up the curbs or stand up from low chairs. My shoulders, with no muscle to hold them in place, are slipping out of their sockets, and I see therapists weekly to help soothe that slow burn of continual pain.

Walking can cause sciatic nerve pain, which moves through my body like lightning, and I've had two recent surgeries on my right hand, my only functioning one, to stem the growing pains of overuse.

I'm all too aware that the time will come when I can't walk from the bedroom to the kitchen, and while our house is adapted for that, I'm hoping I'll be emotionally prepared for it too. That's always the bigger challenge—adjusting to continual loss.

None of this is easy. A body breaking down in slow motion is complicated. I know it and Joel knows it. God knows it. My kids and family know it. And all we can do is walk through it together in hope and trust and expectation.

It's why I look to friends for inspiration.

"It must be so hard that you can't have anything the way you want it to be," I once told Joni. She's been a quadriplegic for more than fifty years and lives in constant pain, and yet she's always radiant.

"True," she said, acknowledging the weight of my words. "But our God sees that, and all those choices, all those things we are giving up, all those will shine in glory one day."

I'll never forget hearing Joni say that when she woke up in pain at night, she was keenly aware that the angels and demons were watching her, learning about God through her response to suffering. That picture has helped me persevere through my daily losses, even when it seems like no one is watching.

Letting go is never easy. But maybe in letting go of the smaller things, like fixing my own coffee every morning, I'm practicing letting go of bigger things. Maybe in the smaller losses, God is preparing me for what only he knows is coming.

When I was younger, I thought I understood the way God operated. I believed that God gives each of us some suffering, but that if we love Christ, the suffering will never be too great or for too long. My view of faith was transactional: I'd been good, and so God owed me a good life in return. I'd made peace with my polio, with the sadness and bullying and pain of my childhood, so it was God's turn to deliver—a happy marriage, loving and obedient children, a thriving ministry, a healthy body, financial security, a successful career. And God did deliver on my expectations for a while, or so I thought.

It wasn't until later that I understood God's ways more clearly. While they were all good gifts, none were God's best gift, the gift meant to satisfy, the gift to be pursued and treasured. God alone had that place, for God himself is the greatest gift.

Suffering—not suffering itself, but turning to God in suffering—gave me an experience of God that was transformative. And breathtakingly beautiful.

Many spend their lives worrying, endlessly asking, what if the worst happens? That question only breeds fear. Rather than asking unanswerable questions, we should turn our doubts into declarations. Even if the worst happens, God will not change. God's grace will be sufficient. God will carry us. And he will never leave us.

I am convinced that suffering is inevitable but despair is not. It's one thing to wish something painful were different but quite another to be hopeless. It's when we turn our hearts away from the Easter that is coming that despair gets its claws into our hearts.

When the worst happened to me, I was at first hesitant to draw comfort from the God who had wounded me. But I hid those doubts and hesitations from others. I feared that my disappointment with life and even with God would damage others' faith. But that was simply not true. I needed to live transparently, showing others that we can't sidestep grief but must honestly go through it.

When I called out to God, I found he was already listening, already present with me, every step of my journey. That presence is as difficult to describe as it is real. It is the peace of a glassy ocean with an undercurrent of powerful, relentless joy. It is breathless excitement and perfect trust. It is bone-deep courage built on the promise that God will never leave or forsake me.

I no longer contrast joy with sorrow because I have found they can coexist. It is *purposelessness*, not sorrow, that squelches joy. When we begin to understand God's purpose—begin to glimpse him working for our good—we can experience true joy even inside our sorrow. After years of walking through fiery trials with the Lord, I can finally understand the truth behind Evelyn Christenson's words that I read so many years ago. Now I know that everything has been working out for my good. That God's will is perfect. That God has made no mistakes. And with that knowledge, even in the fire, I can have joy—deep down joy.

These are the truths that God's Spirit taught me in pain. And they are so comforting, so life-giving, that I would not erase a moment of my pain if it meant unlearning them.

Giving my cruelest suffering to God has softened me. It has worn off the sharp edges of my critical and judgmental spirit and drawn me to the Lord. That process didn't happen overnight. Truthfully, it took closer to ten thousand nights. But I learned that Jesus is enough. I don't need to prove myself to others, to measure up to their expectations, or to define myself by their words. My identity is in Christ.

Long before Joel loved the way I walk, Jesus loved the way I walk.

❧

I turn my neck to alleviate the cramp and stretch my right hand. I rotate my ankles counterclockwise and then back. The sun has almost risen outside, and the sky is lavender. On my desk I see a printout of a writing exercise a friend asked me to do.

It asks, "What would you say to your past selves at different points in your life?" As I wrote my answers, I discovered it was really an exercise in empathy.

I reread my words. They were love letters, really, to who I used to be. Not that who I am today is a perfect example of love, as Joel and my daughters could attest, but that I have been loved perfectly. I *am* loved perfectly.

I move my pen over the printout, noticing themes. I've given my past selves so many gentle admonitions.

> Don't try to walk straight.
> Don't be ashamed of your skin color or having polio or being divorced.

Don't stress about results.

Don't pretend you're okay when you're not.

And gentle encouragements too.

It's okay to take longer.

It's okay to be different.

It's okay to be sad, disappointed, and angry.

It's okay to speak your mind.

It's okay to be yourself.

There's so much I understand now that I wish I had understood then, when I feared other people's judgments and let them rule me rather than resting in God's love and acceptance. Had I securely rested in that love, I could have listened more closely to the girls, been more vulnerable with them, looked past their defiance to see their pain. I'm glad I didn't put them in the middle by criticizing Dave, but I wish I hadn't hidden my struggles behind a perfect picture. While I am imperfect, the cross ensures that God sees me as perfect, so I don't need to earn his love. At this point in my life I know that God fills me with love, overfills me with love, because it's supposed to spill over. It's meant to fill the cups of others.

I place the finished exercise back on the top of my desk and look around the brightening room, then smile. On my bookshelf is a memoir a friend loaned me, which is just *begging* to be savored. Maybe I'll dive into it later today, because I've walled off my morning time with God—Bible and journal, nothing more. But the rest of the day is fair game. I wonder if this book will be one of those stories that takes an unexpected turn. I'm always tempted to flip to the last page to see if everything ends well.

I don't know exactly how my story on earth will end, but I do know *exactly* how my story will ultimately end, because of something I experienced when I was eight.

That summer my parents sent me to a camp for disabled children in Canada. Getting anywhere on my own was a challenge, and I hadn't been walking without braces for long. When we arrived at the camp, I saw that the grounds had been designed for people in wheelchairs and on walkers and crutches. There were no stairs and no curbs. The outdoor areas were level and smooth, and every path was accessible to me. A sidewalk with benches along it wound around the lake, so I didn't need to walk on uneven grass to reach the water. I could go anywhere by myself without worrying about obstacles.

It was wild. My eight-year-old brain couldn't process it. Suddenly I had no limits. There was literally nothing at the camp that was off-limits because of my disability. It was something I had never experienced before and never have since.

But I will.

I will!

My heart nearly bursts when I think of the promise that I will.

Life is a journey, yes, but only if there's a destination. I'm on my way to my Father's house, and I absolutely cannot wait for the party. When I get there I will jog, run, sprint, race, and finally leap into the arms of my Savior.

Then I'll look around. Joel, Katie, and Kristi will be there. So will Shalini, my parents, Jerry and Maxine. My dear friends. Dave. And Paul—my sweet boy whose life glorified God, and who is already enjoying perfect love forever.

We'll all be there. I know it. Because of Christ, despite our failings, we'll all be there together.

And what's a party without dancing? In my glorified body I will take the hand of every person I have ever loved and dance with all my might, throwing back my head in laughter and thanksgiving.

Maybe that's not what everyone hopes about heaven. But this is my story, and it's the only story God has given me so far.

I wipe my cheeks and continue reading Psalm 66:

> For you, O God, have tested us;
>> you have tried us as silver is tried.
> You brought us into the net;
>> you laid a crushing burden on our backs;
> you let men ride over our heads;
>> we went through fire and through water;
> yet you have brought us out to a place of abundance.
> . . .
> Come and hear, all you who fear God,
>> and I will tell what he has done for my soul. (vv. 10–12, 16)

This. This is a picture of my life. Being tested and tried, having crushing burdens and being trampled over, going through fire and through water. And yet God has brought me to a place of abundance, and he has an even richer, everlasting place awaiting me.

After all God has done for me, I will walk through fire for him until the day he calls me home. And when I can no longer walk, I will still proclaim to all who will listen what my faithful Savior has done for my soul.

◈

But enough deep thoughts for one morning! The sun is up, the cardinals are singing outside my window, and my coffee mug is empty and won't refill itself. Before I can text Joel—a civilized mode of communicating suited to our downstairs space—my phone chimes, and I look at the screen. Joel is texting me, and he's clearly on a different, less caffeine-addicted page than I am.

Arise, my love, my beautiful one . . .

I push myself up and stand, then slide my phone into the pocket of my jeans. I take my empty mug in my right hand and walk down the hall and into the kitchen. Joel looks up when he sees me, obviously pleased with himself, and then finishes his text aloud.

. . . and come into the kitchen, for behold I will grind precisely fourteen grams of coffee and brew us each a nice second mug.

"Joel!" I laugh.

"What?" he teases. "Isn't that how the verse goes?"

"Something like that," I say. "You're so good for me, you know that?"

"I do," he says.

I laugh again.

"What?" he says. "I'm just agreeing with you!"

Mocha barks, and we both look out the back windows. A red fox is trotting along on his morning errands. Joel and I watch him while the coffee brews, then we walk to the couch.

"So," he says, settling his arm around me, "what did God show you this morning?"

I begin to tell him. I don't know exactly what the rest of my life will look like—never mind the rest of my day—but I know that God is good.

And so for now, I lean into the fact that I am being held.

"HELD"

MUSIC AND LYRICS BY CHRISTA WELLS

Two months is too little
They let him go
They had no sudden healing
To think that providence would
Take a child from his mother while she prays
Is appalling
Who told us we'd be rescued?
What has changed, and why should we be saved from nightmares?
We're asking why this happens
To us who have died to live?
It's unfair

This is what it means to be held
How it feels when the sacred is torn from your life
And you survive
This is what it is to be loved
And to know that the promise was
When everything fell we'd be held

"HELD"

This hand is bitterness
We want to taste it, let the hatred numb our sorrow
The wise hands opens slowly to lilies of the valley and tomorrow

This is what it means to be held
How it feels when the sacred is torn from your life
And you survive
This is what it is to be loved
And to know that the promise was
When everything fell we'd be held

If hope is born of suffering
If this is only the beginning
Can we not wait for one hour watching for our Savior?

This is what it means to be held
How it feels when the sacred is torn from your life
And you survive
This is what it is to be loved
And to know that the promise was
When everything fell we'd be held

ACKNOWLEDGMENTS

Words cannot express my gratitude to the people who have made this book possible. Not only the people who helped with the actual book, but the countless others who have walked with me for just a part of my journey. You have supported me, loved me, and lived the gospel before me. Thank you.

Jessica Wong and the entire team at Nelson Books who said yes and shared my vision for this book, thank you for believing in me. Austin Wilson, my agent with Wolgemuth and Associates, thank you for your kindness and tireless hard work. David Jacobsen, thank you for helping make my manuscript so much stronger. John Sloan, thank you for your invaluable assistance in drafting my proposal.

Ann Voskamp, thank you for being willing to write my foreword even at a crazy time in your own life. Your words have shaped mine, and you inspired me to start writing.

The staff at Desiring God, thank you for helping me grow as a person and as a writer. Scott Anderson, John Knight, Sam Macrane, David Mathis, Tony Reinke, and Marshall Segal—thank you for your friendship, offering the initial vision for this memoir, and trusting me six years ago by publishing my first article on your website. I'm grateful for each of you. John Piper, thank you for sharing your passion for Christ—your vision of delighting in God changed my life almost twenty-five years ago.

Joni Eareckson Tada, thank you for your quiet example of love and faithfulness. You have modeled how to walk with God in suffering, which has impacted me more than you will ever know.

Christa Wells, I treasure you. Your album for this book is incredible. I'm beyond grateful to you, Ellie Holcomb, Taylor Leonhardt, Jess Ray, and Nicole Witt for all you've done.

Tom Mercer, my pastor and friend, your constant care through difficult seasons has meant the world to me. I am thankful for Christ Covenant Church, for the way people serve and love one another, and for your faithful leadership of this congregation.

Dave, thank you for letting me freely share my story, especially because it is part of your story too. I appreciate that you want to honor God and help others, even at a cost to yourself. I'm grateful that we are friends.

My friends who read early versions of the manuscript—Maggie, Melanie, Su, Karen, Phil, Tom, Ann, Rachel, Dale, Jim, Nik, Margot, Bryan, Sally, Florence, Jennifer, Lisa, Carol, Paula, Bill, Melissa, Matt, Carole, Cheri, Shalini, Mom, and Kristi—thank you for all of your input. Not only did you read, thoughtfully comment, and help mold this book, you helped mold me as a person. As family and friends, mentors and counselors, pastors and writers, you are amazing supporters, and I'm grateful for each of you.

Sara, RuthAnn, Jennifer, Suzi, Ann, and Jeanne, my small group, thank you for praying about this book for two years. We've laughed and cried a lot together, and I love you all dearly.

Jennifer and Lisa, my prayer partners of over two decades, thank you for being my confidantes and friends. You consistently poured into me, even when I had nothing left to give.

My extended family and Joel's, especially Phil, Renuka, and Jan, thank you for listening to me, praying for me, and helping me in endless practical ways.

Ashley and Jeremy, Emily and Chris, I'm so glad we're family. Thank you for being so welcoming to me. I love being part of your lives.

Maxine and Jerry, you are more like parents than in-laws to me.

You have taught me about love and forgiveness and family. I'm so grateful that you are in my life.

Mom and Dad, your selfless sacrifice still amazes me. You are my biggest cheerleaders, and I wouldn't be who I am today without your unconditional support. Our family has been the one constant in my ever-changing world.

Shalini, you are my best friend and go-to person for everything, including my writing. You emotionally, and even physically, have walked through my hardest days with me, even during demanding seasons in your own life. Thank you for always picking up the phone.

Katie and Kristi, I love being your mom. Thank you for generously letting me share your personal stories and for putting up with all my parenting mistakes. Katie, your fierce loyalty, relentless energy, extraordinary generosity, and unwavering devotion to the people whom you love made me, and this book, better. Kristi, you are deeply thoughtful, wildly hilarious, incredibly gifted, and wise beyond your years. Your insightful work on the early manuscript, and all my writing, has been invaluable.

Joel, I love waking up every morning with you by my side. You make my life better in every way. Your deep faith, brilliant intellect, and extraordinary sacrifice for me blow me away every day. Sometimes, like my mom, I wonder if you really do have a birth certificate or if God whipped you up just for me.

Jesus, you have loved me and redeemed me and given me joy in place of mourning. Thank you for giving me these friends, supporters, and loved ones. Everything I have and everything I've been through is because of you. I'm so thankful I will never have to live one moment without you.

NOTES

1. Evelyn Christenson, *What Happens When Women Pray* (Wheaton, IL: Victor Books, 1991), 89–90.
2. Charles Haddon Spurgeon, "Woe and Weal," sermon #3239, delivered at the Metropolitan Tabernacle, Newington, United Kingdom. Published Thursday, March 2, 1911, Spurgeon Gems (website), https://www.spurgeongems.org/sermon/chs3239.pdf.
3. Rita J. Carmack, *Set My Heart Free* (Windsor, CO: Jewel Press, 1984), 43.
4. Frederick Buechner, *The Magnificent Defeat*, quoted in Francis Chan, with Danae Yankoski, *Crazy Love: Overwhelmed by a Relentless God* (Colorado Springs: David C. Cook, 2013), 130.
5. Christa Wells, "This Is What We're Here For," track 5 on *A Rogers/Wells Project: so much to tell you*, Rogers/Wells, 2005.
6. You can find my blog *Dance in the Rain* at https://www.vaneetha.com/blog.
7. Vivian Greene, www.viviangreene.com.